Thetis Down

Also by Tony Booth:
Cox's Navy
Admiralty Salvage in Peace & War

Thetis Down

The Slow Death of a Submarine

Tony Booth

Pen & Sword
MARITIME

First published in Great Britain in 2008 and reprinted in 2009 by
PEN & SWORD MARITIME
an imprint of
Pen & Sword Books Ltd
47 Church Street, Barnsley, South Yorkshire, S70 2AS

ISBN 978-1-84415-859-1

A CIP catalogue record for this book is
available from the British Library

Typeset in 11/13 Sabon by Concept, Huddersfield, West Yorkshire
Printed and bound in England by CPI UK

Pen & Sword Books Ltd incorporates the Imprints of
Pen & Sword Aviation, Pen & Sword Maritime, Pen & Sword Military,
Wharncliffe Local History, Pen & Sword Select, Pen & Sword Military Classics,
Leo Cooper, Remember When, Seaforth Publishing and Frontline Publishing.

For a complete list of Pen & Sword titles please contact
PEN & SWORD BOOKS LIMITED
47 Church Street, Barnsley, South Yorkshire, S70 2AS, England
E-mail: enquiries@pen-and-sword.co.uk
Website: www.pen-and-sword.co.uk

'If blood be the price of admiralty,
Lord God, we ha' bought it fair!'

'The Song of the Dead'
Rudyard Kipling, 1896

'The Admiralty regrets that His Majesty's Submarine
Thetis ... has failed to surface'

First public announcement,
23.00 hours, 1 June 1939

This book is dedicated to the memory of the
ninety-nine men who perished aboard
His Majesty's Submarine *Thetis* –
and to the four who survived

Contents

Foreword

The news that the Royal Navy submarine HMS *Thetis* had sunk numbed the nation. The shock was made worse by the fact that it was peacetime, and everyone knew that the Royal Navy was the biggest, best and most efficient in the world. It had a dozen battleships and battle cruisers, and five more battleships on the way, and its warships provided a symbol of stability in distant oceans. The Royal Navy did not have accidents, let alone disasters.

Britain was a small and somewhat backward society at that time but it was homogeneous; it shared its jokes and its xenophobia and troubles. Even a street accident could, for a brief time, eliminate social and class differences. The Royal Navy was a microcosm of that Britain. When I say the nation was shocked by this agonizing undersea drama, I mean that it affected just about every man, woman and child. I say this with confidence because I was a child at the time and I remember it vividly. At school the teachers whispered together. As the hours ticked away I would hear people ask 'What must it be like for those poor sailors?' The newspapers published photos showing that the hull of the submarine was visible and high above water. 'Why don't they just cut a hole in it and get them out?' everyone asked. In films we had seen masked bank robbers cutting through steel in minutes; we knew it wasn't too difficult for the Navy.

Tony Booth gives answers to the questions that were posed more than half a century ago. Not that there have not been answers provided before. Books have explained it and films have depicted its heroics. There has been an Admiralty investigation, the conclusions of which were kept secret. There was an official public enquiry (oh, how guilty public officials like official public enquiries). It was concluded that no one was to blame.

Some said the *Thetis* was an unlucky ship. Just how unlucky, Tony Booth's painstaking research will tell you. But just to be getting on with, how about this paragraph from his book? What author of mainstream fiction would dare test his reader's credulity with such a Monty Python scene?

> When Lieutenant Commander Bolus gave the order to steer to port, the *Thetis* promptly swung to starboard. Then when he gave the order to steer to starboard she promptly turned to port. By some incredible piece of incompetence the entire steering gear system had been fitted in reverse. Then, when they did attempt to dive, the forward hydroplanes jammed.

Before the Second World War the Royal Navy's Submarine Service had been a dumping ground for 'difficult' officers, alcoholics, misfits and those with ideas of their own. The RAF's dumping ground was Fighter Command and the Army's was the Tank Corps. And yet these were the weapons that proved decisive in the coming war.

The journey to the Royal Navy's top ranks was made on the bridge of the big battleships where well-spoken, ambitious young officers rubbed shoulders with the gold braid. Britain's Admirals loved big battleships, and the Japanese Admirals and United States' Admirals were equally love-struck by these obsolete armadillos. Even in the middle of the Second World War the German Admirals remained convinced that the battleship was the decisive weapon and wanted more. All admirals wanted them as 'Flagships' and used them as command posts. In the Pacific, while the oily-handed United States' submariners were winning the war almost single-handed, the Admirals were deliberately blocking United States' Navy press releases to this effect, in case the cost effectiveness of their precious battleships was questioned.

Although it was the U-boats, and the sophisticated German technology, that made the headlines and almost extinguished Britain's seaborne supply lines, the Royal Navy's far more primitive submarines contributed greatly to the Allied victory. British submarines sank 169 enemy warships and 493 merchant ships but about one in three of the Royal Navy's submarines were lost, one of the highest casualty rates of any service.

As for the sneaky duplicity that the British Admiralty displayed concerning the loss of the *Thetis* in 1939 we should not judge them too harshly. Their behaviour was not unique. When the United States' Navy lost the nuclear submarine USS *Scorpion* in May 1968 they located it on the seabed within a couple of weeks. But it took another four months before they admitted to finding it and even today the true cause is kept secret. (It was sunk with all hands by a torpedo fired from a Russian submarine.) HMS *Thetis* and USS *Scorpion* are two of a long list of submarine disasters that remain shrouded in mystery. The Russian *Kursk* that sank in the Barents Sea in the summer of 2000 was perhaps the most publicized; the least publicized was the Chinese submarine *No. 361* discovered in 2003 by fishermen. It was floating low in the water of the Yellow Sea with its whole crew dead. Who knows what happened? The list goes on, and so do the controversies. The Free French *Surcouf* was, in February 1942 when it sank, probably the largest submarine in the world. And the determination of the governments concerned to keep the story of its last few hours secret was no less impressive. The cause of its ending is still being argued. Navies have always been a law unto themselves and, since the invention of atomic devices, underwater technology is at the top of the world's most jealously guarded military secrets.

Warships of any shape or size are self-contained dictatorships. And self-contained dictatorships shroud their troubles in secrecy. It is not surprising that navies – such as those of Britain, France, Spain and Russia – have in recent times been the focus of mutinies and revolutions.

It is fitting that at last the riveting story of the *Thetis* is told by Tony Booth. Hardworking, dedicated historians – whether professional or amateur – are rare today and Tony Booth is to be cherished. He is second to none in determination and tenacity and respected widely among his peers for his success in digging out hard facts, no matter how long it takes. And he is second to none in making the facts into a nail-biting narrative that reads like a first rate suspense story.

Len Deighton
Southern California
Copyright 2008 Pluriform

Acknowledgements

Barely three days after I started writing this book, my wife, Virginie, and I were invited to a dinner party in the cottage in Guernsey where we now live. While our hosts, David and Maryanne Keys, made us feel most welcome, the dinner conversation turned to the topic of marine salvage, being the subject of my last two books. David said, 'My father worked for the Royal Navy, as a salvage diver before the war. He dived on a submarine in Liverpool Bay called the *Thetis* where ninety-nine men were killed'.

The coincidence seemed too great, and became more so as David proceeded to recount a tale his father told him many years before, one that I had also researched from a completely different viewpoint a little earlier. But such seemingly impossible events are not uncommon when an author sets out to write a book. It is as if the very act of looking for information attracts avenues and leads in directions never dreamed of before. This book is no exception. Indeed, during the four years that *Thetis Down* has been a part of my life, I met, quite by accident, two more people with direct links to the *Thetis* and the disaster that befell her. So firstly I must thank David Keys, for allowing me to interview him at length shortly after his wife Maryanne's lovely dinner, Robert Furniss, for recalling for me his vivid recollections of being given a guided tour of the *Thetis* as HMS *Thunderbolt* in Alexandria, in 1942. Ian Murray Taylor, the grandson of Thomas McKenzie who tried in vain to rescue the trapped men, for taking the time to recount his grandfather's memories of the disaster. And for the use of his grandfather's photograph. Ian Partington for his help.

I must also thank the Archivist, Emma Challinor, for allowing me access to records of the *Thetis* and Cammell Laird shipbuilders held by Wirral Archives Service. Archivist George Malcolmson for all his help at the Submarine Museum archives in Gosport, Hampshire, and for allowing me to quote from the extensive files on the *Thetis*. Thanks also to Submarine Museum Keeper of Photographs Debbie Corner for the use of many images among those held at the museum. I thank The National Archives, Kew, for allowing me to quote from their files, as well as the use of many images in this book. Many of them were actually used during the Public Tribunal, allowing the Court to gain a better understanding of what actually happened. Also thanks to Jennifer Cochrane for all her editorial advice. Many thanks are also due to the Clerk of Records at the House of Lords Record Office for permission to quote from Hansard throughout 1939 and 1940. To the Wirral Museum, especially Ernie Ruffler, for his much appreciated help during several research trips to Birkenhead.

Thanks to *The Guardian*, for permission to quote from an article by David Pallister dated 2 June 1989, covering the story of Liverpool bookmaker Samuel Gothorp and his insistence that the Admiralty purposely refused to breach the pressure hull to free the men exactly fifty years earlier. Material Copyright Guardian News & Media Limited 1989, the *Liverpool Echo* for permission to quote from their newspapers from 1939 to 1946, the *Liverpool Daily Post* for also allowing me to quote from their contemporary editions and the *Daily Mirror* for allowing me to quote from their newspapers published throughout the month of June 1939 and also to their new Mirrorpix online photo archive for the use of the image of Mrs Sybil Bolus, wife of the *Thetis*'s captain, Lieutenant Commander 'Sam' Bolus. Thanks to ITN Stills for the aerial view of the salvage vessel *Vigilant* almost touching the *Thetis*'s raised stern.

Thank you to Lawrence H. Officer, 'Purchasing Power of the British Pounds from 1264 to 2007', www.measuringworth.com, for accurate calculations of currency value based on the Retail Price Index, Stephen P. Ryder for the use of his text on Count Michael Alexander in his publication of 'Der Teufel von Whitechapel' ('The Devil of Whitechapel'), covering Jack the Ripper's alleged Jewish links and Doctor Bill Barker for his clear explanation of the complexities of carbon dioxide poisoning and subsequent death. Please note, despite prolonged and exhaustive enquiries, tracking down some copyright holders has not been possible.

As always I thank Susie Deflassieux and Jane Westcott for their much appreciated help while I was away on several research trips. I must thank my wife, Virginie, for having to share me with yet another book for what has been far too long. Thank you, Vee. It must have felt like a third person in our lives at times. And my two patient little sons, Jack and Hugo, for all their wonderful submarine drawings they have done for me over the past year. Thank you, boys. And finally my thanks for their unconditional patience in sharing their dad with this book, and its tales of submarines and what can go tragically wrong when several minor errors reach a critical mass.

Introduction

In early January 1942 twenty-one-year-old Royal Air Force Corporal Robert 'Bob' Furniss was stationed at Number Two Park 124 Maintenance Unit near RAF Fuka, a small landing ground about 130 miles west of Alexandria. His job was, along with Leading Aircraftmen George Peaker and several others, to sort ordnance into their respective calibres and types for further distribution among the many allied units in the area. After many days of heat, sweat and sand they, along with two other colleagues, were given forty-eight hours leave to enjoy 'Alex' and all that the exotic city had to offer. Upon arrival they checked into a hostel and then visited a barber shop for a proper wash with real soap and to scrape as much of the Western Desert off their bodies as possible. 'The next stop was at the Russian baths, where we were more completely cleansed by incarceration in wooden steam-filled boxes', said Furniss, 'emerging after twenty minutes like boiled lobsters. We were then sprayed with cold water and hosed by stone-faced Russian ladies in white coats. The final indignity was to plunge all naked into an ice-cold pool'.

The following afternoon Furniss decided to visit Greville Young, a friend who worked aboard the 14,000-ton submarine depot ship HMS *Medway*. He added, 'I don't remember how it was that I had this information about Greville being on the *Medway* and can only suppose my father mentioned it in one of his letters'. She was anchored off the main port, ensuring that the First Submarine Flotilla had all it needed to continue disrupting German supply lines. Local fishermen rowed the two men out to the *Medway*. Upon arriving on her deck, Furniss and Peaker saluted the ship when stepping on board, this being service etiquette. 'We waited for the naval officer standing some way off to order some lowly seaman to enquire to our purpose. Duly given and reported to the officer, we were instructed to wait'. Shortly afterwards a rather confused Greville Young appeared and took Furniss and Peaker to the *Medway*'s Petty Officers' Mess where the two airmen were made very welcome. Although Furniss could not remember how he knew his friend was working aboard the *Medway*, now aged eighty-seven he still vividly recalls how they were both invited to see over the T Class submarine HMS *Thunderbolt*, moored alongside the depot ship with three other submarines.

The *Thunderbolt*'s captain was Lieutenant Commander 'Lucky' Cecil Bernard Crouch DSO and Bar. Barely in his thirties, Crouch was called Lucky, a nickname he always disliked, after leaving the S Class submarines HMS *Seahorse*, which was lost with all hands off Heligoland in January 1940, and HMS *Swordfish* nine months later in the English Channel after a mine split her in two. Since Crouch took over the *Thunderbolt* she had become one of the most successful British submarines operating in the Mediterranean, having racked up one Italian submarine sunk off France, five enemy ships sunk and one damaged, all within a year. Many of his crew had been decorated and Crouch turned down a safe desk job to rejoin his men on the front line. Now she was tied up next to the *Medway* for urgent repairs before, again, going into the open sea to continue her successful killing spree.

Furniss remembers climbing down the side of the *Medway* on to the *Thunderbolt*'s deck casing, 'We descended through a hatch into the *Thunderbolt*, which Greville told us was the *Thetis* of tragic memory. We were shown the control room, torpedo room, mess quarters, galley and periscope. The submarine was being serviced and repaired by a number of artificers, using very noisy tools with pipes and cables snaking along at our feet the whole length of the vessel'.

Although an interesting experience that has stayed with Furniss to this day, he really preferred fighting the war from dry land rather than from beneath the waves. In late 2007, looking back to seeing the *Thunderbolt* prepare for another patrol, he recalled how, 'The noise was deafening and Greville had to rely on hand movements to convey his information. I remember the noise, the smell of oil and the heat: but mostly the confined space. After working in the vast desert at Fuka, the cramped conditions in submarines confirmed our belief that we had joined the right service'.

HMS *Thunderbolt* was soon back on patrol, sinking or damaging another six enemy vessels, having already delivered several Special Operations teams into occupied territory. Altogether she completed six patrols. During her seventh, on the night of 12 March 1943 the softly spoken boyish Crouch spotted an enemy convoy and sank the Italian cargo ship *Esterel*. The Italian corvette, *Cicogna*, commanded by Capitano di Corvetta Augusto Migliorini chased the *Thunderbolt*.

Crouch had been chased before, but this was different. He soon became aware that this corvette captain was no ordinary adversary. Unfortunately for Crouch, Migliorini was an ex-submariner who knew intuitively how and where the *Thunderbolt* was likely to be hiding. For two days Migliorini chased Crouch around the Mediterranean, knowing that sooner or later he would have to surface.

The air was getting foul aboard the submarine, but Crouch knew that to surface without caution would mean certain death. On 14 March 'Lucky' Crouch's charmed life took a turn for the worse. Migliorini picked up an echo, in the Messina Straits between Italy and Sicily. Crouch knew Migliorini was closing in, but he had to know from where and at what distance. Standing in the *Thunderbolt*'s tense control room, the smooth-faced, slightly overweight commander hoisted his periscope for a quick 360° scan of the horizon to better assess his true situation. Before Migliorini could respond to the echo, *Thunderbolt*'s periscope was sighted barely 10 feet away from the *Cicogna* on her starboard bow. Just before 09.00 hours Crouch's luck had finally run out. Migliorini's was just beginning.

The corvette captain poured more than twenty depth charges right on target, forcing the sea around the dying submarine to boil in a mass of shattered internal wreckage and oil-stained foam. Within a few minutes *Thunderbolt*'s stern rose out of the sea for the second time in her short life. After reaching a full 90°, she hung upright for a minute or so before spearing towards the seabed like a rapidly accelerating falling dart. Even in time of war, when a ship founders the enemy, as well as the ally, will all too often have pity for those they can see in distress. For the many thousands of dying submariners during both world wars, out of sight, due to the very nature of a submarine's under-water functionality, really was out of mind. Little is known of what really happens, except that hopefully death will be swift. In the case of the *Thunderbolt*, like many sinking submarines, this may not have been the case.

The point where she struck the bottom of the Mediterranean was about 3,000 feet down, or ten times past her certified crush depth. The initial blasts would have killed outright many of her sixty-two-man crew. Others would have drowned while those towards the stern perhaps had time to shut some of the quick-closing watertight doors. Or perhaps, being at battle stations, the doors were already shut and thus more would have survived the initial blast. As she began to descend, all the machinery would have stopped, the lights gone out, and anything loose would now be piling towards the front of each section. Due to her streamlined design her speed would pick up to about 40 mph, and it is doubtful that she imploded at 300 feet. Although her designers rated the T Class boats at that depth they could survive perhaps another 150 to 200 feet more, as a built-in safety margin. That is fine in a submarine fighting to regain control and needing a little more of an edge, but, if it is out of control, the greater depth meant greater pressure and thus a more violent end.

The technical name designers give for the final implosion of a submarine is 'interframe failure'. This rather prosaic term hardly describes what those about to die are going to suffer. Passing 300 feet bolts and rivets would already be popping and the decks would begin distorting, fuel lines would rupture, spraying fuel oil in all directions. For anyone still alive in some sealed area, no amount of cowering and trying to protect themselves was going to help. Weak areas such as hatches, torpedo tubes and any other exit and entry point in the pressure hull, however large or small, would give way to the tremendous external forces now compressing the rapidly failing hull. When a hatch fails under such a sudden pressure blast, the inbound rush is like a solid concrete punch right into the hull like a piston in a chamber, blowing people and equipment to pieces if they are directly exposed to the flying debris.

The effect would then be similar to putting a finger over the end of a bicycle pump and pushing in the handle as hard as possible. The air would heat rapidly after being compressed from one to thirty atmospheres in one, final, heartbeat. In a 1,000-ton submarine, now well past its safe operating depth a wave of solid water would then engulf everything, bringing on welcome death to anyone still unfortunate enough to be alive. Seconds later the devastating trapped compressed air would break the surface as a harmless bubble. Meanwhile the *Thunderbolt* was still a couple of thousand feet from the seabed with a wake of debris running all the way back up to the surface. She was now lost for the second time in her short life, having taken her crew down with her for the second time.

About nine months after the *Thetis* was lost, and a year before she was salvaged and re-commissioned as the *Thunderbolt*, Winston Churchill said, 'All interest in this tragedy has been submerged by the war'. Today, Churchill's statement could just as easily read, 'All interest in this tragedy has been submerged by time'. The first time she was lost, in Liverpool Bay on 1 June 1939 was, and still is, the worst peacetime submarine disaster the Royal Navy has yet faced. Altogether ninety-nine men drowned or suffocated, within 20 feet of the surface, not to mention the suffering of those widowed and orphaned in the aftermath. The disaster became an international media event, mainly because the trapped souls aboard were so near to being saved after her personnel managed to raise the stern a good 18 ft above sea level. Yet to date very little is known about what actually happened during the fifty-hour fight to save those inside. Only three books have ever been published on this tragedy that in its time gripped the world.

The first book came out of Nazi Germany, of all places, where publisher Franz Müller Verlag of Dresden released Count Michael Alexander's controversial book, *SOS Thetis*, in 1944. With a large, red '£' sign dominating the front cover, the book's whole thrust delivers a sordid yarn of how Cammell Laird who, after bordering on bankruptcy by the time the *Thetis* was built, forewent their contractual obligation to insure the submarine to save more than £3,000, the equivalent of about £90,000 today. After all, once delivery was made, she was no longer Laird's responsibility, and what could possibly go wrong on an acceptance trial?

Count Alexander also claimed that while precious air was being used up aboard the *Thetis*, an insurance scam was being hatched between Cammell Laird and the British Government involving Minister of War Sir John Anderson and Lord Hailsham. If Laird's true financial position was ever made public a crash in armament shares would ensue and be catastrophic for the pre-war economy. A very poor position, indeed, just three months before Britain was to declare war on Europe's new and highly aggressive super power.

In 1958 C. Warren and J. Benson wrote *'The Admiralty regrets ...'* which is still considered the definitive book on the subject. At the top of their preface, Warren and Benson both admit, 'Those parts of the book which represent our personal opinions can be clearly seen as such. Those parts which are written as fact are so to the best of our knowledge and ability ...'. Turn the page and they further admit, 'Unfortunately Messrs Cammell Laird and Co. Ltd, and Messrs Wailes Dove Bitumastic Ltd felt unable to assist us'. The part played by both these companies is pivotal in understanding the disaster and its outcome. In the late 1990s a self-published book was released called *HMS Thetis: Secrets & Scandal* by David Roberts. Regarding his own book, Roberts states in his introduction that he relied heavily on Warren and

Benson's book, both as a primary source and as a director for other areas of research. The rest of his book covers many first-hand interviews from family members of those involved, and sheds light on alleged unfair dealing with respect to the *Thetis* Memorial Fund.

Officially a 105-page public enquiry (the mainstay of Warren and Benson's book) was published in 1940, fixing no material blame on any individual, but rather 'a sea of trouble'. Well, a sea of troubles it was, with more than thirty seemingly random events, some hundreds of miles apart, converging to ensure the sea would never let these men go. This rather short report was based on more than 2,000 pages of sworn testimony. Ironically, four days before the official public enquiry even opened the Admiralty had completed their own confidential, in-house investigation, which did proportion blame. Not until 1953 were the people of Great Britain able to sue the Crown, so the injured parties had to content themselves with suing individual members involved in the loss.

Around the streets of Birkenhead in 1939, where the *Thetis* was built, some people had their own version of events. With war imminent, many felt that the Admiralty valued the submarine more than her crew until it was too late. To cut into the pressure hull, as it stuck out of the water, would render her useless against deep diving and depth-charge attack. Thus she would be a very expensive and impotent weapon of war. Other conspiracy theories developed, some with shards of truth, others works of complete fiction.

Seventy years have now passed since the *Thetis* slowly died and a great deal more unpublished information has come to light. In fact, so much information is now available that it is now possible to explore in atomic detail the events before, to a large extent during, and after she was lost. This includes the crucial enquiry transcripts, correspondence and rediscovered files sourced as recently as November 2007. Now, long after her loss, and Furniss's visit to her, as HMS *Thunderbolt*, a much more in-depth account of the *Thetis* disaster is no longer 'submerged' as Churchill once said, within Whitehall bureaucracy and dusty archives up and down the United Kingdom and beyond.

Tony Booth
Guernsey
August 2008

Chapter 1

'Mystery & Mythology'

At 12.30 hours on 29 June 1938 Mrs Amy Power, wife of Captain Arthur John Power CVO, RN of HMS *Ark Royal*, smashed a bottle of champagne across the bow of His Majesty's Submarine *Thetis* on the first swing. Both shipyard workers and dignitaries alike cheered as the all-new T Class submarine slipped slowly down Cammell Laird's ramp in Birkenhead, and splashed into the River Mersey, slowly bobbing and settling on an even keel.

Laird's Managing Director Robert S. Johnson presided over the obligatory luncheon that followed every launch. More than 190 guests were invited to attend the celebration in the Tracer's Room, at Liverpool's prestigious Adelphi Hotel. The large function room, adorned with elaborate stucco plaster mouldings and large brass chandeliers like any other Regency-style function room of the day, was an ideal venue. The Tracer's Room had one small touch that made it rather unique. Every window around the room, be it in a door, or the surrounding walls, were mirrors, reflecting light and movement back on to the guests. The top table dominated the room where the Laird's directors and their wives could see over the six columns before them, of assorted naval personnel, senior Laird's staff, their wives and both local and national press representatives. Among the guests grouped together on one of the long tables were Lieutenant Commander Guy Bolus, the *Thetis*'s captain, and his wife Sybil. Sitting across to his right was Lieutenant Harry Chapman, Bolus's Number One. Lieutenant Antony Jamison, standing by another Laird's T Class build, HMS *Taku*, was sitting five places away from Bolus to his left. Commissioned Engineer Roy Glenn was sitting right next to Jamison. Admiralty Overseers Edward Grundy and Edward Gisborne were sitting at separate tables out of sight and sound of Bolus. Some knew each other while others did not, but within another year all their fates would become intimately entwined in far less cordial surroundings.

1

The guests made small talk and discussed what a fine submarine *Thetis* was while tucking into Cammell Laird's fare, a three-course meal of cold salmon, mayonnaise and cucumber, followed by chicken and buttered potatoes with strawberries for dessert. As the scraping of knives and forks against fine china died away, Johnson stood to give his customary speech. The low buzz of conversation faded, the room slowly filling up with a smoky haze from the many complimentary cigars and cigarettes now lighting up. When Johnson felt that he had his guests' attention, looking across the six long tables, he proposed a toast to the *Thetis* and to Mrs Power before going straight into his usual post-launch banter of light comedy mixed with informative fact giving.

'So we are to be congratulated on the birth of a child', he began. The crowd listened more intently as he went on to explain how the name '*Thetis*' had puzzled him a great deal. 'One had to delve into mystery and mythology to arrive at some conclusion as to naming an Admiralty ship. I had recently picked up a book on ship building in Liverpool – not Birkenhead, but Liverpool'. Some guests laughed and others guffawed at the innuendo reflecting the friendly rivalry between the two closely tied, but still distinctly separate, towns.

'Thetis was a sea divinity', he continued. 'Cammell Laird built the *Achilles* recently, but Thetis was the mother of Achilles so *Achilles* was a bit ahead of his time'. The crowd tittered as Johnson elaborated on his story. 'Thetis dwelt in the depths of the sea with her father, but she brought Achilles up to the surface sometimes'. The guests loved the similarities between Greek mythology and a modern-day submarine. Johnson added how Thetis made her son invulnerable by dipping him in the River Styx, but how she forgot to dip his heel where her hand supported him, thus making one weak area on his body that eventually led to his death. The quips kept coming. 'Thetis', he said with a smile, 'was also reputed to have the power of changing her form – and, I expect, her mind!' The crowd roared.

After speaking highly of Captain Power, and the sea trials of HMS *Ark Royal*, another Cammell Laird's build, Johnson turned to Mrs Power and explained how she had just travelled at great inconvenience from the south of England to launch the new submarine. The guests applauded as she stood to say how she felt sure that the *Thetis* would be a lucky ship. 'This was a most unexpected honour. I have had the chance of seeing a number of ceremonies, but there was nothing quite like the launch of a ship, a chance that came to very few naval officers' wives'.

HMS *Thetis* was the first of three T (or Triton) Class submarines built at Cammell Laird from the original 1936 programme. Plans for a new British submarine had begun two years earlier, but any new design was heavily constrained by the 1930 London Naval Treaty. The Treaty was an international pact signed by Britain, France, Japan, Italy and the United States with the intention of limiting submarine warfare and warship construction. Britain's submarine fleet was restricted to only 52,700 tons, with a limit of only 2,000 tons per unit, and maximum deck armament of 5.1 inches. The 'T boats' were only 1,095 tons, thus enabling more units for the agreed overall tonnage, yet capable of packing a harder punch.

The 'Ts' almost never happened at all. By the early 1930s the Government and the Admiralty were at odds as to the future of the submarine. Prime Minister Stanley Baldwin wanted a total abolition, or at the very least a reduction to units of only 250 tons. This would be totally inadequate for Britain's defensive and offensive needs and plans for a new submarine continued in earnest. Although any new design had to be smaller than the Odin, Parthian and R Class boats already in use, Baldwin's assessment was overthrown in the wake of another arms limitation treaty in 1936. The way was now paved for the 'Ts' to leave the drawing board and become a three-dimensional reality with HMS *Triton*, the first of her class having her keel laid at Vickers-Armstrongs of Barrow-in-Furness in August 1936.

Originally known as the 'Repeat Ps' the T Class was revolutionary in the extreme, taking all the best features of the previous three classes and adding a great deal more. All three older classes had eight, eight and six torpedo tubes respectively. The T Boats carried ten torpedo tubes, six below water, two above in the bow and two amidships also facing forward. Her submerged speed was also faster than her predecessors, as well as much improved surface and underwater handling capabilities. One drawback was that, because of the Treaty's displacement limitations, they were slower on the surface. This was considered a small price to pay for so much added firepower.

The 1936 programme included four vessels, three to be built by Laird, being HMS *Thetis*, which was laid down Christmas week in 1936, and HMS *Trident* three weeks afterwards and HMS *Taku* in November the following year. Laird almost lost the *Thetis* to another yard after submitting a tender quote that was considered too high. The original design had called for Admiralty engines to be fitted, but Laird believed that they could reduce costs and win the contract by installing Sulzer instead of Admiralty engines, also reducing the *Thetis*'s size by one frame, or 2 feet. Still the Admiralty thought Laird could beat their original price of £270,500 (or £12.6m today) even with the twin Sulzers. Director of Naval Contracts (DNC) E. C. Jubb did not mince his words when he told Johnson, 'The price quoted for fitting this machinery appears high and it is hoped that you will be able to reduce it appreciably when forwarding your further offer'.

Being determined not to lose the *Thetis* to a competitor Laird took the none too subtle hint. Within five days of Jubb's pointed letter, Johnson submitted a new quote. After receiving no reply from Jubb, he telephoned the DNC two weeks later with his new offer. 'We have again looked at the tender and in view of the length of the ship being reduced by 2 feet and in the hope that we will be able to build the Sulzer engines cheaper'. He then told Jubb that he could, indeed, beat the original price. The new price was £267,000 (or £140,000 cheaper today) with a delivery time of two years.

The Admiralty had an added incentive. The output of the Admiralty engines was 2,500 BHP and the Sulzers was 3,300 BHP and as speed was not governed under the London Treaty every ounce of power was priceless, especially in combat. Jubb still waited a further two months before informing Johnson that Cammell Laird had won the tender, but emphasizing, 'The Admiralty desire that the vessel be completed in all respects by 10 May 1938 (i.e. twenty-one months from the date of receipt of the building drawings). It is proposed to insert this in the contract accordingly'. This meant a launch date in October 1937. When the Admiralty later pressed Johnson as to why their submarine was not ready to launch on time, he politely informed Their Lordships that the delays were due to non-delivery of essential machine parts that needed to be built into the hull. Now it was the Admiralty who took the hint and immediately quickened the delivery.

The day after the *Thetis* slipped down Laird's ramp Johnson was once again attending another post-launch luncheon. This time the celebration was for the 5,000-ton merchant ship *Jonathan Holt*. To be in a position to launch two vessels in two days may seem like the results of an extremely prosperous yard, but Johnson knew that for many years, long before he fought to win the *Thetis* tender, British shipbuilding was in dire straits. Unlike the previous day, when he made the guests laugh at his *Thetis* quips, this time Johnson stood up in his usual manner before a hushing crowd and without smiling, or delivering his usual quick humour he stared at the 215 guests before him. He admitted what he really thought, both of the state of British shipping, and the full effects that Government apathy was having on the industry. Indirectly he was making a strong plea for Government intervention to save his yard. 'In my opinion, the shipping and ship-building industries are definitely on the downgrade in this country' he began. 'We in this country were pushed aside by foreigners, who were using their brains, subterfuge and subsidies to capture the trade of the world.'

'What,' he added, 'is the good of war ministers and air raid precautions if you have not sufficient ships to keep the country alive? We must remember we nearly lost the last war through lack of ships'. Since 1913 more than twenty yards with a combined building capacity of producing 1,250,000 tons of shipping a year had already closed down and Johnson knew that Laird was not far from becoming just another statistic. In a direct plea to the Government he added, 'I see no prospect of getting merchant ships in this yard unless the Government step in and subsidize shipping and shipbuilding in the same way as the foreigners do it'. He warned that if the situation did not improve his yard would have to cut their workforce from 10,000 to a mere 2,000 with all its disastrous repercussions on the local as well as the national economy. Four years later his appeal would lend credence to Count Michael Alexander's allegations of a conspiracy between Cammell Laird and the Government to ensure that both their financial interests were protected, at the cost of those trapped aboard the stricken submarine.

By the time Johnson gave his pessimistic speech, HMS *Thetis* had already begun her fitting-out programme. Within a couple of months members of her officers and crew arrived at Birkenhead in advance of her final acceptance trials. This was mainly to familiarize themselves with the new vessel from the earliest possible stages and throughout the working-up period. Walter Charles Arnold joined the *Thetis* six days before her launch and was present throughout her year-long fitting out programme and sea trials. As Leading Stoker, his position was in the engine room while on the surface, and in the machinery space in front of the forward escape chamber when dived. As the inside of the *Thetis* grew into a recognizable submarine, more members of her crew joined to watch and learn how their future workplace and home was put together.

At 5 feet 11 inches tall, twenty-five-year old Lieutenant Frederick 'Freddie' Greville Woods was more than a little too tall to work in

5

submarines. Still, he joined his first submarine in 1936 and HMS *Thetis* was Woods' second when he arrived in October 1938 to become her Torpedo Gunnery Officer. A great deal of the torpedo room assembly had not yet taken place, such as many external fittings to the tubes, and the fitting of the bow cap operating mechanisms. This was a unique opportunity for any young submarine officer to see the machinery he was eventually to operate actually being assembled.

He could also examine the machinery and make suggestions to Laird's regarding slight alterations to the way some aspects of the equipment would be ready for use under his control. Woods later recalled one such incident, 'I noticed that the clips on the watertight door in the bulkhead between the tube compartment and the torpedo compartment made the shutting of the door more difficult, because they hung down and prevented the door shutting on to the coaming. I pointed this out to one of Cammell Laird's officials who went down with the submarine and he said he would see what he could do about it'. In fact the design showed all eighteen lugs on which the butterfly nuts as being all of equal length, but on the finished product they certainly were not, making some harder to close than others. Not being able to close this door was a large contributing factor to the disaster.

The preliminary torpedo trial tests took place between 6 and 10 March and were solely to assess her torpedo firing systems and capability. This included checking the torpedo tubes, bow caps, bow shutters (the shaped openings built into the boat's hull that open prior to firing a torpedo) and actually firing dummy torpedoes, or bursts of air out of the tubes. Retired submarine officer Commander Alfred Maguire was valued for his many years experience, and he was invited to assist with submarine torpedo trials. Laird was to work all the equipment under Navy control. After that, the tube builders (in this case Chatham Royal Dockyard) sent a party to examine and test all the tube fittings ready for Maguire's trial. The whole of the firing equipment was worked in his presence, including the loading of a torpedo into each tube. After the preliminary trials, only about thirty minor items were found to need attention, including the fact that Numbers Three and Four bow caps were leaking.

Again the minor faults were eclipsed by further bad luck. Maguire reported, 'The trial was seriously handicapped by the presence of an excessive amount of dirt in and around all the working parts; and in the fore end, and also by the unprepared state of the gear, many pipes being disconnected and several not even made. If an excessive amount of dirt which really handicaps our work is found, we bring it to the notice of the firm in this manner so that it does not occur again, because we are continually going to this firm'.

Maguire noted that the hydraulic bow cap indicator system, also mentioned by Woods, was still very much incomplete. The clips requested by Woods to be fitted to the door in Number Twenty-five bulkhead were either still missing, or dysfunctional. There was a recommendation to fit gauges to each bow cap telemotor receiver to show the pressure on each. When Maguire left, he wrote a rough report of these small jobs for Cammell Laird to carry out before her final dive trials. It was the custom to leave a rough report, so work could begin immediately, before the final typed version was sent to the shipbuilders, which could take another fortnight to arrive.

Another major factor began in March 1939, early on in the various practical trials of both the boat and her equipment before official Admiralty handover. The trials included submerging safely in an enclosed environment as well as undertaking underwater and inclining experiments to determine individual draught and trim characteristics. The first of these trials was held in Cammell Laird's Wet Basin. In order that this condition should be fulfilled, the submarine's gross weight must be known, even before she is fitted out and loaded. This is determined by knowing the weight of torpedoes, stores etc. and adding cast-iron ballast and extra water to her tanks to temporarily make up for the deficiency.

The object of the preliminary trimming experiment was to determine whether the ballast, which had been fitted on board as the result of the design calculations, was sufficiently accurate. If it was not, then it was necessary to establish any important alterations to the permanent ballast already built into the boat. Assistant Naval Constructor George John Stunden took part in all these trials. He remembered how the *Thetis* was taken down until her bridge, gun and periscope brackets were just above the water. Draught boards were placed above the submarine's own draught marks, then simply by looking through the periscope it was possible to measure the actual depth under the keel to get an exact reading for her first trim.

Three weeks later the final ballast and trimming experiments were carried out. Stunden said, 'It is possible to make very precise adjustments – a submarine requires it – and this final trimming experiment is carried out very carefully in order that figures we get from it may be as reliable as possible.' At the same time three inclining experiments were undertaken. These were a submerged inclining experiment, then a low buoyancy and finally a surface one. This was to get the three-dimensional transverse stability of the *Thetis* to ensure she floated on an even keel. During her second experiments some of the ballast did have to be shifted, including 6.1 tons from the bow and a further 4 tons distributed further back in the submarine. When all alterations were finished, she was 2.7 tons light of her 'main ballast trim', the much-needed point at which she could submerge using the hydroplanes alone. Such a deficiency was a built-in safety measure to ensure that she did not plummet during her first real-time dive in the open sea.

Any minor teething problems the *Thetis* had since experienced were about to be eclipsed by a run of ill fortune from this early in her trials right up to the end of her life. On 14 April 1939 she undertook her machinery trials in Liverpool Bay. Such a test was considered a preliminary full sea trial, but the engines were only to be run for eight instead of the mandatory thirty hours required before formal Admiralty acceptance. Leading Stoker Arnold took part in this trial, which was cut short after, in his own words, 'A very unusual occurrence'. During the *Thetis*'s engine run, her lubricating oil system choked. Arnold explained that he thought dirt had got into the different systems because so much time had elapsed between when the engines were fitted and when they were actually used.

What actually happened was that the circulating water to the port engine failed because the 2 feet or so pump spindle shattered through metal fatigue, accentuated by an electric current created between the spindle's metal shaft coming into contact with a bronze impellor to draw in the salt water. It was a design flaw made somewhat worse after Vickers reminded Laird, 'A much better solution would be to make the whole shaft in a stainless quality, as was originally suggested by Messrs Sulzer'.

The trial had to be postponed for a few days, then bad luck struck again during her return to Birkenhead. On 18 April she had completed her eight-hour engine trials and on entering the Wet Basin at 22.00 hours her starboard side struck the 6,980-ton United Molasses tanker *Athelduchess,* moored alongside the Wet Basin's North Wall. Above the waterline no immediate damage was noticeable, but a further survey showed damage to both vessels. The *Athelduchess* had two damaged blades and the pitch was out. On closer examination the *Thetis* had written off one whole propeller and shaft. She needed to be dry docked where the shaft and propeller were removed from the Cammell Laird's build, HMS *Taku*, to ensure the *Thetis* was fit for delivery. The cost to make good all repairs was £534.15.2. That, and a bill from United Molasses for £252.7.9 and repairing the old shaft, came £1,102.3.2, or in today's value a little less than £50,000 for the shunt.

The submarine now had one small formality to undertake before her dive trials. She needed her certificate of seaworthiness, even though not all the work needed to meet that criteria had been completed. The certificate stated that the vessel, 'In respect of strength, stability, seaworthiness, and every other matter on a fit condition for leaving our premises for these trials. Further, that the vessel will not, in any condition of lading [loading], be in an unsatisfactory condition as regards stability. Seamanlike precautions will be taken on each occasion of a sea trial, and provision will be made in this connection, including items mentioned in the clause relating to trials in the hull specification'.

A senior Laird's representative signed the certificate, then the wording was added, 'We see no reason to doubt that the vessel will be, by the date named [30 April, the proposed date for the dive trials], in all respects in a satisfactory condition for leaving Contractors' premises for the purpose stated'. Principal Ship Overseer Lieutenant Albert Hill, inspecting his first T Class submarine, and his assistant, Frank Bailey, were responsible for the *Thetis* and were on board for the trial. Lieutenant Commander Bolus, Glenn, Hill and District Electrical Engineer Bowden countersigned the certificate. She was now considered safe and seaworthy, although this would later become heavily contested. By tradition the final trials were nearly always conducted in Gareloch on the Clyde, Scotland. It was protected naturally and trial dives took place only about a mile offshore.

HMS *Thetis* steamed up from Birkenhead carrying out engine trials and other tests when bad luck struck once again. According to C. Warren and J. Benson in their book '*The Admiralty Regrets ...*' when Lieutenant Commander Bolus gave the order to steer to port, the Thetis promptly swung to starboard. Then when he gave the order to steer to starboard she promptly turned to port. By some incredible piece of incompetence the entire steering gear system had been fitted in reverse. Then, when they did attempt to dive, the forward hydroplanes jammed. Warren and Benson said, 'this state of topsy-turvydom became, for the duration of the trial, a fixed hazard for the officer-of-the-watch and helmsman to negotiate between themselves. While at the outset it caused unbelievable merriment among the crew, the incident did not pass unnoticed by the more sober-thinking persons on

9

board. It seemed strange that acceptance machinery tests, supervised by Admiralty overseers, should have failed to detect so obvious a mistake'.

Eventually the time came for the dive trials. She raised her after hydroplanes, to dive, which worked fine. When dipping her forward ones to increase the angle of dive, they jammed. She was completely unable to dive. If that was not unfortunate enough her after periscope hoist press jammed rendering it, too, useless. Hill's main duty as Principal Ship Overseer was to ensure that Laird fulfilled their duties as far as the Contract was concerned and to ensure that every operation on a trial, however minor, was carried out to the letter. Hill and Bailey jointly decided, along with Bolus, that it would not be suitable to continue the diving trials at this time. Just before leaving Gareloch, Bolus, Hill and Bailey asked Henry Bremner to fetch a chart. The three senior men then decided between themselves that the best place to carry out the dive trials would be Liverpool Bay

The *Thetis* then returned to Birkenhead for further repairs and for a date to be set for another attempt at her real-time dive. On 1 May Maguire re-visited the *Thetis* and found that many, but not all, of his recommendations had been carried out, especially the hydraulic indicators that would show a light once the bow cap was fully open. He later recalled, 'I do not think they could get it to work satisfactorily', adding that Number Six bow cap also now leaked, but it was thought this was due to an obstruction, probably a piece of flotsam jamming its recess. The water in the Wet Basin was not too clean, and a small piece of wood, or something similar could easily jam in the bow cap, causing a leak. Maguire did not think it very serious, but he still noted it in his report, thinking that perhaps a faulty rubber jointing might also have been the problem.

The inside of the torpedo tubes had to be coated with a bitumastic solution, then a hard layer of enamel was added that was finished with a blow lamp to ensure it was fully bonded. This process was essential to ensure the torpedoes had a smooth run into the open sea. The work was sub-contracted with Admiralty approval to the Wailes Dove Bitumastic Company Limited, an experienced firm in this type of specialized work. In fact the tender went out to three firms, but the other two never knew that there was no intention to give the work to any other than Wailes Dove, regardless of price. On 14 May Wailes' employee Hughes spread the bitumastic solution inside all six tubes. As Hughes finished one tube, he went on to the other while John Henry Stinson prepared the enamel. This was no easy job. The solution was a solid glass-like mass that needed a great deal of heat to make it into liquid form. He said, 'We have to gradually render it down until it gets into a liquid state. Should we try to rush the enamel, we are apt to burn it. We completed the whole lot, commencing on the Friday; we completed everything, both enamel work and blow lamp work by Monday night'.

Several weeks later Assistant Admiralty Overseer Edward Grundy testified that the rear doors were *not* coated with enamel when he checked Stinson's work. He was quite clearly under considerable pressure at the time. Not only was it the first time he had ever been tasked with checking bitumastic enamel, but he was concurrently over-seeing different parts of four other submarines and two warships in yards around the country. Unable to stay on one job until its completion, he only got to see the *Thetis* about twice a week. The true events surrounding this one small detail became one of the most hotly contested during the whole official public inquiry culminating in Stinson and Grundy directly contradicting each other. With the court having to believe either the worker or the Admiralty overseer, their decision would have a major impact on the outcome of the inquiry's findings.

A further setback struck on 23 May when the *Thetis* was being re-fuelled for her second attempted dive trials. While the fuel oil was being pumped aboard under high pressure, a relief valve on the oil pipe line located in the control room blew off, forcing high-pressure fuel oil to spray all over the control room. As the sticky, black mass oozed into every possible crevice, it seeped into her Number Three battery space necessitating the removal of both cells and a full survey of the insulated space to ensure no lasting damage was done. The rosbonite (a bitumastic waterproofing and sealing agent) coating in the battery flat was damaged and the whole of the batteries in this space had to be removed, taken out of the submarine and placed on the quay, the full job costing another £256.15.10, or about £12,000 today. So far Laird had put in insurance claims for about £70,000 in today's value and the submarine had yet to make her first dive.

The following day Laird submitted to the Admiralty their amended fourteen-day diving trial and completion programme, which was covered by an insurance claim for the first failed attempt in Gareloch. The most important of these trials was to begin on 1 June and included diving and diesel electric tests, adjust compasses and proceed to her pre-designated dive position about fifteen miles due west of the Bar

Lightship in Liverpool Bay. Along the way she was to carry out trials on the after hydroplane, on secondary power and local control. Auxiliary steering trials were also planned at full power on both her telemotor system and local control. After that she was due to start her diving trials before returning to Birkenhead at about 22.30 hours. A detailed cleaning, storing, gunnery inspection and embarkation of naval stores were next. Then the *Thetis* would be ready to hand over formally to the Royal Navy, ready to leave Cammell Laird for operational service as part of the Fifth Submarine Flotilla at 08.30 hours two weeks later on Thursday 15 June.

One of the last speakers at the *Thetis* launch party exactly ten months and twenty-eight days earlier was Commander R. A. Hawksworth of HMS *Ark Royal*. He stood up and proposed the health of Cammell Laird, wishing he could put into adequate words the loyal co-operation between the civilian shipbuilder and the Royal Navy. In reply, naval architect Mr F. G. John said, 'We are proud of the fact that [Laird] is one of the few selected firms to build submarines for the Government and have been for more than twenty years'.

John continued, 'My engineering friends tell me that ship construction has not improved since the time of Noah, but the best reply was to sail in the ship that was launched today. Not that I want to belittle Noah, but Noah was the first builder, the first owner and the first officer'. John concluded somewhat ironically, 'I suppose that the first submarine officer was Jonah, although whether he was in full command was doubtful, but he came out all right. We hope that those who go to sea in HMS *Thetis* would come out all right, and that her commander would become as famous as Jonah himself'. Comparing the *Thetis*'s commanding officer to Jonah was unfortunate. With Jonah being a symbol throughout the world as the bringer of ill fortune, the *Thetis*'s run of bad luck was about to change from the irritating to the tragic.

Chapter 2

Morning Departure

Alfred Ernest Godfrey had been the master of various Liverpool Screw Towing & Lighterage Company tugs for more than thirty-five years and had been in command of their 169-ton tug *Grebe Cock* for the last two. She carried a standard complement of seven men, including master, mate, able seaman, ordinary seaman, chief engineer, second engineer and fireman. On 31 May 1939 the *Grebe Cock* was moored in Liverpool's Alexandra Dock when Godfrey received orders to be at Cammell Laird's Wet Basin at 09.00 hours the following morning. All he knew was that he had to attend a new submarine called HMS *Thetis*, which was due to undertake her diving and equipment trials before Admiralty acceptance as a fully-fledged weapon of war.

Later on that day he was further instructed to carry a small boat to disembark surplus civilian personnel after the equipment trials and before the *Thetis* made her series of test dives. Cammell Laird's Fitter James Lauder had already closed down the three port torpedo tubes and left them in the 'shut' position with the power turned off a few days earlier. Instructions were then given for no one to touch them. 'They were absolutely sealed for the last time', he said. Although they were sealed, this was a figure of speech used at Laird to mean that they were shut down tightly and not to be used without express orders. Assistant Head Foreman Frank Miller Black ensured that the three starboard tubes were also locked and – metaphorically at least – sealed.

Leading Stoker Walter Arnold rose early on 1 June. The morning was already promising to develop into another scorching summer day across Liverpool, the River Mersey and out into the Irish Sea. During the previous week the weather had been getting gradually warmer, with temperatures reaching 70°F later that day. After washing and putting on his naval uniform Arnold walked the short distance north from his house at 30 Park Side Road, Tranmere, to Laird's Wet Basin.

The *Thetis* was moored against the Basin's Boiler Shop Wall, a berth on its east side. He arrived at 08.00 hours, climbed the wooden gangway on to the submarine, and descended into her pressure hull. The smell of oil, grease and new paint filled his nostrils as he edged past the myriad of people, making last-minute preparations before her morning departure. Crouching his way through the watertight door into the engine room he spent the next four hours there, getting the fuel tanks prepared and filled before Bolus gave the order to start the main engines.

While Arnold was busy in the engine room, Lieutenant Woods and Cammell Laird's Assistant Foreman Shipwright John Rowe arrived at the *Thetis* about an hour later. Rowe ordered a dinghy so he could take her draughts before she was due to sail about forty-five minutes later. He asked Cammell Laird's Forman Engineer, Arthur 'Archie' Robinson, to blow the external tanks. This was necessary to ensure that no water had crept back into the supposedly empty tanks to give a false draught and thus a wrong trim. Once they were blown, Robinson informed Rowe that he could take the draughts.

Foreman Engineer Frank Shaw was employed exclusively in Cammell Laird's outside engineering department. His job was fitting the main propelling machinery on the *Thetis* as well as the auxiliary machinery just outside her engine room. She was the fourth submarine he had worked on, making him well experienced in his field. Shaw had also been on board for all dock trials, preliminary Mersey and official Clyde trials and was well aware of the minor teething problems the *Thetis* had suffered since first trying to put to sea several months before.

Thirty-year-old ship fitter Archibald Craven left his house in Lansdowne Road, Birkenhead, for his brief walk to Laird's yard, having said goodbye to his ten-year-old son, John, and wife Mabel. His colleague, twenty-seven-year old fitter David Norman Duncan, was un-married and had no children. A Scot from Edinburgh, David's only close family was his seventy-one-year old mother Rose whom he barely saw these days due to his work in Birkenhead. Gilbert Henry Dobells, was a sixty-three-year old caterer who, along with his colleague, forty-seven-year old William George Bath, was employed to prepare and serve food to all the extra men embarked for the trials. Both men had worked for Liverpool City Caterers for many years and had served lunch on numerous Cammell Laird shipping trials and this one was set to be another routine set-up-and-serve affair.

14

Dobells had no children, just his wife, Jessie, to whom he said goodbye before heading for the Wet Basin. Bath said goodbye to his wife, Bessie, and his only child, eight-year-old Elsie, but others, like twenty-seven-year old Laird's engine fitter Cornelius Smith, had Marie, aged fifteen, right down to little Edith, aged just nine months. Lunch would be presented on specially erected tables and chairs extending through the forward torpedo stowage compartment and adjoining crew mess area. All the extra furniture and boxes made the already cramped space even more restricted and would, within a few hours, greatly hamper any attempt to seal off the rapidly flooding area from the rest of the submarine.

Godfrey sailed as ordered on 1 June to arrive at the *Thetis* for 09.00 hours. As he steamed down the Mersey a haze hung in the air and the rising temperature enhanced the typical port smells of salt, iodine and fuel oil drifting through the air, the brackish bleach-like tang forever changing on the rising heat. Passing the Princes Landing Stage Godfrey looked up at the Royal Liver Building's clock and adjusted his watch to its time rather than his own. For all his experience of towing every type of sea-going craft, from warships, to luxury liners to cargo vessels, even accompanying submarines clear of the Liverpool Bar Light, a submarine on her dive trials was a first. Having not been informed in any way of what his duties would entail, Godfrey tied up near the Wet Basin, went ashore, and approached Cammell Laird's Dockmaster, Taylor, to make further enquiries. The Dockmaster could only tell Godfrey that he would be taking a small party with him aboard the *Grebe Cock*, additional to his standard seven-man crew, but could give no other information.

Shortly before the *Thetis* was due to leave, Godfrey was still very much in the dark as to what he was actually supposed to do. He remembered, 'Mr Taylor then said that Mr Watters, who I understood was the Assistant Shipyard Manager, would be at the *Thetis*, and I said I would walk up to see him. Mr Taylor replied, "I'm going up that way, I'll come with you." Just as we arrived at the gangway of the *Thetis* a Naval Officer – whom I later learned was Lieutenant Commander Bolus, the Captain of the *Thetis*, arrived.' Taylor met Bolus and introduced Godfrey as the master of the attending tug. Bolus greeted Godfrey with a cheery 'good morning' and the two men shook hands. The tug master then admitted to the commander, 'I've never attended a submarine on her trials before, so what do you want me to do?'

Bolus replied, 'Well, you're in Laird's hands, but I'd like you to keep in touch with the *Thetis* during the whole trial'.

'What speeds will you be doing?'

Bolus said, 'About 15 to 16 knots'. This was more than a little too fast for the *Grebe Cock* to keep up.

'Our full speed is only about 11½ to 12 knots.'

'I'm glad you mentioned that point,' said Bolus, 'I'll accommodate you regarding the speeds'.

Godfrey had every reason to want the *Thetis* to match his speed. 'I told [Bolus] of a case of accompanying a submarine away where she was doing 13 knots, and the boat I was in could only do 10 knots. The submarine ran away from us and I never saw her again'. Godfrey still did not even know where the dive trials were going to be, but while talking to Bolus, he noticed Mersey Pilot Norman D. Wilcox on the submarine's bridge. 'I saw him with the chart in his hand, so I asked him where he intended to do the diving trials. He replied, "Away in the direction of the Calf", so I took it was the Calf of Man'. The Calf of Man is a one-mile² island just off the southwestern extremity of the Isle of Man. The rather apt name refers to the Danish word 'kalfr', meaning a small island near to a bigger one.

Still unsure of his role in the day's dive trials, Godfrey asked Bolus if the *Thetis* needed to be towed out of Laird's Basin. After all it was a job he had been tasked with doing so many times before. Bolus gave a firm 'no', as the submarine would pull out of the Basin under her own steam. The two men then, literally minutes before setting sail, worked out a rough idea of what the *Grebe Cock*'s part was going to be that day. Bolus wanted her at the dive site by 13.00 hours, asking Godfrey whether they could agree a rendezvous point. He suggested the Bar Lightship, northwest of Birkenhead, to which Bolus agreed. Godfrey then walked back to the *Grebe Cock* and prepared her for sea.

One of the extra personnel Godfrey was instructed to carry was Lieutenant Richard Evelyn Coltart. He had been in submarines for five of his thirteen years in the Royal Navy. Bolus had told Coltart that he was to go in the *Grebe Cock* for the diving trials, as he was standing by on her sister ship, the Cammell Laird's build HMS *Trident*. 'I asked him what kind of communications should we have', said Coltart. 'We discussed it and came to the conclusion that there were only two methods we could have used; that was by tapping on the hull of the tug and by explosive charges dropped overboard'. Bolus decided to dismiss both ideas. Instead he would have a good look round with the periscope before going below periscope depth, and would not be there long enough for a vessel to approach.

Apart from that, Coltart's duties were pretty clear-cut. '[We] were to keep an eye on her periscopes, the mast and the red flag; to follow-up while she was at periscope depth at a reasonable distance, and when she had gone below periscope depth, I was to look out for any surface vessels, although I should not have been able to communicate with her had there been any, owing to Lieutenant Commander Bolus saying that he would take a good look round before he went deep'.

Captain Harry Percy Kendall Oram was commander of the Fifth Submarine Flotilla located at the submarine base at Fort Blockhouse, Gosport, Hampshire. He had very little to do with the acceptance of a new submarine, except with supplying stores and ensuring Navy discipline. On this occasion Oram decided to accompany Bolus and his officers for this dive trial, not so much to assist in the operations, but to assess the officers for competence and possible promotion. He had always felt that all too often recommendations for promotion were based solely on third-party reports and he was keen to see for himself in real time just how competent officers under his overall command really were. At 09.30 hours on Thursday, 1 June he arrived at the *Thetis*, casually dressed in civilian clothes and boarded her to make his officer assessments.

More than 100 men were now aboard. As well as her normal crew of fifty-two official Naval personnel, the others were a further eight officers posted from other T Class submarines, there for the experience. Thirty-seven assorted civilian technicians were aboard to check and operate essential machinery, according to Admiralty contract, who in turn were watched by seven Admiralty overseeing officers. The remainder were Pilot Norman Wilcox, Captain Oram and the two Liverpool City Caterers, Dobells and Bath.

Rowe climbed down the ladder into a dinghy and rowed across the mirror-calm water around the *Thetis* to read her draught marks on both port and starboard sides on her bow and stern. The forward end, portside was 13 feet, 3¾ inches. The starboard bow was at 13 feet, 1½ inches. The after portside was 14 feet, 8¾ inches and the starboard after end was at 14 feet, 6¼ inches. Taken altogether these figures showed she had a 2½ inches port list. Not a good way to start any voyage, let alone a first dive trial. He then took his dinghy to the wall and climbed a ladder to report his measurements to Assistant

Overseer Edward Gisborne. Rowe said that after getting his draughts they would trim the ship ready for going out in the diving trial. This would include removing the 2½ inches port list through blowing or filling tanks as a counter measure.

For Gisborne's benefit, Rowe again took the draughts when she was ready to leave, 'We walked to the gangway and Mr Hill and Mr Bailey were standing there with a piece of paper'. The paper showed that her four draughts had now changed to portside forward 13 feet, 8 inches, starboard side 13 feet, 4¾ inches. The after draughts had also altered to portside 14 feet, 7½ inches and starboard side to 14 feet, 4½ inches. All put together this meant that instead of reducing the list it had, in fact, crept up to 3¾ inches. Bailey had also taken the draughts, well partly at least. Rowe continued, 'I drew his attention to the fact that he only took the portside. The portside of the ship was to the quay. I drew his attention to the draught on the starboard side, and he mentioned to Mr Hill they could fill the starboard tubes'.

Lieutenant Woods was standing on the casing. One of his first jobs before the *Thetis* left was to remove the gangway. As Woods ordered the last solid link with the quay to be dragged off the submarine, all those below heard the distinct scraping and clatter as it left the *Thetis* and they knew they were on their way. The gangway was being taken off so quickly that Rowe had to jump on it and then ashore in two moves, before Woods cast it off, Rowe looked back to see his three superiors, Hill, Gisborne and Bailey, descend into the submarine's interior.

Once the gangway was clear, Bolus gave the order to release the mooring lines and start engines. HMS *Thetis* slipped smoothly away from the quay with Bolus shouting departure orders through his small, highly polished, brass megaphone. She nosed out directly opposite Liverpool Anglican Cathedral across the River Mersey, her grey hull and casing looking almost white against the bright sunshine and low summer mist. She turned left towards the open sea, gliding past the Three Graces, the Liverpool Port Authority Building, the Cunard Building and the Royal Liver Building dominating the skyline on their starboard side. The hazy sunshine made all three Liverpool landmarks look bleached of their natural stone colour as the *Thetis* slid by and onwards into the glittering open sea.

At 10.25 hours the *Grebe Cock* finally let go her moorings in the Wet Basin and steamed out towards the rendezvous point. She arrived at the Bar Lightship at about 12.00 hours, *Thetis* and *Grebe Cock* running neck and neck, until the submarine sailed past the tugboat with ease. The weather was very fine, with a light east-south-easterly breeze, the Irish Sea was mirror-calm, and the tide had just started to ebb.

Woods stayed on deck until about forty-five minutes before the trial dive. Just prior to her proposed descent, he entered the submarine through the forward hatch and struggled through the torpedo room and stowage compartment. He had to negotiate all the tables and chairs where the men were about to eat, politely excusing himself to the many extra personnel, who had formed into small groups and were getting in his way. For his own interest Woods looked at the trim chit, which he believed Laird had given to First Lieutenant Harold 'Bert' Chapman. The trim chit was a piece of paper with all tanks printed in blurred, blue ink down the left margin with leader dots running half way across the paper. Numbers representing how much each tank held were written in pencil at the end of each line of dots. The state of the torpedo tubes was scribbled on the bottom as an afterthought. All tubes were said to be empty except Numbers Five and Six, the two lowest tubes that had been filled to complete her trim.

During the journey out to the Bar, a vacuum test was also put on the pressure hull to check for any leaks. This required dropping the internal air pressure to help draw any outside water through possible leaks in the pressure hull. At sea level any leak found would not be that much of a problem, but at her full diving depth, under considerable depth-charge attack, any weakness, however small, could be disastrous. When the *Grebe Cock* was about 200 yards off the submarine, Godfrey said to Lieutenant Coltart, 'Supposing she submerges altogether, shall we see any trace of her? If she goes under water, shall we see any air bubbles or any track like a torpedo makes?'

'No', replied the Lieutenant, 'there will be nothing at all to be seen if she submerges'. Coltart then ordered Crosby to signal Bolus to discover if she would, indeed, be diving below periscope depth. Victor James Crosby had been a wireless telegraphist in submarines for seven years. He had been standing by in the *Thetis*'s sister ship, HMS *Trident* when his First Lieutenant instructed him to join the *Grebe Cock* and to take a lamp and batteries for signals. His primary duty was to send and receive all messages to and from the *Thetis* as well as to keep an accurate log of times and messages sent. The *Grebe Cock* did not have an official logbook, so Crosby had to record his messages on scraps of paper and create an official log later on.

19

After the *Thetis* had received the signal, Bolus replied, 'No, we will have you in view with our periscopes and red flag showing above the surface'.

'Very good, Sir', Godfrey answered, as he remained stopped until the *Thetis* was at a safe distance of about 300 yards ahead. After the *Grebe Cock* had fallen about half a mile astern, Bolus ordered a signal to be sent, saying that he was adjusting compasses. The Bar Lightship was a common place to carry out these trials, although the location was kept secret, as a submarine was very vulnerable to enemy attack at this crucial time because it required the vessel to be stationary for part of the time. Godfrey noted that at about 13.30 hours the *Thetis* signalled that she was about to carry out full speed turning trials, which meant careering around at full speed in all directions. He tried to keep his tug as near as possible following astern, but on some occasions the *Thetis* got well ahead.

Aboard the submarine preparations were being made to secure her for diving in slow time. Although the crew was highly skilled, a virgin dive was never carried out at speed so that men and machine could be broken in with ease, without risking any possible human or mechanical failure. They were nearly ready. Bolus spread the word throughout the submarine for anyone leaving to get to the bridge at once. No one did. He then gave instructions down the voice-pipe for the diving signal to be sent to Fort Blockhouse. First Lieutenant Chapman informed Bolus that the submarine had been shut off, that is, all external vents were closed and the engine room exhaust secured.

Bolus then raised his brass megaphone, pointed it towards Godfrey and squinting into the dazzling early afternoon light, he delivered his four, clipped sentences that within two hours would play such a key role in the death of the *Thetis* and those aboard her. He took a deep breath, 'We are about to dive', was the first sentence. 'No one is leaving the *Thetis*. All are accompanying us on board for the dive. My diving course is 310°.' Bolus then issued instructions as to how Godfrey was to be of use. He shouted, 'I want you to follow on my port quarter, Captain, at a distance of half a mile'.

Oram, Bolus, Leading Telegraphist William E. Allen and pilot Norman Wilcox then went down through the lower conning tower hatch, which was closed behind them. As soon as Bolus landed in the control room he ordered the main tanks to be flooded in slow time. Within seconds water was rushing first into Number One tank in the bows and Numbers Four, Five and Six pairs down each side of the hull.

Twelve columns of air and water mixed together and rose about 20 feet into the sky from the tanks, screaming like a jet engine as tons of water were sucked into the void. The noise was so loud that Coltart and Godfrey could hear the roar half a mile away. Cammell Laird's representative Ernest John Randles was also present aboard the *Grebe Cock*, on behalf of the shipbuilder, and he was to act as a liaison officer between Godfrey and Coltart if the need arose. He told Godfrey that Wilcox would be leaving the submarine at the Bar to board the pilot boat there.

Godfrey replied, 'It doesn't look as if the pilot is leaving, as she is already passing Number One Pilot Boat at speed and has made no signal'.

'Randles answered, 'Well, that was the instruction'.

In fact Wilcox had definite orders to leave the *Thetis*. On 31 May the Superintendent of Pilotage issued a memorandum to Number One, the *Charles Livingstone*, that Cammell Laird wished Wilcox to be discharged at the Bar before the dive trials took place. The Superintendent added, 'It is hoped that nothing will interfere with this request being carried out'. Pilot Ernest Bibby was Second Master aboard the *Charles Livingstone* who, when in position, saw that the *Thetis* was not flying a flag to show that Wilcox was, indeed, disembarking. Bibby got the pilot boat to within 100 feet of the *Thetis*. He could clearly see Wilcox on the bridge with two naval officers. Bibby hailed through his megaphone, '*Thetis* ahoy, I have special orders to take you over board'. Seeing Wilcox, Bibby knew perfectly well the pilot was addressing him. Bibby received no verbal reply, but saw Wilcox wave his arms in a way that meant he was not leaving. He again hailed Wilcox, 'Are you coming over board?' Again Wilcox just waved his arms. 'There was no indication that *Thetis* was slowing down and I accordingly ordered hard a port and rang "slow" on the telegraph and let *Thetis* proceed'.

Normally Bolus would sound the boat's klaxon to speed all hands to their dive station, but as this was a trial dive, every stage was being undertaken virtually in slow motion to maximize on safety and maintain control if anything should go wrong. Woods stayed in the torpedo compartment right forward and tube space along with Able Seaman Stanley Crombleholme, who was stationed watching Number One main vent and auxiliary vent in the tube space. He had to crouch high up between Numbers One and Two tubes to maintain his diving station. Torpedo Gunner's Mate Ernest Mitchell was near the telephone

21

chatting to engine room artificer Harold Howell, on the after side of Number Twenty-Five bulkhead, leading out from the torpedo space into the stowage area where Dobells and Bath were preparing lunch. Leading Seaman John Turner was watching Number Two main vent at the after end of the torpedo compartment as the dive commenced. Everyone throughout the submarine was now in position.

Once the tanks were full, the *Thetis* should be at neutral buoyancy when the slight tweak downwards on the forward and upwards on the after hydroplanes were enough to glide her effortlessly beneath the surface and on her way. Now, with everyone in position – and the hydroplane blades correctly pitched – she refused to dive. Being a first attempt, it should have taken about fifteen to twenty minutes at the most to find neutral buoyancy. After that something was most definitely wrong. Twenty minutes later auxiliary tanks were flooded. Still nothing. Some 250 tons of water had now filled her throughout and still she refused to leave the surface.

Until the submarine reached her diving station, Engine Fitter Frank Shaw's duty was to attend the port engine, and then for the dive he was to remain in the control room in case he was still needed. Just prior to the dive he was ordered to proceed to diving stations as planned, and he immediately left the engine room and went forward into the control room for further instructions. All hatches were again checked and the routine vacuum test was put on the ship to ensure that nothing was left open before she dived. The test took five to ten minutes during which time Shaw took part in the examination within the control room.

When the order for diving stations came, Arnold went to his place at the forward pumping controls. 'My orders there came through either on an indicator or by telephone, the indicator for pumping and the telephone for flooding'. There was a good half hour between when the engines stopped and the dive was attempted. Arnold remembered First Lieutenant Chapman going through the boat to check on different valves connected with the dive, trying to discover what had gone wrong. The next thing Arnold recalled was the main vents opening, albeit for a short time, but not long enough to take the *Thetis* right down. Still she was hovering just on the surface refusing to go down.

During the attempted dive, Arnold got orders to flood the tanks forward. He opened three valves. This did not admit water to the tanks, but only to the main line. Once Arnold allowed the water to flood in, the tanks were filled independently by crew members in individual compartments. Then he was told to look for leaks. Arnold found one above his pumping station and climbed up to see where it was coming from. He located the leak in part of the humidifier pipe where the water was seeping in around it. Not a major leak, but one that needed notifying.

Captain Oram remained in the control room. He said, trying to justify the problem, 'During the next quarter of an hour it was quite clear to those of us in the control room that the amount of angle on the hydroplanes or horizontal rudders, which were trying to take the submarine under water without success, gave us the clear impression that the submarine was very light. This would be quite normal as, to err on the side of safety, the trim was probably made out on the light side'. She then went down a little, but like a massive air bubble she kept fighting to reach the surface while the hydroplanes strained to take her down. The effect was of a submarine bouncing across the surface. After about half an hour of this relentless juddering it was clear to Oram that the lightness was in the forward end of the ship, and, as the majority of the tanks had already been filled, he could see that First Lieutenant Chapman was just a little puzzled.

Oram turned to Bolus, 'I wonder if Number Five and Number Six tubes are full?

'I don't think they should be full', came a voice from somewhere in the crowded control room. It was never determined from whom.

'They should be by the trim statement', Chapman confirmed to the voice. The *Thetis*'s log also read, '10.55 flood 5 & 6 tubes. 10.56. 5 & 6 tubes flooded'. During the next few minutes, it did not really matter anyway. Confusion soon broke out across the control room. Whatever the condition really was, they most certainly needed to be filled right now, or at least confirmation received that they were, so another reason could be investigated as to why they could not dive. Throughout this episode there is no recorded reference as to whether the *Thetis*'s log was consulted independently of the trim chit, or professional opinion taken to accept their true position.

Woods returned to the forward tube space and ordered hydraulic pressure to be put on to the bow caps should the tubes need to be filled. This meant opening two small wheels on each side of the bow cap-operating lever only, and would not open the bow caps themselves. The effect was similar to turning a car ignition, so the engine is ticking over. Then it is just matter of putting it into gear to transfer the power to the wheels, or in this case the bow caps. He then checked to see if they were full by opening a small test cock on the tube's rear doors.

Number Six tube gave a small dribble, indicating it was at least half full. Number Five gave no dribble, squirt of water under pressure, or puff of air, indicating there was not even any pressure in the tube, let alone water. Woods returned to the control room and asked Chapman again to confirm if Five and Six tubes were meant to be full. Chapman consulted the trim chit and said 'yes'. Woods later testified, 'I said I did not think they were full. He asked Mr Robinson of Cammell Laird whether Numbers Five and Six tubes were meant to be full. Mr Robinson said "No".'

For all his experience on the high seas, Godfrey had never seen a submarine dive before. Still, her efforts to get below the surface seemed more than a little odd. She appeared at times to be rolling from side to side, or going down slightly by the bow or stern before bobbing back to the surface. At one point she even veered to port for no apparent reason, her laboured attempts looking all the more striking as both he and Coltart watched the light-grey submarine fight to submerge. Instead of the usual minute to go down, she struggled for nearly an hour while her hydroplanes fought a losing battle against her far from neutral buoyancy. Godfrey turned to Lieutenant Coltart, 'She seems to be making a long job of it. I thought a submarine can dive in a minute'.

'Yes, that's the usual time,' said Coltart, 'a crash dive only takes about thirty seconds'.

Meanwhile Woods inspected the mechanical bow cap indicators for all the tubes to make sure they were closed. All six indicators were located in the centre of the 4 feet, 6 inch space between the port and starboard tubes, on the forward bulkhead. They were all positioned vertically, but not in numeric order. From top to bottom the sequence ran in twos like a mirror image, so what was read on the upper indicator appeared opposite for its partner. Number Two was uppermost, mirrored with Number One below, so open and shut were opposite to each other. Then came Numbers Four and Three and finally at the bottom, Numbers Six and Five. Woods was adamant, 'I remember repeating in my mind, as I looked at each indicator, the words "Shut", "Shut", "Shut", looking at Number Five first [at the bottom] and then progressing upwards. I was satisfied at the time that it did show me shut'. He did not look at the hydraulic indicators as they were still not working properly, and they would only have shown when the bow caps

24

were fully open. Woods started with Number One tube. He opened the test cock. A faint hiss of air escaped. No water.

Leading Seaman Walter Hambrook was assisting with the rear doors. He was a very accomplished submariner with more than four year's experience operating torpedo tubes. Both men knew each other well after serving together aboard the Oberon Class submarine HMS *Osiris* about three years earlier, where the tube lever layout was identical to the *Thetis*. Confident that only Number Six tube held water, Woods wanted to open each one in turn to ensure no caps were leaking. Hambrook was standing by the lever of each rear door as it was opened, Woods had to stand on the bottom rear door handle to reach the top tubes. He then repeated the procedure for Number Two tube. The same hiss of air escaped from the test cock and, again, upon opening the door the tube was dry. The same procedure was carried out for Numbers Three and Four tubes, missing Number Six, as he already knew it was at least half full.

Woods later remembered, 'I opened Number Five test cock in the same manner previously and there was no sign of air or water. Then assisted by the rating mentioned [Leading Seaman Hambrook], I commenced to open Number Five rear door'. The door was so stiff that Hambrook had to kick the lever upwards with considerable force before the door began to move. At first a small amount of water trickled out from behind the rear door's bottom. Woods continued 'I thought this was just a little that had not been drained away. I have seen this happen before'.

Watching from the bridge of the *Grebe Cock*, Leading Telegraphist Crosby noticed that the *Thetis* seemed to have difficulty in diving as though she was rather too light. Her bows did submerge and her stern rose. She then levelled up so that her guardrails were awash then her stern went up again for a short time and after a little while she levelled up again, this time awash up to her gun and half her bridge. He said, 'She remained like that for a very short time, and then dropped down bodily with very much the same effect as you would get if you pushed a round stick into a deep pond straight down'.

Godfrey also saw her trying to go down, at one point she was partly submerged. 'Then she seemed to level up a bit. She then went down by the head and appeared to me to be in trouble. I thought she was trying to make surface again. She then went down by the head again and this time disappeared completely. She appeared to me to go down like a stone'.

Chapter 3

Trials & Errors

The rear door Hambrook was trying to kick open had blown back in an instant under the explosive force from tons of inrushing seawater. Woods shouted, 'Get out of the compartment!' He then turned to Petty Officer Mitchell, who was still standing stunned by the telephone and screamed, 'Tell them to blow for Christ's sake!' Meanwhile Jamison, and Crombleholme had already struggled out of the rapidly flooding area, leaving Woods and Howell to follow on behind. Within seconds the level had reached the test cocks in the middles of the two lower tubes, Numbers Five and Six and was rising rapidly.

Woods was convinced that the inrush was not due to an open bow cap. His instant assumption, being so certain that the bow caps were shut, was that there must be a fracture at the forward end of the tube. For this reason he did not try to get at the bow cap levers on the starboard bulkhead. They were grouped in threes on both sides about 5 feet up from the deck, levers Two, Four and Six being on the port side, and Numbers One, Three and Five in the mirror position on the starboard side. Had Woods done so, he could well have stopped the inrush almost immediately and averted the unstoppable, disastrous chain of events now unfolding.

Frank Shaw was still in the control room after being relieved of duty on the port engine and was making general conversation with his colleague, Arthur Watkinson. Suddenly the still air became a strong gust as it blew through the control room on its way to the after end, sucking dust, and loose papers in its wake. Only seconds had passed and the *Thetis* was already taking a sharp bow-down attitude. Shaw was flung bodily against the Number Sixty-nine watertight door, leading forward into Bolus's cabin and the officer's wardroom while other men were flung against each other, or the equipment normally used to control the submarine's every movement.

27

Oram turned to Bolus and told him to blow main tanks immediately. As the compressed air forced its way into the tops of the tanks the water was pressed out at the bottom and her bow began to rise, albeit very slowly. She was now fighting against the laws of physics. The water was being forced out of the tanks at about two tons per second, while the inrush through the now gaping Number Five torpedo tube was pouring in at about three-and-a-half tons per second. She did rise and her bow did break the surface. Oram, Bolus, Woods and the other 100 men aboard must have felt relief that such a near miss could just have easily gone the other way.

Items not sucked into the stern-bound air-rush soon slid along tables and counter tops towards the bow this time and everyone knew that the submarine's battle to beat the inrush was lost. The bow ever so slowly tipped downwards, gaining speed with every passing second, forcing more water through the tube and into the *Thetis*. More than half the submarine's reserve of high-pressure air had just been wasted. Bolus stopped blowing to save the precious compressed air for another perhaps more needy use. All he could do for now was order all unnecessary lights to be switched off to save battery power and, without knowing the full extent of the damage, to close all five watertight doors throughout the submarine.

Back in the rapidly flooding fore end, the water was passing the test cocks on tubes two and four, meaning twenty-three tons of water had already flooded the compartment. Woods could see that the force of water blasting through the open tube was throwing Hambrook about the tiny compartment, as he crashed and bounced off all the valves, pipes and other steel fittings like a rag doll. 'I had to stand at the side of the compartment to assist him and haul him up', said Woods. Although he later admitted, 'It occurred to me that what I ought to do was to close the door on him, but I preferred to wait and assist him. I had to assist him out of the compartment, which meant that some time was wasted before the port watertight door could be closed'.

Only about eight seconds had now passed since the rear door was opened. The water had now reached the top two tubes, meaning thirty-three tons was inside the pressure hull and about to enter the torpedo stowage compartment. Woods' admission that 'some time was wasted' was an understatement. Altogether the compartment needed only forty-five tons of water to completely fill the space – or about twelve seconds. However noble Woods' actions were, every second spent trying to pull

28

Hambrook out of the churning vortex allowed another two tons of water to pour in.

Had Hambrook been left behind, the other three men would have had many more precious seconds to prevent the flood from spreading to the next compartment, which ultimately sealed the fate of nearly all those on board. Eight days earlier the United States Navy submarine USS *Squalus* had also sunk on her dive trials due to a massive inflow through her engine room. Closing the watertight doors ensured that thirty-three men survived, but they did so knowing that locking men still alive in the rear half of the submarine was their only chance of survival. The practice was not uncommon aboard stricken submarines of all navies.

Like many submarines and ships, the *Thetis* was designed for an optimum amount of accidental or combat related flooding above and beyond her normal operating conditions. The effect, known as Archimedes' principal dictates that the buoyancy of a floating mass pushing down on a liquid equal to the force it is pushing against, it will float because of the amount of liquid the weight displaces. In theory, if the maths are right any weight or size of ship can be made to float, but alter its buoyancy through flooding and the Archimedes Principal will be no more.

The effect was similar to what ultimately sank the 45,000-ton White Star liner *Titanic*. She could survive with four compartments flooded, but when water entered the fifth she was doomed. In the case of an early 1,090-ton T Class submarine this was only one compartment, specifically the Torpedo room from the tip of the bow to Number Twenty-five bulkhead. Should she be flooded beyond that point, then trying to surface under normal conditions was impossible. In such a dire situation if it was a choice between drowning men in a compartment and saving the submarine, the men had to be sacrificed. That was it, however cruel, it was the sacrifice of a few for the many and every submariner knew it.

When most of the men were out of the torpedo room and into the stowage compartment, Lieutenant Jamison and Howell still tried to shut the watertight door to prevent flooding that section any more. The original Admiralty design had specified a quick-closing door controlled by a central wheel, that, once spun, could lock the door all the way round in one quick, smooth action. Bearing in mind that this was a collision bulkhead, a later revision of the plan changed this to a cheaper and less complicated type that was opened and closed with the eighteen butterfly bolts all round the door, each needing to be screwed into corresponding hasps welded on to the surrounding bulkhead. It took considerably longer to shut, and as a first line of defence against severe bow damage, it was in retrospect totally impractical.

Howell and Jamison tried to shut the door and screw in all eighteen bolts, but they faced several major problems. A latch held the door firmly in its 'open' position and they had to get round the door, back into the vortex and let the latch go. This was no easy task with tons of icy water pouring in. The further the submarine dipped down, the increasing angle made the door heavier and thus harder to release from its latch because it was designed to open towards the bow rather than away from it. Woods added, 'I do not think that the clips for securing the door were being held up in their stage position by the spring fittings which I have previously mentioned, and thus the clips hung down and jammed against the coaming when the door was shut'. Water and foam were now flowing into the torpedo room up to Number Three and Four tubes and now free flowing into the next space where Dobells' and Bath's boxes, tables and chairs started to float in the swirling torrent.

They struggled in the bitterly cold water for what felt like hours instead of seconds as they tried, time and again, to frantically align the bolts with the hasps and lock the door shut. With their hands almost numb with cold, just as they thought they were winning a butterfly bolt hanging down jammed at the bottom of the door and its surround ensuring that there was no airtight seal. As if the situation could not get any worse, the lights flickered and went out, plunging the men into icy, disorienting darkness. Eventually Howell did manage to get just one clip on as best he could when it became patently obvious that too much water had, and was still, entering the torpedo stowage compartment. One clip was simply not enough to hold back the force of the water, as it bent the door back against the one clip and kept on bubbling in. One clip at the top had the effect of compressing the watertight rubber seal at the top of the door, forcing the bottom outwards, which allowed the water to warp the door inwards due to the pressure against it.

They were now faced with a serious dilemma. They could either stay to try to stop any more water from entering the second compartment and cling on to Archimedes Principal, or they could give up this section to save the next, knowing that the submarine was not likely to surface again. Not being able to surface again was not now the most immediate problem. Losing the third compartment carried much larger far reaching problems than not ever resurfacing. Housed in this section were the forward crew space and wardroom, but underneath the deck plates was the submarine's battery stowage areas. Had seawater reached the terminals, all the crew would be aware of was the distinctive pineapple and pepper odour of a deadly cloud of chlorine gas. Very shortly their eyes, throats and lungs would burn before a violent and painful death ensued for everyone. They decided to lose the stowage compartment and save the batteries – a decision albeit with the power of hindsight, would later be heavily criticized.

Once Howell and Jamison decided to give up the compartment, getting out proved to be rather more difficult for Petty Officer Mitchell and Lieutenant Woods who were still in the stowage area, trying to close the door in Number Twenty-five bulkhead. While making a valiant last-ditch effort to get just one more clip on the door another attempt to save the *Thetis* at the cost of whoever was still in the compartment was made. Leading Stoker Arnold reached the watertight door between the stowage compartment and the battery space. He, like Woods, later admitted, 'I guessed what had happened and tried to shut the bulkhead door'. Woods and Mitchell now gave up the attempt to close the door and decided to save themselves, but Arnold had already decided to close the door and drown the men. He later explained, 'People were still in the torpedo stowage and tube compartments at that time, [and] they were trying to close the fore-end door, but the water was coming in so quickly they had to get into the accommodation space to where I was'.

Mitchell and Woods must have seen what was happening, but their bid to stay alive was further hampered, as they now had to climb up rather than walk along the deck to the next section. 'I found great difficulty in climbing out of the compartment', said Woods, 'due to the angle of the ship and the fact that tables, stools and boxes were falling from the aft end of the compartment on top of us. I slipped back several times, as my shoes were wet and slipping on the corticene. Mitchell was ten seconds behind me'. Corticene was a dark brown type of linoleum used throughout the Royal Navy and although hardwearing and weatherproof, it was notoriously slippery when wet.

Their will to live, and Arnold's reluctance to lose the compartment soon clashed, but as Arnold continued, 'Leading Stoker Cunningham, Engine Room Artificer Howell and myself tried to shut the door. We had several attempts, but as fast as we tried to shut it people were

31

pulling it open to get through. We were going to shut them in, but they kept coming aft one by one to pull the door open and get through, so that we could not get the door shut. Eventually they all got through and we got the door watertight. These people eventually all got out. We had some difficulty in shutting the door owing to the steep angle of the boat', and the fact that the door weighed nine hundredweight.

Exhausted after trying to haul himself out of the stowage compartment, Woods now had to take a short rest in the forward crew space before reporting to the control room what had just happened. The next watertight door was Number Sixty-nine bulkhead, which Shaw had crashed against on the control room side a few minutes earlier. With the five watertight doors now shut, Woods hauled himself up to shout through a ventilation duct what had just happened. Once Bolus knew that the fore end was secured he ordered all the watertight doors to be opened, so the senior officers could assess the full extent of the damage. Just in case it might help, Bolus gave another order to run the engines half-speed astern in the hope that the *Thetis* would surface. The movement only increased the angle of the submarine and he had no choice but to give the order to stop the main engines, leaving the *Thetis* to float in the water like an arrow frozen in its descent.

Chapman, Glenn, Oram, Bolus and Admiralty Overseer Bailey discussed at length ideas to remove the water. Two methods were put forward, either to pump or blow the water out through Number Five torpedo tube and back into Liverpool Bay. They did have one piece of good fortune. A connection from the ship's high-pressure air system was located on the dry side of Number Forty bulkhead that would allow air to be blown into the torpedo compartment. However, a hatch at the top of the stowage compartment on deck, which was used in harbour for loading torpedoes, was designed to take immense external force, but only a marginal rise in internal pressure. It was held down by the weight of water outside rather than dogged down from within.

The five men feared that if they put too much pressure into this compartment, the air would bubble out of this torpedo hatch and so waste their limited air stock and cause more water to pour in. At 120 feet they believed that the external pressure was about $60\,\text{lb}^2$, but the amount of pressure needed to blow out the water was around $65\,\text{lb}^2$. The difference was only marginal, but 5 lb would still be enough to make the plan fail. There were other considerations. What if the force of the inrushing air slammed shut the door to Number Five torpedo tube? This would cause a rapid and very dangerous pressure build-up. What if the bow section emptied too quickly? With so many tanks already blown, this sudden loss of water, which in effect had now become ballast, would cause the *Thetis* to become very unstable, perhaps causing her bow to shoot up or veer to one side or the other.

About half an hour later the acute angle had largely disappeared as she settled on the seabed, making life much more bearable, for a short while at least. Later on Woods knew it could only have been an open bow cap and not a fracture that caused the flooding, and became increasingly concerned that someone under his command might have blundered. He asked Leading Seaman Hambrook to again confirm that all the bow cap levers were parallel to each other. If this had been so, it would indicate that Number Five bow cap-operating lever, as well as all the others were all shut. Hambrook was adamant that they were definitely all parallel and 'correct'. With nowhere else to go, Woods returned to the watertight door on the escape chamber, leading into the flooded torpedo stowage area, to help all he could.

Once the *Thetis* settled on the seabed, Bolus ordered both the fore and after indicator buoys to be released. These were 27 inches in diameter wooden floats, weighing 3 cwt, coloured red and yellow with a red flag on top and visible for about three miles. Captain Oram went forward to the escape chamber to see for himself how bad things really were. 'I, personally, went into the foremost escape chamber, and with a torch, which I shone through the glass scuttle, observed the water to be in the torpedo compartment, filling it to, approximately, three-quarters full, and whilst I watched I saw the level still rising'. Quite clearly, although Howell had achieved an incredible feat by getting one clip on the Number Twenty-five bulkhead door, it was really having little real effect on the *Thetis*. She was, clearly, slowly sinking.

Their only option was to pump rather than blow the water out. There were two pumps on the submarine's main line water service, both located in a non-flooded compartment, but before the compartments could be emptied, it was necessary to close Number Five torpedo tube. This could only be achieved if a man passed through the Number Forty bulkhead escape chamber and back into the icy cold, flooded compartment to close the rear torpedo door and open key valves to ensure the water could be removed.

If the plan worked then it might be possible to start the main ballast pumps, get rid of all the water in both compartments with ease, and it was back to the surface for everyone. Woods remembered, 'Lieutenant Chapman said he would make an effort to get through and close

Number Five rear door. I told him two men were necessary for a job like that. He insisted on going alone.' The plan was not only to get Number Five rear door closed, but then to return to the after end of the torpedo stowage compartment and open up the two bilge suction valves, which would suck water, one from the torpedo compartment and one from the torpedo tube space. Rubber torches capable of withstanding any amount of wetness had been allocated and delivered to the *Thetis* for use in the escape chamber, but they could not be found anywhere on board. Ordinary torches wrapped round with electrical tape had to be improvised. Lieutenant Chapman, wearing his normal clothing and weighted with heavy eyebolts to stop him floating prepared to go in.

Putting on his DSEA (Davis Submarine Escape Apparatus) he entered the escape chamber. The DSEA set was first pioneered in 1903 before becoming standard naval kit in 1929. It was similar to a lifejacket with a supply of compressed air to aide the wearer until he broke the surface. The set included goggles, a nose clip and a rubber breathing/buoyancy bag containing a cylinder of compressed air. The breathing bag was connected to a mouthpiece by a flexible corrugated tube; breathing was through the mouth only, the nose being closed by the clip. The breathing/buoyancy bag was fitted with a non-return release valve, which allowed air to escape from the bag as the user ascended towards the surface and the water pressure decreased.

The pure oxygen then passed through a soda lime filter as he breathes it in and out, thus removing the dangerous carbon dioxide. The flask of oxygen lasted only twenty minutes, but these were boosted by two smaller 'oxylets' giving the wearer a further five minutes each and thirty minutes altogether, but if a person was at constant rest and breathed without any effort this could be pushed to up to two hours.

It sounded like the perfect answer to get a man into position and prepare the submarine for removing the water. DSEA instructor Lieutenant Commander Evelyn Roberts Churchill Macvicker was the instructional officer for Davis Escape Apparatus for Home Flotillas. As well as being responsible for the installation and maintenance of DSEA sets aboard submarines, he also oversaw the training of submariners in its use, and saw many types of submariners pass through his training programmes. After the *Thetis* disaster he reflected on how men were trained under his command 'They pick it up easily. I think it should be remembered that men in submarines are above the average intelligence, and I presume the same is true to a certain extent of any workmen sent out in a submarine. We find no difficulty whatever in instructing men. Some are a little more backward than others, but there is no very definite dullard with whom we cannot deal'. But now the DSEA sets were about to be used like a miniature aqualung under constant high pressure, which was fine in principal, but largely beyond their design capability.

Chapman's eyebolts chinked against the steel entrance as he clambered into the escape chamber. Commissioning Officer Glenn closed and locked the small circular door before he flooded the chamber. Chapman heard the valves open. The cold water rushed in from the open sea. His only light source shone in through a small spy hole from the comparative safety and warmth of the submarine. He felt a sudden chill spill over his shoes and up his legs before the light fell on the rising black mass. For all a submariner's escape training, trying to fight back the sense of panic and claustrophobia at this point was a heavy mental strain. On came the water, creeping passed his knees, waist and chest, while he breathed heavily as the sudden raw, cold gnawed at his more sensitive areas. In a flash he began banging on the door to be let out, not so much through any feeling of being trapped, but through severe pains in his chest and ears.

Even if he could stand the severe, albeit temporary pain, there was another more sinister threat to face. Inhaling oxygen under pressure for too long causes oxygen poisoning and eventual death. The effect is greatly enhanced as the pressure increases and the less time available before the onset of poisoning. To be trapped in a submarine and have to escape from about 200 feet wearing a DSEA set could affect the user, but he would be on the surface before harmful effects took over. To enter the flooded compartment at about 120 feet gave the user about fifteen minutes before he became unconscious and possibly dead. About three minutes were needed to flood the escape chamber up to sea pressure, and about the same for draining it again after the man's work was done. Only about seven minutes were now left to find and carry out the necessary work, in near total darkness, dressed in normal clothes, and wading through freezing seawater.

The chamber was drained down and Chapman crawled out, glad to be relieved from the pain, but at the same time disappointed at his failure. Woods immediately volunteered to make the second attempt, but only if another crewmember accompanied him. Ernie Mitchell agreed to go, his job being twofold. Firstly Woods would enter the flooded sections with a rope secured around his waist, mainly to find his way back, but also to communicate with Mitchell through an agreed code of tugs. Woods was later much more candid about his more human wish to use a rope. 'I felt that it would give me more confidence if I could maintain contact with someone'. Having said that, the second reason was that if Woods was not back after an agreed amount of time, Mitchell was to give him up for dead and close the door facing into the flooded areas to ensure another attempt could be made. Quite simply, if Woods had perished alone, the door would have been left open and both sections could never be entered again.

After the chamber had been flooded they were to open the door on the forward side, go through and close it. Petty Officer Mitchell was then to secure the other end of the rope to an eye-plate on Number Forty bulkhead. Woods was then to make for the rear door and close it. On his return Mitchell would open the valves with a wheel spanner then both men would re-enter the chamber, close the door, drain down and enter the safety of the crew mess. Pumping could then begin, the two sections would soon be empty, and it was home before dark.

Both men were weighed down with heavy eyebolts, just like Lieutenant Chapman, and were fitted with their DSEA sets. Woods said, 'We entered the compartment and it was flooded from outside. When the water had reached our eyes Petty Officer Mitchell was drumming on his ears to say he was in great pain. I allowed the flooding to go on for a few more seconds hoping that he would overcome it, but he still exhibited signs of great pain so I gave the signal for them to drain down'. Woods really thought that his ability to withstand such a sudden pressure change was nothing out of the ordinary, and he was quite confident as to why Mitchell could not cope. The chief pain when under pressure occurs in the ears and is most frequently felt when a person is unable to clear what is known as the Eustachian tubes. This is usually done by holding one's nose and blowing through their ears.

Yet another attempt to seal the torpedo room had failed. Although shivering and exhausted Woods again volunteered to re-enter the escape chamber for a third try. After he had recovered his strength a little, Woods went though the whole procedure again, with Acting Petty Officer Cecil Smithers to assist him this time. Both men, weighed down with eyebolts and wearing their DSEA sets, entered the escape chamber. The small hatch was closed. They stood facing each other,

36

listening to the hiss of water entering the cramped, darkened room as it slowly crept up their bodies.

'We carried out the same procedure as before,' said Woods, 'but Petty Officer Smithers showed signs of distress and after waiting for a few seconds I again gave the signal to drain down. Petty Officer Smithers afterwards said that he felt his heart was paining him'. He was in so much pain he actually said he thought his heart was 'going wrong'. Again Woods felt no ill effects and although two engine room stokers, Matthews and Cunningham wanted a fourth attempt Bolus refused to allow them to try. They had to look at other ways to get back to the surface, including masterminding a plan to get outside help.

The normal carbon dioxide content of air is about 385 parts per million. A saturation of about ten per cent in a confined space is lethal, but this depends largely on the individual's age, state of mental and physical health and general endurance. By 22.00 hours the levels had reached about 2.3 per cent, which was still not too noticeable. The atmosphere was still breathable and the temperature maintained a balmy 60°F. Although the submarine was very overcrowded, conditions aboard at this stage were still quite pleasant. That is, apart from condensation dripping from the ceilings, or forming into rivulets like rain on a window as they flowed down the fresh paint into small puddles on the deck plating. Some minor leaks were found and plugged, but the steering gear and the periscopes leaked continuously. Rather annoyingly nearly all the food was lost in the first two compartments, but there was very little appetite, as all efforts were focused on getting to the surface.

Although her own ASDIC (Anti-submarine Detection Investigation Committee, an early form of Sonar) was severely damaged on impact with the bottom, Bolus knew that Subsmash, the Royal Navy's crack submarine rescue procedure, must have been ordered by now. Subsmash was designed, in theory at least, to locate and save a downed submarine's crew. It was only a matter of time before at least a dozen warships would be swarming all over the sea above them. Not knowing when they would arrive, or just how damaged his system really was, Bolus ordered that a constant ASDIC watch still be kept. Just in case they heard something, anything, or were able to perhaps make contact with a warship. Hopes rose after a telegraphist reported the propellers of a ship, but when another went to listen, they both came to the conclusion the echo they were receiving was a pump running at the submarine's stern. It was now 23.00 hours. Eight hours had passed since she first nose-dived to the bottom of Liverpool Bay. Some of the older and less fit men like Bath and Dobells were starting to pant. They were becoming flushed and headaches were beginning to get worse. The early stages of slow carbon dioxide poisoning were already taking effect.

Chapter 4

Subsmash!

Godfrey turned to Lieutenant Coltart literally moments after the *Thetis* had disappeared and said quite bluntly, 'I didn't like the way she dived. She appeared to be in trouble to me'. Looked at objectively, by the more experienced submarine officer, the event was completely different. Yes, the *Thetis* had dived suddenly. Her periscope and red flag were not visible above the surface, but neither had any smoke signals or indicator lights been released to show that she was indeed in distress. Coltart's first impressions were that she was quite manageable, and that she would speed up, or blow tanks, and reappear at periscope depth somewhere ahead. In fact, he said that the lack of any emergency signals, 'Went far to allay my anxiety altogether'.

But, as the minutes passed, the tension was clearly mounting on the tug's bridge. Coltart was young, fresh and far more aware than anyone aboard the *Grebe Cock* as to what the *Thetis* was likely to do next. Godfrey, who had worked the Liverpool waterways since before Coltart was born, just intuitively knowing something was amiss. With no land visible, the Master asked the Lieutenant if he could at least steam the tug in the direction in which they all knew the *Thetis* had been ordered to proceed. Perhaps they might just see something, anything, to show that he was over reacting and there was nothing to fear.

'No', replied Coltart, 'if the *Thetis* was in any trouble she may circle round and break surface anywhere in the vicinity and if we were moving through the water we might strike her and do her serious damage'. Godfrey then suggested that he could steam into the tide to try to keep position for which Coltart agreed. He then steamed back for fifteen minutes, being sure that they had drifted a quarter of a mile since the *Thetis* dived. To keep countering the drift Godfrey repeatedly cut engines before steaming back on the same course to roughly, very roughly, the same place.

On the bridge, telegraphist Crosby was looking out ahead, Coltart was looking out astern, Randles and Godfrey were keeping a general lookout all round, ensuring a constant 360° scan out to the horizon and back. The visibility from the *Grebe Cock*'s bridge that day was about eight miles. Steaming into the tide with so many pairs of eyes glued to the sparkling, blue sea – if something was there they would see it. Smoke candles could be seen from about three miles and the buoys for about the same, so they had an extremely good chance of seeing where the submarine was. The *Thetis* also had twenty-five indicator lights aboard. They played two roles in submarine practice. Their main job was to be attached to a dummy torpedo to act like a tracer, which enabled the weapon to be recovered more easily. The second function was as a distress signal because they could be attached to special wooden floats and shot out of the submarine's smoke candle ejector. Not one person aboard the *Grebe Cock* saw the couple of smoke candles and many more indicator lights, which were released at least every two hours from shortly after she went down until after sunset, nor the two marker buoys.

As the afternoon wore on, there was still no sign of the *Thetis*. Coltart's next decision, and its later impact on unfolding events, has long been regarded as a major contributing factor to the eventual tragedy. Through a freak twist of fate, what really transpired was one of the few events that greatly helped to alert the Admiralty that the *Thetis* was, indeed, in serious trouble. Neither Godfrey nor Coltart knew the duration of the *Thetis*'s proposed dive, and neither could the *Grebe Cock* leave her position and steam back to Liverpool to find out.

Unbeknown to Coltart and Crosby the *Grebe Cock* was fitted with a radiotelephone in Godfrey's cabin, just below the bridge, albeit with only a thirty-mile range. They were about thirty-eight miles from the nearest land-based station, Seaforth Radio just north of Liverpool, so they might just be able to get some form of communication through. Both Coltart and Crosby worked out a simple message designed specifically not to arouse anxiety. Then Coltart instructed Crosby to send the signal, asking Fort Blockhouse what was the duration of the *Thetis*'s dive. Straight away Crosby ran into problems. He was trying to get Seaforth for about twenty-five minutes and although conditions were good as far as the *Grebe Cock* was concerned, on several occasions Seaforth Radio told Crosby to alter his frequency, due to interference. The message did eventually get through, but instead of taking about twenty-five minutes to reach Blockhouse in Gosport about 250 miles away, the message took a great deal longer.

By 16.45 hours Godfrey was becoming more anxious that perhaps they were drifting further away from the spot and recommended that they drop anchor. Coltart agreed, but releasing the anchor and allowing it to free-fall down its hawse pipe into the sea was not going to be easy. Liverpool Bay in that area was about 130 feet deep at high water, and each anchor chain, or cable as it is properly called, would not reach the bottom, let alone run out enough to hold the *Grebe Cock* in place.

All this time Godfrey's tug was drifting farther away from his original position. Finally he secured the tug to the seabed about 2 ½ hours after the *Thetis* went down. 'It was a very difficult job', Godfrey later recalled, 'I only had two men to spare. One had to be down in the locker, and then I had to unshackle the chain from the keelson [the inboard side of the keel] and then connect up with the other one before I dare let go'.

Barely thirty minutes after Coltart's message was sent, he was ready to accept that perhaps something was wrong and he should update Fort Blockhouse with his concerns. This action was intended to induce his superiors to launch Subsmash, but again the *Grebe Cock* had difficulties getting the message through. The eight-mile difference between the *Grebe Cock*'s position from Seaforth, and her radio's maximum range, now proved to be too far to get this single, most important, signal. Crosby tried repeatedly to inform Blockhouse that Coltart was now genuinely concerned. '[But] I could not get through to Seaforth', he said. 'I called the pilot cutter at Port Lyness with the intention of asking the pilot cutter to pass the message for me, but had no luck with the pilot cutter either'.

All submarine movements at Fort Blockhouse were recorded on a large blackboard, which listed the names and numbers of every Royal Navy submarine diving, as well as their dive times, dive position, and the time at which they were supposed to surface. Two further copies were kept on a signal pad, a special form distributed to the Wireless Office and the Signal Distributing Office under the control of the Chief Yeoman of Signals who handled all incoming and outgoing messages. His duties also included informing the Duty Commanding Officer if a submarine had failed to signal on time.

In overall command at Fort Blockhouse was Rear Admiral (Submarines) B. C. Watson. On 1 June he was sick at his home in nearby Hambledon. Below him was the Duty Staff Officer; on this day being Commander George Barney Hamley Fawkes. He would only be notified of a delayed surfacing signal once it had passed through the chain of command to ensure firm action needed to be taken. Further down the chain was a Duty Submarine Commanding Officer who saw to the day-to-day workload. He was chosen from a different Flotilla leader each day. Should the Flotilla leader be unavailable the duty would then fall to an available submarine commander.

Ironically the duty submarine commanding officer on 1 June was Fifth Flotilla Leader Captain Oram who was at that precise moment trapped aboard the *Thetis*. He had already arranged for his second-in-command, Commander Lancelot Milman Shadwell to take his place. Unfortunately Shadwell was aboard HMS *Winchelsea*, a destroyer attached to the Fifth Submarine Flotilla, which the *Thetis* would have joined. The *Winchelsea* was, at that time, being mock-attacked during a submarine exercise in the English Channel. On this, of all days, the pecking order fell all the way down from Rear Admiral Watson to Lieutenant Commander Lipscombe, of the submarine *L-26*, until Shadwell returned later that day.

With only routine signal traffic to deal with, Lipscombe was having a pretty quiet time. Just after lunch the Chief Yeoman of Signals passed on to him the *Thetis* dive signal, one of many messages going through the Department that day. Bolus's brief message told Blockhouse the time, duration and heading for his dive. Lipscombe then settled into overseeing the updates on the board and ensuring that copies of all signals were ready in Shadwell's office, in an orderly pile, for his return. Shadwell came back from trials aboard the *Winchelsea* at about 16.15 hours, some twenty-five minutes before the *Thetis* was due to give her surface signal at 16.40 hours to inform Blockhouse that all was well.

Since 1934 an Admiralty Fleet Order laid out concisely the exact procedure to follow should a submarine go missing in Home waters, that is, if she was lost in a clearly defined boundary around the United Kingdom down to a depth of 300 feet, the standard operating depth of many British submarines at the time. The *Thetis*'s surface time passed with no surface signal. A few minutes later, at about 16.45 hours the Chief Yeoman of Signals told Shadwell that the *Thetis*'s signal was a few minutes late. Shadwell telephoned the Admiralty Operations Division in Whitehall to notify them that the submarine was slightly overdue and did they know something that he might not. The Admiralty confirmed that they, too, had not been contacted. Shadwell then called Cammell Laird, but like everyone else they had heard nothing either.

A signal that late, or indeed a good hour afterwards, never created a sense of concern within the Admiralty's submarine nerve centre after such a short period of time. There could always be a rational explanation. Perhaps the submarine's wireless had broken. After all, she was on her first dive. It had been known to happen before and sometimes it took time to send a signal if the radio mast was too wet. Still, just in case, the Wireless Office at Blockhouse was instructed to call the *Thetis* every ten minutes and Shadwell thought it prudent to at least inform his superior, Duty Staff Officer Commander Fawkes.

At about 17.30 hours, in the absence of his direct superior, Rear Admiral Watson, Fawkes considered it his responsibility to take further action. He got out a chart of Liverpool Bay and after studying how far she would get during the time she was diving, he decided to inform various other Naval authorities. Naturally his first call was to the Admiralty to tell them that one of their submarines was overdue. He then told Watson, who was still sick. Fawkes then tried to telephone Watson's Chief of Staff, Captain Ian Agnew Patterson Macintyre, at his home in nearby Southsea. Macintyre was aboard the Bittern Class Admiralty sloop HMS *Enchantress* with First Lord of the Admiralty James Richard Stanhope, Thirteenth Earl of Chesterfield (and direct descendent of William the Conqueror) earlier in the day. Stanhope had been visiting various naval establishments around the country since late May and he just happened to be near Plymouth on 1 June. After repeated calls to Macintyre's house failed to locate the Chief of Staff, Fawkes had to take control.

The time was now 17.38 hours. Gosport Post Office had just received an odd telegram originating from a tugboat in Liverpool Bay. It was not marked 'urgent' or 'important' like most Admiralty signals relating to submarine actions. Considered routine traffic, the message's final few miles were yet to be covered by a delivery boy on a bicycle who, to make matters worse, had a puncture along the way. Fawkes got through to Plymouth Duty Officer Bayne at about 17.50 hours and told him the whole story to date. He added, 'I am definitely not assuming that an accident has taken place yet, but naturally I am anxious'. Bayne distinctly remembered his conversation with Fawkes in a somewhat different light. He remembered the Staff Officer actually saying, 'There

43

was no cause for anxiety' as they were 'expecting a surface signal at any moment'.

Bayne knew that the B Class destroyer HMS *Brazen* was in the area after she had attended gunnery trials off Belfast and was now homeward bound to Plymouth. She could be re-tasked to help locate the *Thetis* if need be. Bayne added, 'I then told him [Fawkes] HMS *Brazen* was in the Irish Sea. I estimated then, roughly sixty miles away. "There is no need to take action", he [Fawkes] replied. I gained the impression that he was not keen on any action to be taken then, and he said to me, "If you make any signal, make it code".' The destroyer had another advantage. She was fitted with the latest ASDIC submarine detection system and could, if deployed properly, locate the *Thetis* very fast indeed.

The *Thetis* was now exactly one hour and ten minutes overdue. Although Fawkes was not stopping Bayne making the signal he did not feel justified in re-tasking *Brazen* on his own initiative, so he rang the Admiralty in Whitehall to get more up-to-date information. Whitehall still had nothing to add, so Bayne decided that the *Brazen* must be re-tasked and sat down to draft the signal, asking her to re-direct to the submarine's last known position and attempt to make contact.

At about 18.10 hours the Duty Officer brought Coltart's message to Fawkes with Shadwell left to send a reply, back by telephone this time to Seaforth, stating very briefly that the *Thetis* had dived at 13.40 hours for three hours, just what Coltart wanted to know. He decided not to allay his concerns to Lieutenant Coltart – a decision he was later to be heavily criticized because Coltart had no idea how concerned Plymouth and Fort Blockhouse were now becoming.

In reality Coltart did not need to know the general mood of his superiors. As a seasoned submariner he was well aware that they knew she was overdue and the matter was out of his hands. Shadwell had other valid reasons for being so brief. He later said in his defence, 'When I telephoned Seaforth Radio, the Dockyard Exchange, Portsmouth got me through very quickly, considering the distance, but the line was exceedingly bad. I spent about five minutes trying to explain to the operator, who was very willing, but finding it very difficult to hear, first the destination of the message, that is to say, a tug at sea. He could not get hold of the name, and then had considerable difficulty in understanding what I wanted him to pass on. I think that, to a great extent, influenced me in getting a message of some kind through in a simple form, which I thought would get there'.

Meanwhile, due to the wealth of circumstantial evidence piling up over the previous two hours or so, for Fawkes, Coltart's attempt not to create anxiety did just the opposite. The telegram in itself was not proof of an accident. After all Coltart sent it at least an hour before the *Thetis* was due to officially surface. Fawkes recalled, 'I therefore said, "Well I have got no proof, but I must assume an accident has taken place", and therefore I took action at once accordingly'. He notified Bayne, explaining that he considered the situation was now serious and that action should be taken. Bayne quickly scribbled another signal to HMS *Brazen* ordering her to now proceed at top speed, inferring that the last locate-and-communicate order was no longer enough and it might now be a rescue mission.

At Fort Blockhouse Fawkes rang the Duty Commander at the Admiralty in Whitehall, stressing that he was assuming an accident had taken place and why. The Duty Commander contacted the Air Ministry to arrange for an airborne search of the area. The Admiralty Fleet Order laid out what action to take in just such a situation stipulating that the Commander-in-Chief of the Home Port in whose area the sinking took place was to assume full command of the rescue operation. In this case Commander-in-Chief Plymouth, Admiral Sir Martin Eric Dunbar-Nasmith VC was now in overall command of the situation above and beyond Fawkes, Macintyre, Bayne and all others so far involved in the operation.

As an experienced submarine commander in his own right Nasmith was awarded the VC in 1915 while in command of the submarine *E-11*, one of the most successful submarines operating in the Dardanelles Campaign. While on patrol in the Sea of Marmara, he sank eight enemy vessels, including two transports an ammunition ship and three supply ships.

Fawkes explained to Nasmith that he considered the Admiral should, in accordance with the Fleet Order's Paragraph Five, launch a pre-set, full-scale search and rescue operation, Subsmash.

The Sixth Destroyer Flotilla was sent as part of Subsmash, which still had the capability to conduct an underwater search, using ASDIC like HMS *Brazen*. Unlike the Anti Submarine Flotilla, they had the edge on speed, so were clearly the better option for the job. A similar signal was sent to the First M/S, or Mine Sweeping Flotilla and the Royal Navy's dedicated diving vessel HMS *Tedworth*, which was moored on the Clyde with no coal aboard. This was the first time the Fleet Order had been deployed since becoming part of Admiralty practice four years earlier. The time was now about 19.00 hours on 1 June.

Captain Macintyre finally arrived at Fort Blockhouse at 19.40 hours from spending the day with First Lord Stanhope. After agreeing with everything his various subordinates had done to that point, Macintyre's first executive action was to have the duty destroyer HMS *Winchelsea* ready for sea as soon as possible, having only just returned from submarine attack trials in the Channel. She would be his command post for the long journey up to the *Thetis*'s dive site, should he need to be present. Like a well-oiled machine, under Admiral Nasmith, Plymouth Command was now in full control of the rescue operation, with Fort Blockhouse as its support. Barely six hours had elapsed out of the twenty-four deemed necessary to effect a successful Home waters' rescue operation. Nineteen hours later – or twenty-four hours and ten minutes after the *Thetis*'s surface signal was overdue – the Admiralty's crack rescue operation failed completely in its objective to save the very lives it was designed to rescue.

Back in Liverpool Bay Godfrey remembered, 'We remained at anchor, still with all men keeping a good lookout. I was leaving Lieutenant Coltart to suggest any step he desired to take, and which I could, of course, have fallen in with, but we agreed that the only thing we could do was to remain at anchor to mark the position and to continue to keep a good lookout for any traces of *Thetis*'. But there was one more useful asset in Liverpool that Nasmith was well aware could greatly help the trapped men over the coming hours. For all the effort the Admiralty were putting into getting to the spot there were many resources already located in Liverpool, barely twenty-five miles from the *Thetis*'s last known position. Nasmith knew personally Liverpool's Water Bailiff and Marine Surveyor, Commander Hubert Viner Hart. Hart was also responsible for salvaging sunken vessels within Liverpool's waterways to ensure that the approaches to the Mersey were always kept clear. He appeared to be the ideal man for the job. Indeed, Hart had an impressive salvage record, having cleared fifty-one major and 251 minor shipping casualties from in and around the Mersey so far during his twenty-three-year career.

Hart was at home at about 20.30 hours on 1 June when he got the call from Commander Bayne. Hart recalled, 'The gist of the message was to this effect, that the C-in-C Plymouth [Nasmith] feared that an accident had happened to this submarine; that as he knew me personally, and he also knew that I possessed salvage vessels and facilities always available, would I immediately go out and render what assistance I could'. Hart telephoned Liverpool's shore superintendent to request that the port's Wreck Master, Charles Brock, and other key figures including professional divers, to join the Mersey Harbour's vessel, *Vigilant*, at Liverpool's Princes Landing Stage. The *Vigilant* was technically a hydrographic tender, buoy tender and salvage vessel all in one with the pulling power of more than four average cargo ships. It was normal practice to have only half her crew aboard when alongside, while the others were ashore. So urgent was Nasmith's request that Hart was prepared to sail with or without a full crew.

The Port's other, smaller salvage vessel, the *Salvor* was also deployed, and the tug *Crosby* was used to ferry the *Vigilant*'s crew who missed her sailing, out to the vessel to bring her up to full crew strength. Hart also gave orders for steam to be got up on Camels number Three and Four, and later the smaller Camel Five, ready to be towed out to the *Thetis* should they be needed to lift her. A camel was like a dumb (meaning they had no engine power of their own) barge, fitted with an array of salvage gear necessary to lift a sunken vessel. They worked by being on the surface, on either side of a wreck, with wires strung between the two via the underneath of the wreck at low tide. As the tide rose, the power of the natural lift ensured the camels could raise the wreck off the seabed. The camels were then towed as far as possible towards the shore until the next high tide. The process would be repeated enough times to get the sunken vessel above the low tide line for permanent or temporary repairs. Should the *Thetis* be down, and should she need such support, they really were the big tools for the job.

The three vessels were well under way within a couple of hours, but the camels could not be sent so easily. Although steam could have been raised en route, it would take twelve hours. They were all locked in by the tide in the Albert Dock on Liverpool's waterfront until the midnight high tide. They were not even taken out then and made ready. Hart explained, 'The position, of course, was in my mind, but at that time we were not even certain that an accident had happened to the submarine. In any case she was absolutely un-located, and a camel is no use for any purpose whatever, unless wires have already been placed under the vessel for the camel to work on'.

The *Vigilant* actually left Princes Landing Stage at 21.45 hours, only an hour and a quarter after the Plymouth call. A diver was on board, Frederick Orton, Brock the Wreck Master, Commander Eric W. Harbord from the Mersey Docks & Harbour Board, as Hart's deputy. Everything that could be done was now implemented with precision, both in Liverpool, and according to Admiralty procedure. All emergency services were rushing to the scene with enough hardware, due to arrive well within the Admiralty stipulated twenty-four-hour time frame. Since Subsmash would take some time to arrive the search went out across Liverpool to find two submarine officers, Lieutenant Commanders T. C. C. Lloyd, captain of the submarine HMS *Trident* standing by at Cammell Laird, and R. N. Garnet captain of the other Cammell Laird's T Class build, HMS *Taku*. They were somewhere in the city and should they be found the two men could, at least, offer key advice until the full force of the Admiralty's search-and-rescue mission was on site. Now, the next of kin had to be informed that their loved ones were overdue.

Lieutenant Commander Bolus's wife, Sybil, decided to go to the cinema in Liverpool with her friend Mrs P. C. Comper, at the time her husband was diving. She drove with her friend from their family home called Oakfields in Hooton Road, Willaston for the forty-odd mile drive northwest to Liverpool. The two women escaped the hot after-noon sun and sat in a dark cinema, the projector beaming a smoky shaft of light on to the screen where the American submarine USS *Squalus* that had sunk during her test dive off New Hampshire eight days earlier was on show. The Loss of the *Squalus* still dominated inter-national news, all the more so due to the innovative way the crew was saved, using a diving bell. Sybil and her friend looked at the dramatic flickering monochrome images of a salvage ship lowering an empty diving bell down to the *Squalus*, and it returned to the surface with relatively healthy, rescued submariners.

Perhaps more than anyone during that Thursday afternoon matinee, Sybil alone must have empathized with the anguish the loved ones of the *Squalus*'s crew had – and were – still going through. Married to a submarine commander, she was well aware of what could go wrong, and what the outcome might be. After the main film had finished Sybil drove back to Willaston, dropped her friend off and went back to Oakfields to wait for her husband's call to say that the test dive went well and he would soon be home, perhaps they could spend the week-end with their nine-year-old son Martyn. When she got home, Sybil opened her front door and saw a small, white Admiralty telegram waiting for her. She picked it up, opened the envelope, and her mind must have flashed back to the smoky cinema auditorium and the downed *Squalus* she had seen a few hours before. The clipped, single sentence, said only that *Thetis* had failed to surface from her test dive.

Sybil ran out of Oakfields, jumped back into her car, and sped back to Birkenhead.

Chapter 5

Escape!

Canadian-born Flight Lieutenant John Avent was off duty and resting in the Officers' Mess at 269 squadron, Abbotsinch Aerodrome (now Glasgow Airport), about a mile from Paisley, Scotland. His superior, Wing Commander Frederick Laurence Pearce, walked into the mess and told Avent that a signal had just arrived from Coastal Command regarding a submarine missing off Great Ormes Head in Liverpool Bay. Within thirty-five minutes three twin-engined, RAF Anson aircraft, code-named 'H', carrying Avent as the leader, as well 'T' and 'X', were fully crewed with pilot, navigator, wireless operator and observer scrounged from around the base. The sun was due to set at about 21.00 hours on 1 June. Leaving Abbotsinch at about 20.00 hours, flying at 130 knots, at 3,500 feet for the 140-mile run to the area meant they arrived dead on 21.00 hours. The sun dipped below the horizon four minutes later, leaving the western sky a blend of reds and oranges and the sea akin to a lake of molten copper.

Avent's chances of a positive sighting were diminishing every minute as darkness slowly crept over the sky and sea from the east, but his three Ansons were not alone. Four, twin-engined Oxford training aircraft from Number Five Flying School based at RAF Sealand in Flintshire, North Wales, were added to the search. At some point over the Irish Sea, Avent decided not to go to the last known location as ordered. 'We set a course to a position ten miles to the west', he explained, 'so when we arrived there we would be up sun of the last reported position'. Flying 'up sun' means to fly in the opposite direction to the sunset, thus allowing the aircrews to make the most of every last dying ray of light.

Avent ordered his accompanying planes to spread out at half-mile intervals, so that they could cover approximately a mile-and-a-half sweep. To improve their field of view all three planes reduced speed to 90 knots and dropped down to about 400 feet. They searched the area without luck before turning eastward for twenty miles and a new search area. Although the sun had now gone the rest of the night remained unusually light with a visibility of ten to fifteen miles. The height, speed, sea conditions and abnormally bright night sky meant that any oil or distress signals should have been clearly visible to all seven planes from some distance.

Aboard the B Class destroyer HMS *Brazen* Lieutenant Commander Robert Henry Mills altered course immediately he received the signal to steam towards the *Thetis*'s last dive position. He could only make 13 knots because just one boiler out of her three was lit, a cost-cutting measure introduced across the Royal Navy to save coal. Frustrated with their progress Mills increased speed to 17 knots, the maximum possible on one boiler. He wanted more speed regardless of measures to save fuel and about twenty minutes later his second boiler was connected before increasing speed to 26 knots. Shortly afterwards he received Bayne's second signal, based on Coltart's dive time concerns, ordering Mills to proceed with all haste this time. When the third boiler was put on line, the *Brazen*'s speed jumped up to 30 knots, and forced her through the waves like a modern-day hydrofoil.

At about the same time Avent reached the area, the *Brazen* spotted the *Grebe Cock* in the same vicinity. He closed her to about 800 feet, and, by Aldis lamp, signalled to her, 'Are you in position where submarine last dived?' Crosby replied 'No; only approximate position'. Mills had already decided that for thoroughness to search an area of approximately three miles in each direction of the *Grebe Cock*, and if he had no luck to enlarge the area all round. Mills then asked Godfrey what the submarine's diving course was and what time she dived. He replied that it was course 310° at 15.00 hours [sic] Mills remembered, 'I started investigating to the westward because my information from the *Grebe Cock* was that the submarine's diving course was 310°'. His information came from Coltart, who suggested that there was a better chance of finding the *Thetis* to the west of the *Grebe Cock* because that was the direction the submarine was actually heading.

The *Brazen*'s search pattern followed a grid whereby every part of a given area could be fully covered. An arc of 45° on each side of the *Brazen*'s course line was swept and if nothing was located the ASDIC dome on the bottom of her hull was rotated a few degrees and the process repeated. The sky was clear and still quite light, giving the watches ample opportunity, like Avent's aircraft, to spot any surfaced distress signal. With her ASDIC beam radiating out from beneath the hull, Admiral Nasmith calculated that the *Thetis* would be located by 22.00 hours that night. Only four miles away from the *Grebe Cock*, the *Thetis* was still settled on the seabed well within Mills' original search plan, but as the *Brazen* steamed to the west – the *Thetis* was lying to the east.

Shortly before 22.00 hours Avent spotted a small object in the water on his port side. 'We altered course and flew over to this, and it appeared to be a buoy, and also a long, dark object underneath the water, a dark shadow, more or less cast on the surface of the water. The shadow looked about 25 yards long and narrow, probably 2 to 3 yards wide'. Avent descended to only 50 feet above sea level to take a closer look. As far as he could tell it was a yellow conical buoy, one side was in the shadow of the setting sun and the colour could not be determined for sure. His navigator saw a flag on the top of the buoy, giving every indication that this originated from the *Thetis*. Avent saw a trawler about two miles west of the buoy. His wireless operator fired four green Very lights, a recognized distress signal, but the trawler either did not see the signal, or decided to ignore it.

Aboard the *Brazen*, Lieutenant Commander Mills did see the Very lights and shortly afterwards he received a signal to investigate the area. Just before widening his ASDIC search pattern that would very soon have found the *Thetis*, he headed for Avent's signal. Had the *Brazen*'s stayed a little longer, or Avent spotted the buoy an hour later, the night would have turned out very differently indeed. Aboard Avent's plane his navigator realized he had made a navigational error. He corrected the buoy's position, which was passed on to Mills, but made no real difference because he was already steaming further away from the *Thetis* with every passing minute.

Shortly after 22.00 hours Avent decided it was too dark to continue his air search, and all three Ansons headed back to Abbotsinch. No sooner was Avent heading back to Scotland, than he received a signal for all three aircraft to land at RAF Sealand and resume the search at daybreak on 2 June. Aircrafts 'T' and 'X' failed to get the message and flew on, but 'H' did and Avent turned his Anson south towards Sealand where an airstrip was marked out with flares to guide him safely in.

Aboard the *Thetis* Oram, Bolus and other senior personnel knew things would get much worse before they got any better. They discussed whether to let the men use the DSEA sets to make them more comfortable, but by the early hours of the morning the decision was taken not to issue them. The reason was one of long-term survival, rather than short-term comfort. Had they been used, simply to sit around and breath a little easier, not only would precious air in the sets be used, but the all-important soda lime filters would become exhausted and thus escape impossible. Soda lime is made from mixing lime with caustic soda and the filters converted the carbon dioxide breathed out into the set's oxygen bag back into breathable air. But after four hours it would be saturated and any amount of top-up from the submarine's oxygen manifolds would be, like the sets themselves, quite useless.

After the aborted attempts to enter the flooded compartments and close the rear door on Number Five tube had failed, Captain Oram and Lieutenant Commander Bolus, along with other senior personnel met to decide what to do next. Two actions were decided upon. Firstly, they did not abandon the idea of blowing out the water from the front two compartments, but this time they would do it with outside help.

Secondly, with an average depth of about 130 feet, and a submarine with a length of 275 feet, she could be re-ballasted to push the stern above sea level. This was for two reasons: to lessen the distance necessary for men to escape, especially after the experiences earlier that afternoon while trying to pass men through the forward escape hatch. And, most importantly, what better way to attract search and rescue craft than have the stern sticking up out of the water.

The senior officers centred in the control room to hammer out the best way for outside help to get air into the flooded compartments. 'Our idea was that the plan so written out should be taken to the surface by a man escaping with his Davis Safety Escape Apparatus', explained Oram, 'so that it would be possible that when the connection had been made on to the ship, and the air compressor of the surface vessel pumping air down the hose pipe, the men inside the submarine would be able to cooperate and open the necessary valves to allow the high-pressure air to be passed through Number Forty bulkhead by means of the salvage blow'. The air would not refresh the exhausted atmosphere in the hull, but would go directly into the submarine's high-pressure air system and could then be easily channeled into the flooded compartments.

The plan relied on having skilled men on the surface connecting an air-hose to one of either two connections – the gun recuperator just forward of the conning tower on the port side, or the whistle connection on the bridge. The recuperator was the preferred choice simply because it was easier to find. The officers knew that the divers who would probably be the first to arrive would not be skilled in submarine work. To help them to understand and locate where the airline needed to be fixed they drew rough diagrams with notes to show exactly where the point of entry on the casing was. But pumping the air in was not going to be enough. Just like their attempt to blow the torpedo compartment from inside the vessel, the fore hatch would still blow open with the force of the inrushing air. To combat this, the rough notes also gave diagrams of how and where to secure the fore hatch to ensure there was no leakage.

To ensure the salvage plan was found a man would have to reach the surface through the escape chamber with the plans strapped on to his body in case he did not live long enough to be rescued alive. Dawn was at about 04.00 hours, eight hours away and about thirteen hours after they went down. At 04.15 hours on 2 June Avent was back in the air and flying towards the last known position of the buoy. Although he was in constant radio touch with the *Brazen*, they both had clearly different views on the surrounding area. 'Visibility was very bad then,' said Avent. 'There was very little wind, but what there was, was from the east, which blew out the Liverpool smoke haze over there and the visibility was down to less than a mile'. He again was not alone. Four more Ansons were deployed from Abbotsinch during the night and three seaplanes from 209 Squadron Armament Training Station at RAF West Freugh, five miles east of Stranraer, Scotland. They flew to Holyhead to augment the search, or act as a shuttle service out to the wreck site as needed. Altogether eleven aircraft had been airborne for thirty-two hours and forty minutes; they failed to locate any real sign of where the *Thetis* was.

Although time was precious, there was still plenty of air left to ensure enough hours to find and rescue everyone, had the Admiralty plan worked. Engineering Officer Glenn did not get the final plan to the control room for approval until after midnight – its success relying solely on whether the rescuers were well equipped. 'If the gear was available they could save the ship', explained Oram.

While Glenn and his men worked on the salvage, focus was shifted to getting the stern above sea level. First of all Arnold was ordered to pump out the three fresh water tanks, which reduced the submarine's weight by ten tons. It was not much, but a start that was frustrated by the *Thetis*'s design. The tanks were not fitted for pumping out so a manhole door had to be taken off one tank to drain the other two down into it, then pump it out through the bilge suction to the open sea. The next stage was to pump out four of her six fuel tanks, two of which were located in the stern. This, like trying to remove the fresh water, was no easy task. The design of the submarine did not allow for fuel to be handled through her main line pumping system. To overcome the problem the fuel lines from both pairs had to be connected to the main line. Laird's men, who worked unceasingly throughout the night, removed copper pipes from the main engines then had to bend them by hand before joining the pieces from the fuel tanks to the main line system.

After hot and exhausting work, that clearly used up a great deal of air, the pump was put on the stern fuel tanks at about midnight and to their relief the trapped men could hear the fuel bubbling through the system and into the open sea. By 03.00 hours this group was emptied and Bolus estimated that the ship had been lightened by fifty tons, lifting the stern to an inclination of about 18°. At first this small rise was thought to be due to the rising tide, but pretty soon it was realized she was, indeed, going up by the stern. They were on their way back to the surface, but another inevitable problem was beginning to sweep through the submarine.

By the early hours of the morning the carbon dioxide levels were up to about five-and-a-half per cent. The older and less fit men were suffering from headaches ranging from mild to severe. These were no ordinary headaches. The carbon dioxide build-up in the body led to pressure in the skull across the whole cranium. The pain was so bad it induced vomiting, made worse by having to bend down or move to any great degree. Many were panting as if having done hard exercise. In fact it is the carbon dioxide in the body that triggers the action to breath, so they were panting as if having undergone heavy work. However, when one has panted after exercise the body soon re-adjusts. For the men in the *Thetis*, they kept on panting more and more, as the air became more poisoned. Soon the involuntary muscle jerks would start and obscuration or sudden loss of vision when changing posture. The carbon dioxide was causing acid to build up in body tissue. If they did not get out soon, the acid would cause the vital organs to shut down, followed by death.

Lieutenant Woods was all too aware of the effects on the crew. Since trying to enter Number Forty bulkhead he had been resting, trying to warm up and get his strength back. Once he felt better he got up and went to the control room to see if he could help. 'An order was given to shut Number Three port and starboard Kingstons [telemetry-controlled tank valves separate from the main line]', he said. 'A rating was endeavouring to do this job. It consists of working a ratchet spanner, which fits on a spindle, but he seemed to be in such a bad way that he was unable to concentrate on the job so I did it myself.' Arnold remembered this time a little more humorously, if that was possible under the circumstances. 'First thing in the morning everybody was struggling for breath. While I was lying down alongside another leading stoker, I asked him what he was panting for, and he said, "you aren't doing so badly yourself!" I did not realize I was panting so much'.

Oram more seriously caught the moment when he later said, 'As no sign had come from the surface vessels we presumed that we had not been found, but at the same time it was apparent to the commanding officer and myself that in view of the length of time it was going to take to pass all the men through the escape chamber it was imperative that the escapes should commence at the earliest possible moment as there was a danger of the last men becoming unconscious before they had a chance to escape'. If the men left in pairs it would now take about a quarter of an hour to get them through the chamber, if nothing went wrong. To get all 103 off would take nearly thirteen hours. The air was due to run out in about nine.

Bolus and Oram could see the situation was becoming dire. Even Bolus was beginning to suffer. As the stern rose he had to wedge himself between the chart table and a bulkhead behind Shaw to try to stay upright. He was having great difficulty trying to shout orders but still managed to maintain command and control. Another effect of carbon dioxide poisoning was a laryngeal spasm, a sudden constriction of the vocal cords, making breathing and talking temporarily impossible. During the night one of Bolus's strained orders was for readings of the after depth gauge. Eventually the gauge read zero, meaning the stern should now be above water. His next almost strangled order was for Z tank outboard and inboard vents to be opened. This should now allow fresh air into the submarine's high-pressure air system. If the blower was run, air would also be sucked through the tank, through the inboard vent into the after compartment, and some of the foul air would be expelled.

Oram was sure that there must be a fishing boat or merchant vessel standing by on the surface and to delay escape could be catastrophic. It was now or never. Somebody had to go to the surface with their plan to clear the flooded compartments. If a ship was there they could all be saved; if not the freezing water and strong tides could carry them deep into the Irish Sea and the plan, as well as the messenger, would be lost. Oram now made a decision that changed the fate of every man on board. 'I then offered to make an attempt to reach the surface', he later recalled. 'As a precautionary measure I called for a volunteer to come with me so that there was a chance that someone with inside knowledge would be found on the surface if I failed.

Lieutenant Chapman passed the word through the submarine for a volunteer. The men, all lying down where they could, propped up against bunks, chairs or piping, passed the word down as best they could. Two seaman and Lieutenant Woods, who was seated on the deck at the forward end of the control room immediately volunteered. But, as Woods later admitted, 'I did not know what it was for at the time the call was made'. Oram chose Woods from the three volunteers, his reasoning being that the young lieutenant knew a great deal more about the internal workings of the submarine and could be of help to the rescue teams long after the salvage plan had been delivered. Little did Woods know at the time, but his blind decision ultimately saved his life.

Before leaving the control room to climb up to the stern, Oram told Bolus that he would make for the submarine's indicator buoy or tail, if the tide was not too strong, and hang on for as long as he could. He also told Bolus not to delay in getting men out of the submarine. It was daylight now, and although there was a chance of them being swept away, drowned or dying of exposure the situation aboard was now too acute to risk staying where they were. The men, he insisted, should escape in pairs, one naval rating, who all had practical training in the Davis Escape Apparatus and chamber, and one civilian worker who only had a short lecture on the theory of escape prior to embarking for the dive trials.

Oram and Woods now had to turn towards the control room's after door, squeeze past the many men now slumped in every available piece of free space and, with strained and laboured breathing, make the slow and distressing climb up to the after escape chamber. Although all the men they climbed past were deteriorating much faster, now, the two officers found them in a cheerful state and, while lying on the bottom plates, were always willing to hold out a hand to pull the two officers ever closer to the escape hatch and ultimately escape for the sake of everyone.

Such a trip should take no more than a minute or two. On this occasion Woods and Oram needed forty-five minutes to cover the forty or so feet to the chamber. When they got there, the two men were so distressed that it took them a good fifteen minutes to recover before they could crawl into the chamber. Before doing so Oram stripped down to only his trousers to avoid any clothing getting caught on the way out. Both men were smeared in thick grease to try to improve their chances of survival against the bitter cold. They then put on their DSEA sets, pressing the cold, sticky grease into their bodies. Lieutenant Chapman wished them both 'good luck'. He and Glenn were there to work the escape chamber. Woods asked Glenn how he was feeling. He replied that he had strong pains in his chest. Woods looked around at the men suffering in the cramped and stifling conditions. Before he entered he saw one man who was unable to get up. 'I remember estimating in my mind what was the latest period the men could hold out', he said, 'and that time was six o'clock in the evening. I think I might have been probably rather optimistic'.

Both officers climbed into the escape chamber through the steering compartment entrance. This made sense due to the submarine's angle whereby the engine room door on the other side would prove too hard to operate with the men in such a sick state, as it opened towards the bow and would be dead weight hanging down. Once inside Oram wrapped the rescue plan in plastic and tied it to his wrist, should his lifeless body be found. For the third time in less than twenty-four hours Woods was again inside an escape chamber as freezing water again slowly worked its way up his body. Oram was finding it progressively harder to concentrate on the Davis escape drill that he knew so well. Every simple instruction: *put on the nose clips, adjust the goggles, open the exhaust vent, turn on the oxygen*. It took all his concentration to focus on the drill, then what seemed like forever to execute the instructions.

When the water reached their waists the inflow was stopped and the chamber drained down. Chapman opened the door and said something to Oram, but he was temporarily deafened from the sudden pressure change and did not catch what the Lieutenant had said. Just like the day before, Woods did not have the same ill effects. He asked Chapman what the matter was. The Lieutenant replied that he thought the escape hatch was above the water. If so, they could all literally just walk out of the submarine. Unfortunately it was about 20 feet below the surface. Before Chapman slammed the door again Woods asked for the air compressor to be switched off until they had escaped. The machine was making so much noise, both Oram and Woods could not hear themselves speak and needed every opportunity to communicate freely until the last possible moment. Ultimately the opening of the Z tank valves and the compressor made no difference anyway.

As the water poured into the escape chamber, up over their bodies and they could wait no longer to start breathing the sweet fresh oxygen from within the DSEA set's own compressed air supply. For the first couple of minutes their breath burned against their lips as the soda lime carbon dioxide filters worked so hard to clear their poisoned breath. Just before Oram opened the escape hatch, the two officers heard nine charges explode above the submarine and around it. The *Brazen* had eventually found them, well within site of where the search started more than eleven hours earlier. Sixteen hours had now elapsed since the *Thetis* went down. Liverpool, with its abundance of manpower, rescue shipping and equipment, was well on the way to the area. Before they left, Oram and Woods heard the collective cheer from all the men in the after compartment, as the *Brazen*'s charges exploded around the submarine, knowing that finally their rescue was imminent.

Sybil Bolus arrived in Birkenhead late on 1 June to see hundreds of relatives and friends of the trapped men standing around Cammell Laird's gates eagerly waiting for news that was not forthcoming. All she could see were looks of fear, pain and anguish in the gaunt faces and reddened eyes of the wives, sweethearts, parents and children of the men under her husband's command. Regardless of her own fears, Sybil made herself known as the wife of their loved one's captain and immediately took control of calming people's fears. Gathering as many around her as possible, she explained in a cool, slow, but commanding voice just how their men would be found. The soothing effect was instant. She then persuaded many to go home and get some much-needed sleep before seeing their men the next day.

Although she had already twice driven to Liverpool that afternoon, a total of about 160 miles, Sybil still volunteered to drive each anxious person home, not finishing until about 03.00 hours on the morning of 2 June. She, like all the other relatives, was back at Laird's gates at daybreak to continue their vigil. At 08.45 hours Laird announced that the *Thetis* had been found and all aboard were safe. The effect was electric as cries of anguish turned to sobs of joy. Sybil was beaming.

Dressed in a light-blue skirt, check blouse with a scarlet flower pinned on the front, her hair immaculately braided, she looked much fresher than the hours of angst really showed. Sybil explained to the waiting mothers how their loved ones will soon be escaping using DSEA equipment, adding, 'I am certain that everything will be all right with all of them. Now why don't you go home and rest.' She took the nearest telephone numbers of each waiting relative and promised to call them when there was some news, while still finding time to play with young children, not really quite sure of what was going on, or where their daddies all were.

Thetis crew member Leading Seaman Walter Luck from the Wirral had parked his motorcycle and sidecar in Laird's car park early the morning before. His father, Walter Luck Senior, was relieved to hear the submarine was found, but could still not accept his son was safe. He said that he would believe it, 'When my son takes me home in the side car of his motorcycle'. Walter Senior admitted that it had been a very anxious night, but he had never doubted that everything would be all right. 'He had every faith in his officers, and had said many times that they were a fine set of men'. Walter's mother, Jessie, was one of those who had kept a vigil outside Laird's gates. When the news came that her son was safe, she said through tears, 'What wonderful news. Luck by name and Luck by nature. Thank God!' Walter Arnold's wife was one of the last distressed loved ones Sybil had ferried home about five hours earlier. Mrs Arnold was now back at the gates along with four generations of the Arnold family: Walter's son, Derek aged twelve months, his mother, grandmother and great-grandmother. Walter's wife was putting young Derek to bed the night before when she heard the shocking news on her radio that the *Thetis* was down. 'It was a terrible shock', she said, 'thank God they are safe'.

The wife of Leading Telegraphist William E. Allen had left their baby with her landlady and rushed down to Cammell Laird's gates late on 1 June. Allen's last words to his wife and child the previous morning were, 'Expect me when you see me'.

'I didn't know then', she joked, 'that it would be after such a terrifying night'. His wife's fears had now clearly turned to elation, as she jokingly explained how her husband was the tallest man in the ship at 6 feet, 3 inches – not exactly cut out for the cramped conditions of submarine life, especially a telegraphist's wardrobe-like operations room.

The wife of Commander Reginald Hayter, one of the extra officers aboard to observe the trials, was also overjoyed when she got the news at their family home in Woking, Surrey. 'Thank God!' She exclaimed. 'It has been a terrible ordeal, and I can hardly believe that all is well. Since we heard about the *Thetis* we have hardly known what to do'. Captain Oram's wife only knew her husband was safe when a reporter knocked on the door of their home in Cosham, Hampshire. 'Naturally the anxiety has been very great', she said', 'and I am very relieved at the news. What about everyone else?' She asked the reporter. When he said all were safe, She replied, 'I, and all the other wives, I am sure, have been waiting every moment for that assurance'.

Chapter 6

'I Bide My Time'

A few square feet of the blue-glaze sea surged with white bubbles, as two figures burst out of the foam in full view of the *Brazen*'s bridge. She had been on her way east, to investigate a large patch of oil sighted by the Irish cargo ship SS *Meath*. For the frustrated Mills it was just another wild goose chase, but before she even reached the *Meath*'s recorded oil position he sighted the *Thetis*'s stern about three miles away on his port quarter sticking a good 18 feet out of the water. Twenty minutes later the *Brazen*'s whaler was lowered, rowed across to Woods and Oram and the two men knew they were safe.

While Woods was given a hot bath and a good breakfast, Oram wasted no time in delivering his salvage-cum-rescue plan to Mills. After sending for Lieutenant Coltart whom he knew was aboard the *Grebe Cock*, Oram peeled the grease and water-soaked package from his arm, took the crumpled sheets of notepaper out of the make-shift waterproof packaging and laid them out for Coltart to see. They certainly did not look like very much, just a few ragged pieces of paper with roughly-drawn diagrams and a few notes, all composed in thick pencil lead: hard to believe that the lives of 101 men and a state-of-the-art T Class submarine now depended on them. 'I gave him the plan', said Oram, 'explained the general situation to him, and told him that he must look out for men escaping from the after escape chamber'.

Oram then made a signal through to the Commander-in-Chief, Plymouth, Admiral Nasmith, giving him the general situation and explaining about their recovery idea. Oram was still suffering from the effects of carbon dioxide poisoning, as well as nervous exhaustion, and now he had to lay down and let the symptoms pass, happy in the knowledge that he had delivered their rescue plan, its application had already begun, and he could now, finally, rest. The *Thetis*'s DSEA escape equipment had worked perfectly and the chamber had operated as it was designed to do, quick, efficient and perfectly safe. Mills immediately informed the Admiralty that the first two men had escaped and the rest were alive and would be coming up in the same manner as the two officers. By the time Oram and Woods reached the *Brazen*, the next two men were due to burst through another cloud of bubbles at any moment. It was now 08.30 hours, nearly seven hours before he thought the air would run out.

As soon as Mills saw the *Thetis* he signalled the *Grebe Cock* to up anchor and follow him. Godfrey saw the tail before he even had got his anchor up, but he did not link it with the *Thetis*. 'I took it to be an aeroplane. There had been an aeroplane reported missing the night before from Ringway Airport [now Manchester Airport] and I thought it was her sticking up'. Godfrey calculated that he had been barely two miles from the *Thetis*, stationary at anchor, the whole time and had still failed to see her. He later explained why, with so many eyes scanning the morning horizon, this serious oversight had occurred. 'I think the *Brazen* and the *Vigilant* would possibly hide it from us'. This was quite possible. Mills reported he was only three miles away and eventually spotted the tail with the naked eye. He should have seen it much sooner, but the track of the sun moving with him obscured it for some time.

Commander Hubert Hart, aboard the *Vigilant*, saw the tail about the same time as Mills, arriving on the scene to see Oram and Woods break the surface. He lowered a boat at once, in case anyone else escaped in the same area, because both the *Grebe Cock* and the *Vigilant* were ordered to keep away from the immediate area. This was by no means a callous act. 'It was obvious then that you were only going to kill people if you put anything other than boats alongside', said Hart, 'if people were coming up'. Quite often, when a submariner broke the surface wearing a DSEA set, the velocity of his ascent would throw the man out of the water up to his waist before crashing back down into the foam. Slamming into a steel hull at that speed head first, directly in line with his escape route, would mean certain death.

Hart was a key figure in arranging for the necessary equipment for Oram's plan to be sent out from Liverpool. Even before these arrangements were made he decided from his own initiative to get burning gear sent out at once. The time was exactly 08.53 hours when he sent the message to Mr Rowland at the Mersey Docks & Harbour Board saying:

SEND BURNERS AND BURNING GEAR OUT AT ONCE WITH TUG

He had no instructions to do this, but as a professional salvage officer, he wanted it there. 'I think, at the time, the position in my mind was this. There was no immediate question of all the crew being lost, or indeed any of them, but as a measure of precaution and absolute necessity in the salvage of the submarine, we may require burning gear and, therefore, it is to be sent out at once'. The cutting gear was in their buoy stores, where all navigation buoys were repaired and overhauled, at a place called the Dingle, about two miles from the Princes Landing Stage. Even allowing for getting the gear from the Dingle and loading it on the tug *Crosby*, the two-hour run to the *Thetis* took five hours and seventeen minutes.

Not until a little after 09.30 hours did Hart finally put through the signal, asking for the air pipe, compressors and diver necessary to begin putting Oram's plan into full effect. Once the gear arrived, it was loaded on to the *Vigilant*, which was now a joint diving and salvage platform. Hart also decided to run a wire underneath, the *Thetis*'s stern in front of her rear hydroplanes and back to the *Vigilant*, just in case the stern again sank below the surface. All the time the salvage operation was going on, rowing and motorboats from the *Brazen* and the *Vigilant* loitered around the area waiting for others to escape, being careful to avoid the place where Oram and Woods disturbed the calm blue surface about two hours earlier. At least twelve more assorted ratings and civilian men should have surfaced by now. Woods asked Brock to bang on the submarine's raised hull to let those inside know that it was safe to come out. After enough hammer blows fell on the steel plating to justify a sound response, Brock said, 'We gave repeated bangs, like an ordinary series of knockings, and there was no reply, so we spelt out "come out" [in Morse Code] a number of times so that they would know someone was waiting outside'. There was no reply.

Arnold, Glenn and Chapman saw the tell-tail shaft of light, shining down through the flooded escape chamber spy hole, showing that the two officers had been flung to the surface. Although no more than a speck in the vastness of the trapped submarine the tiny beam meant their plan was by now in safe, competent, hands and the men could start immediately to escape the foul and now dangerous conditions building up within the submarine.

Glenn and Arnold moved forward to re-set the escape chamber for the next two men to leave. Glenn, who was clearly the more distressed of the two, did what he could to help. Arnold later explained what happened next, 'We drained down the chamber again and owing to the angle of the boat the water just ran over the coaming of the bulkhead door into the main motors. This caused a short circuit and there was a cloud of smoke, which came into the Stokers' mess [steering compartment]. We shut the bulkhead door and those that had gas masks put them on and the others used DSEA gear without being ordered to. The smoke was thick and white, and choking'. The smoke enveloped the men, some of whom were now in the early stages of dying, indiscriminately burning their eyes, throats and lungs. Due to the running dehumidifier, the smoke eventually soaked throughout the whole submarine. This, at least, thinned the smoke down and made life fractionally more bearable. Morale was rapidly declining when Lieutenant Chapman decided on a drastic step with just as drastic consequences.

If the air was becoming too foul to breath before the small fire, the smoke pollution had made matters very much worse. Chapman knew time was running out, and there was no way that all the men were going to escape before the air ran out. To speed up the process he ordered four men into the escape chamber that was only designed for two. The interior of a 1930s T Class submarine escape chamber measured 6 feet 9 inches high and barely 3 feet across. Two fully-grown men, complete with breathing sets fitted into the tiny steel vault quite comfortably. But four men shoehorned into the tiny space, their breathing sets pressed into one another, had considerably less room around them than in a coffin. The four chosen men were already very weak. The now monumental effort to put on the breathing apparatus, then put one foot in front of the other and drag themselves closer and closer to the chamber was considerably more than gruelling.

Jamison and Glenn felt that four men were two too many, but had to obey their senior officer. Two Royal Navy personnel, Leading Stoker Thomas Kenney and Stoker Wilfred Hole along with two Cammell Laird's men including Cornelius Smith, showed no signs of fear as they forced themselves into the chamber. The tough square-jawed Kenney had once already failed his escape chamber training at Fort Blockhouse, which was a very rare occurrence. He was not the best choice for such a chance escape idea. Stoker Hole had every incentive to get out. The day was his first wedding anniversary with his wife, Caroline and he already had a six-month-old baby daughter called Eugene to provide for. Each man only had a few inches of space around himself and his rather bulky DSEA set. Standing upright this would be bad enough, but as each man crushed into his companion due to the steep 35° angle the *Thetis* had gained, exhaustion, discomfort and fear were bottling up.

Once the four men where squeezed inside, Arnold closed and locked the door. He then opened the inlet valve and the water gushed into the bottom of the chamber. Arnold explained, 'We shut the door on them and flooded up exactly as we did in the first instance. The place flooded up all right – it went in quite fast, really'. Inside the chamber the occupants slipped and jostled for position within each one's tiny space. One of the Royal Navy men was tasked with opening the escape hatch once it had been flooded up. It was a simple two-part action – with only two men that is. A wheel on the hatch was spun round to the 'hatch free to revolve' point on a dial then it was a simple motion to remove a clip on the hatch – a slight push – and it would fly open into the open sea and freedom.

In the darkness Hole, Kenney and the two Laird's men could not see, only feel the ice-cold liquid move over and between them. Whatever they thought at this moment, relief from the cramped conditions was now only minutes away, as they, too, would soon shoot out of the chamber, burst on to the surface and be saved. Before the water reached the critical point, where the pressure equalled to free the hatch, an attempt was made to open it far too soon. They might as well have been trying to push through a brick wall. Nothing happened. Another attempt was made and still the hatch was firmly locked shut.

The escape time passed and Arnold still could not see the welcoming shaft of sunlight indicating that the hatch had opened and the four men were gone. Inside the chamber Hole, Kenney and the two Cammell Laird's men were far from escaping to freedom. The calmness they had displayed only minutes before while entering the chamber was now eaten away with a will to live at any cost. As the fear and panic spread, each man kicked and fought his neighbour, limbs and heads banging and slamming into each other and the steel walls, as they all fought to hold on to life.

Arnold and Glenn gave them plenty of time to make their escape, but after what seemed far too long they drained down the chamber and opened the door. 'We waited and waited, and it came to a quarter of an hour and still no sign of the hatch opening', said Arnold. 'Nothing happened, so we drained down, and three were dead and the other one was very near it'. To everyone's horror the four men were twisted and gnarled together in their final death agony. The fourth man, Cornelius Smith, was only barely alive. 'Their mouthpieces were just torn away from them', added Arnold. 'They were all foaming from the mouth when we brought them back. We dragged the three bodies back into the boat and helped the other chap out, and he was just about finished, when we brought the three bodies back it broke the morale of the men; you could see it on their faces. You could not speak down there – but you could see the look in their eyes.'

Cornelius Smith who was just hanging on to life could hardly speak. He was one of Shaw's men. Shaw had entered the compartment to try to get away from the smoke and ended up helping Arnold to remove the dead. He knelt beside his colleague who was trying to talk, but finding it incredibly hard to say what had just happened. Shaw put his ear closer to Smith's mouth. Smith muttered a few inarticulate words before Shaw grasped what had happened, 'I asked him why they had never got out and he said, or he tried to tell me, that they could not open the hatch'.

Regardless of this tragedy the men had to keep trying to escape or they were all doomed. Jamison and Glenn now suggested openly what they felt before, that only two at a time should now go out. But there was every chance those trying to escape would also be drowned in the confined space, if a fault had developed in the hatch. Looking around at the utter despair among the more lucid men, Glenn called Arnold and Shaw to one side and said, 'For God's sake try and get out and buck these lads up!'

Shaw had no practical experience of using the Davis Escape Apparatus or the chamber but, like the Laird's men present on the dive trial, he had at least attended a lecture. Arnold was very confident of his fate. 'From the very first moment I was down there it never dawned on me for one minute that I was going to stop down there'. He took control of his and Shaw's escape, coming across as the experienced escape chamber user, but he was hiding a secret unknown to Shaw, or even his own crewmates. He later testified, 'I had never been through the escape chamber [training] at all, it was the first time I had been in it. The last time I went to go through was when Kenney collapsed at the bottom of the tank (at Fort Blockhouse), so they drained it down and I never went through the escape chamber'. Shaw, believing he was with a rating experienced in submarine escape, let Arnold take control of his life.

Arnold slowly put Shaw's breathing apparatus over the man's head and tried to wrap the straps around his body twice as recommended. Shaw was too overweight and Arnold had to settle for doing it once and tying the rest of the straps the best he could. Arnold then told Shaw that he must open his exhaust tap on the side of the apparatus as he left the chamber. This was essential. Poison gasses could build up in the mask, or worse still the apparatus could burst under the pressure differential between their depth and the surface. Either way if Shaw did not open the cock, he would perhaps surface dead, or suffer serious injury.

As the two men entered the chamber, Lieutenant Chapman, as with Oram and Woods, wished the two men good luck. Arnold closed the door and started flooding the chamber from the inside this time to ensure he had control over his own life, albeit without the full training. Arnold remembered the state of the men long after he left. 'The air was in a terrible state by then. It was just exhausted'. Before Shaw entered the chamber he took one last look across the steering compartment. About eighteen men were lying around the room in various stages of carbon dioxide poisoning, slumped over, vomiting or twitching while others were motionless. The stench of sweat, vomit and urine made the choking atmosphere even harder to swallow. He reckoned only about six were still fit enough to escape under their own abilities compared to many more Woods had seen about two hours earlier. He described how the air was very thick. Speaking was very difficult and a choking feeling gripped his throat. The two men climbed into the chamber as Hole, Kenney and the two Laird's men had done so half an hour before. When the door was locked both men did not put on their mouthpieces until the last possible moment. Forty-five minutes had passed since the fire broke out and as Arnold left he could still see men still wearing their DSEA sets and masks, which would soon become empty.

Now, as the cold water poured like it had during the previous failed attempt, for all Shaw had learnt in theory during his lecture, nothing could have prepared him for what happened next. He later captured vividly what Hole, Kenney and the others went through before dying so violently. 'When you step into the escape chamber and the water begins to fill up, when you put this mouthpiece on, the first time, speaking from experience the water covers your head; you can just barely see. You have a pair of goggles on; you have a feeling that you are trapped, and your instinct is to put your hand up and shove the hatch off. If you do that right away it will not open'. When the chamber was flooded quite high Arnold signalled Shaw to lift the hatch. They both knew that there was every chance it would not work and they, too, might be dragged out dead or dying a few minutes later. Shaw did what he was told, pushed on the hatch clip to open it, and braced himself to be shot out into the open sea. Nothing happened.

Arnold motioned to him to wait a little longer. Both men stood calmly for a few tense moments as the water rose ever higher in the confined blackness. Shaw tried once again. This time the hatch flew open, propelling him up and out very fast indeed – but he forgot to open his exhaust vent. Arnold, realizing what had happened, was just able to twist it open as Shaw's body shot passed him hitting two stays on the way up. Arnold, unlike Oram who had stripped to his trousers was still fully clothed including his boots, was right behind Shaw, but got caught on the hatch clips because of the submarine's angle. A few hard kicks and he too was free. Apart from hitting the same two stays as Shaw, in a matter of moments both men were on the surface being pulled into boats, safe and well. Both men were taken to the *Brazen*. Along the way, after all the breathing difficulties they had suffered, they both enjoyed a good smoke in the clean fresh air of a calm Liverpool Bay still bathed in the early morning brightness of another particularly hot summer's day. On boarding the *Brazen*, Arnold was asked if any more were coming up. He said that they most definitely would be, in pairs, and to watch out for them.

When Arnold and Shaw managed to escape, the tell-tale shaft of light told those aboard the *Thetis* that the two men were safe. The hatch had worked fine. The next Navy rating and Laird's man donned their breathing apparatus and slowly crawled into the tiny chamber. Ever so slowly, someone who still had enough strength closed the door. The two men were flooded up, most likely thinking that it was an unequal pressure that caused the others to fail and they would not now make the same mistake, trying as hard as they could to keep mind, body and rational thought together. The valve was turned to 'ready to open'; when the moment was right the clip was removed and the hatch flew open.

The bubbles rushed out, as daylight poured in. Just as they could taste freedom the hatch jammed only 3 inches up from the closed position. All they could do was hammer on the hatch as hard as their exhausted bodies would let them, and slide their fingers into the open sea, but that was as close as they would ever get to escaping. For some

70

mysterious reason the hatch had jammed, just another rotten episode in the *Thetis*'s relentless bad luck.

The chamber was drained down, they crawled back out, broken, demoralized and much nearer death than they had been only minutes before. Two more volunteers dragged their half lifeless bodies into the chamber. Again it was flooded up and again the two men pushed the hatch up, and again just as it opened and daylight shone through the hatch jammed at about 3 inches, enough for them to glimpse the sunlit surface beyond their dark, steel prison. After a few futile hammer blows, all the two men could do was go back into the foul interior and hope that help would now come from the outside.

The *Brazen* and the *Vigilant* kept nearby while their tenders continued to stay in position around where the other four men had escaped. Shortly afterwards another cloud of bubbles was rushing to the surface – but no heads appeared. Brock saw very clearly what had just happened, and what came next. He said he clearly heard, 'A distinct knocking, like hammering in the submarine. There was nothing continuous; it was just a case of ordinary hammering. It was purely and simply as if a man was hammering at something, and then he would stop a bit and hammer a bit more.'

A little later another cluster of bubbles rushed to the surface. Again Brock heard the frantic hammering, and again no more men escaped. No more ever would. All those still trapped aboard could hear and feel each hammer blow like a nail in their own coffins. By this time the effects of poisoning were getting too great. Men were giving up now and were lying down wherever they could. The next stage of carbon dioxide poisoning was taking its toll. Many were suffering from confusion. Others would become argumentative and fighting each other for no reason as the poisoning took its toll on the brain.

Some would be suffering from hallucinations and many were too far gone to even cry out, or even cry for that matter. Shortly thereafter some, and gradually more and more, would slip into a coma noticeable by the heavy panting slowly ceasing. Just as they are dying they may start to breath heavier again. That had nothing to do with the carbon dioxide. It is a reflex action to grab on to the very low levels of oxygen still present. Those who were still alive looked on at their comrades, possibly thinking that they really were fine after all, still alive, so there was hope. But such a reflex is only reached at the very terminal stage and death came shortly afterwards. No one still alive had the strength either to escape, or help to conclude Oram's plan.

Although there were no other escapes the general mood among the rescue craft was good. So good in fact that a signal to Managing Director Robert Johnson aboard the Laird's built RMS *Mauretania* off Scotland on her sea trials, 'Good prospects of saving majority and also good prospects of salving submarine after rescue of crew ...' Regardless of the foul conditions now badly affecting those trapped aboard the *Thetis*, Hart distinctly remembered, 'We were told most definitely that everybody inside was quite happy, and that they were all expected to escape from the Davis Escape'. He could not remember from whom the message came, but he believed it originated from the *Brazen*.

After trying to locate the source later on, he drew a complete blank. But he was adamant that the message, and its contents, '[were] definitely agreed upon by everybody who was there, as far as my own staff were concerned'. During the next two hours there was very little activity at the wreck site, apart from keeping vessels away should others escape and arranging the necessary equipment to put into effect Oram's plan. Ironically the motto of HMS *Thetis* was 'I Bide My Time'. About twenty vessels waited for the expected escapes. But the dying men they were led to believe were still quite happy were, biding their time, knowing that their only hope now lay in those on the outside – who were, according to Admiralty policy, thinking just the opposite.

Chapter 7

The Slow Death of a Submarine

About 300 miles northeast of Liverpool Bay, Chief Salvage Officer Thomas McKenzie was trying to raise the 26,000-ton German battle cruiser SMS *Derfflinger* in Scapa Flow, Orkney. He had many years salvage experience, which included two years with the Liverpool & Glasgow Salvage Association, three-and-a-half years with the Admiralty Salvage Section during the First World War, then seven years salvaging the scuttled German Imperial High Seas Fleet in Scapa Flow under salvage engineer Ernest Cox. Then he spent a further six years salvaging the German fleet under the firm Metal Industries who bought out Cox in the early 1930s. McKenzie was without doubt one of the United Kingdom's most experienced marine salvage officers.

The *Derfflinger* was well and truly dug deep into the mud at the bottom of the Flow. Even with dive times down to only one hour the operation was dogged with many minor cases of the bends, and trying to find the fine balance between lifting her level, which was now eluding even this highly accomplished salvage expert. Operations to reclaim the *Derfflinger* started in autumn 1938. About eight months later on 2 June 1939 she was still far from being on her way to the surface.

At about 10.00 hours that Friday morning McKenzie was walking down to his office when a Boom Defence officer stopped him and said that he had just heard on a wireless that the *Thetis* was missing. There was only a handful of divers in the whole country qualified to descend to the depth of the stricken submarine, most of whom were already employed on the *Derfflinger* that day. After getting the news McKenzie continued to his office to offer the help of his crack divers. 'I went in and I asked them to clear a line for a priority call straight away' he said. In actual fact he made one phone call through to the Admiral,

73

Rosyth, and sent two telegrams, one to the Admiralty in Whitehall, saying succinctly, 'Can be of assistance sunken submarine with deep-sea divers and salvage ships specially equipped for compressed air work'. To be certain that he had the ability to help, McKenzie sent the same telegram to Cammell Laird, only adding, '... and fitted with compressed air chamber'.

He had to wait around his office for nearly three hours for the telegram from the Admiralty saying in so many words, thanks, but no thanks. Cammell Laird, said, 'Many thanks for your offer. Ship has been located and all reported safe'. All he could do was to leave his office, for the three-mile boat trip back out to the *Derfflinger* and another hard day's work trying to win her back. Shortly after McKenzie sent his two signals Captain Nicholson aboard HMS *Matabele* arrived at the *Thetis* dive site leading the Sixth Destroyer Flotilla. Under the terms of the 1934 Admiralty Fleet Order Nicholson was now the senior ranking officer on site, assuming overall command of the salvage and rescue operations. When the *Matabele* dropped anchor, Lieutenant Woods boarded her to report on what had occurred while Nicholson was en route from Plymouth. They met on the destroyer's bridge where Woods showed deep concern, not only for the health of those still trapped aboard, but also for the fact that no more men had escaped since Arnold and Shaw several hours earlier.

He was clearly very anxious by this time and emphasized to Nicholson that in his opinion the situation must by now be somewhat serious. Nicholson later recounted, 'At the time I was trying to get a grasp of the situation. Having suddenly arrived up there, I did not know what steps had been taken or what had been done. What was going to be done, and what should be done now'. His and others' confused approach was to dog the remainder of the rescue operation and contribute significantly to its tragic outcome.

Mersey Docks & Harbour Board diver Frederick Orton was an experienced man, whose main work ranged from recovering lost equipment to minor salvage operations. He had only ever worked at depths of about 40 feet – not about 130 feet where the *Thetis* now lay. His first job upon descending to the *Thetis* was to locate the forward torpedo hatch and try to screw it down so more pressure could be pumped into the flooded compartments without the compressed air blowing it open. He had never dived on a submarine before, so Wreck Master Brock drew a rough sketch of where the hatch, whistle and gun recuperator were in relation to the conning tower. To ensure Orton did not miss the submarine on the way down, Brock dropped a four-pointed grapple on her forward end so he could follow it right down on to the *Thetis*'s deck casing.

Orton climbed awkwardly over the side of the dive launch, down a small ladder and was soon below the surface and gliding down to the bottom in a steady slow-motion free-fall. Holding on to Hart's shot line he passed the steeply angled *Thetis* all the way down. In his other hand was a thin rope to tie near the gun so he could glide right into position on his next dive. But the grapple was not the only line snaking into the depths. Right next him, like a thin, black shadow was a galvanized wire, no thicker than a length of twine. As the submarine came into view the fine wire was wrapped all around the conning tower, and the gun, like an erratic steel spider's web. He said, 'There was so much of it; there were yards and yards and yards of it. One part came down from the buoy and that was fouled right round the conning tower, and then there were all these other bits wrapped round and round and round'. The wire came from one of her marker buoys and the thin, but incredibly strong wire was extremely dangerous for any diver.

The visibility was an impressive 40 feet or so in all directions, giving ample opportunity for Orton to find and execute what he was instructed to do. First of all he tied the line to a ladder on the port side of the conning tower and immediately signalled his attendant that he was about to surface. Closing his air outlet, Orton floated to the top without the need to decompress. He later explained, 'I reckon to do far more work doing it in short spasms like that, than staying down for an hour'. He had a point. The longer he was down the longer he would have to decompress and being the only diver on site at the time the more time he was able to stay on the *Thetis*, rather than decompressing, just looking at her far below him.

After only two or three minutes of fresh air he was on his way back down. This time he followed Brock's grapple before sliding down the submarine's jumper stay (a short forward mast support) right next to where the forward hatch was supposed to be. But, even with such good visibility he could not find it, or the gun recuperator for that matter. All Orton could do was return to the surface yet again before making a third dive to set in motion Oram's plan. If he could not find them, the whole plan was doomed. Orton surfaced, intending to only stay for another few minutes and grab a wheel spanner to screw down the fore hatch, should he find it on the submarine's fore end. While he was looking for the spanner, Brock was called to the *Somali* for yet another of the day's many, many conferences. He told Orton not to descend this time until he returned, or sent word of what to do next. Orton was already on the ladder to go down. To save the effort of trying to get back into the dive boat in all his cumbersome dive gear, and wait for his next move, he decided to stay where he was. Shortly afterwards Brock hailed Orton's attendant and shouted across to him. 'Call the diver in, finish diving'.

Somewhat confused, Orton replied, 'What about our ropes? Shall we buoy them or cut them?

'Cut them', Brock shouted back. 'They may get in the way of the release buoy and upset the operations'. It was about 11.45 hours – dead slack water. Orton had a good hour and fifteen minutes dive time left, more than enough to complete one of the two main tasks he was ordered to do. Too much emphasis was being placed on not getting in the way of escaping men, but Orton, being no where near the after escape chamber was more than happy to continue.

Nicholson and the other senior officers aboard the *Somali* were beginning to realize that Oram's plan was very quickly becoming impracticable. Its implication was taking too long. The all-important strongback to secure the fore hatch was ready at Cammell Laird for midday, but it would still not be at the scene before 15.00 hours, and Orton had yet to locate where to put it, or given the chance for that matter. Oram remained in the *Brazen* and he was still clearly not very well. He had to rest frequently, and was unable to write his signals, having to dictate them instead. Even though he was informed of what was happening he still had no clear idea of what was going on, blindly believing that his rapidly disintegrating salvage plan was the only way forward.

In theory it was a great plan. Had it succeeded it is highly unlikely that anyone would have died. In practice it was severely handicapped by lack of time, know how and tools for the job. About twenty hours had now elapsed. Nicholson's first move, as the now fifth commander of the rescue operation, was to go to the *Vigilant* and talk to Hart about what the best action was to take. They decided to force the *Thetis*'s stern higher out of the water and secure it there so a hole could be cut in the stern to release the crew. At 13.10 hours the *Vigilant* was heaving the stern higher in the water, running with the rising tide. The angle of the stern had increased to about 60° after two tugboats helped the inclination by towing the *Vigilant* astern. This should, in theory, have secured her higher in the water. Inside she was becoming very unstable, as well as making life for the trapped men intolerably harder.

Now lacking the strength to move, many men tumbled into each other, or solid steel fittings as they piled towards the bow end of the engine room and steering compartment, bumping, scraping and twisting their exhausted bodies along the way. Although the air was just about exhausted by now, and some of the men were already dead, it was quite clear to the rescue craft that a few trapped aboard were still very much aware of what was happening. Nicholson was later questioned about the efforts of the men inside the *Thetis* to make their presence known around this time. He replied, 'In fact tapping did occur ... but there was too much to do. One was too occupied to follow up [and] we had no time. It was reported and we left it like that; I never followed it up'. One wonders why Nicholson could not have had someone, anyone, of the hundreds of men now under his immediate command just tap on the raised tail from time to time to give the dying some feeling of hope.

By early afternoon at last an inspection plate into Z tank could be removed and perhaps air could finally be fed into those still barely alive. A whaler rowed out to the stern where Brock jumped on to the submarine's tail and hauled himself up to where the inspection plate was located. He planned to open both an outer and an inner plate to gain access to Z tank up to bulkhead 146 where the men were on the other side. Even if he did succeed in gaining entry through the hatches, inside was more than a little cramped. There were hydroplane shafts and the steering gear shafts towards 146 bulkhead. Then there were very heavy, large rolled steel stiffeners to support the compartment, very much like large steel pillars welded to the bulkhead for added strength. Narrowing down to only 9 inches at the tightest point near the rudder head there had been very little room in which to move.

Three tugs had since been dispatched from Liverpool with cutting gear and would be arriving at any moment, so removing the plate was now an absolute must. At 14.40 hours the tug *Crosby* was the first on scene with cutting gear and the Liverpool & Glasgow salvage vessel *Ranger* was not far behind, along with the tug *Holm Cock* with her gear. The *Somali* came near with her drilling equipment to put in the airlines to feed fresh air into the dying men. With the ebb tide starting to run, Brock had to wedge himself into position as the tide pressed against the tail, trying to force her down. He slowly removed the outer cover, which, when freed slipped over the side, splashed into the water and was lost. The inner cover had four large bolts, firmly securing it into the submarine's hull. They turned with ease, but as they were loosened a large volume of air gushed out of the crack, under considerable pressure.

Nicholson ordered the plate to be screwed back down tightly until they could confirm if this was normal or not. Oram said that the plate could be removed, but with the *Thetis* balancing precariously on her stem, and the tide pressing her down, just as Brock was again unscrewing the bolts the *Thetis* started to cant over and he had to jump clear. She naturally swung into the ebb tide, losing nearly all of her buoyancy in the tail with the *Vigilant* hanging on for dear life. The more she was at right angles to the tide the more the pressure built up against her. The tide swung her right round into its own line. Hart said, 'It would have been possible to lash the *Vigilant* to the stern of the submarine and not to try to get it more out of he water. That was my idea, as I told Captain Nicholson, but to raise the submarine slightly in order to get low enough to cut the hole, and the mere fact of holding on to her did not raise her sufficiently to let us do that. We were advised we could not possibly burn a hole low enough in her through which the crew could get out'. A grave error. The time was 14.40 hours. About sixty minutes before carbon dioxide levels started to become more lethal.

In his own words Nicholson knew the situation was 'desperate' and although more than eighteen rescue ships were now above the *Thetis*, the trapped men were no closer to being rescued. Nicholson, who was supposed to be in command, had no idea what to do next and again turned to Hart for an answer. Quite clearly the commander did not like what the salvage man had to say. Hart insisted that they hold the *Thetis* in the same position until low water because once the tide ceased ebbing she could be hauled up higher and thus it would be easier, and safer, to cut a hole. He later remembered, 'Captain Nicholson again repeated that the position was desperate and asked me if I realized it, and I told him that of course I did. He then suggested, after talking to his staff, apart from me, that we should endeavour to raise her higher, to cut this hole, by placing tugs in the reverse direction, namely, ahead of the *Vigilant*, and pull her up into the tide. That was his exact expression "desperate".'

Nicholson had relied heavily on the advice of Doctor G. Ramsay Stark for what he did next. Stark who had arrived a little earlier from Holyhead, as medical adviser, had already diagnosed carbon dioxide poisoning as the primary problem, judging by the condition of the four survivors. He told Nicholson that the chances that anyone would be alive after 18.00 hours were 'slight'. This was the clinching piece of information that made Nicholson decide to take such drastic, but futile measures, to save the trapped men. He also informed the Treasury Solicitor a few weeks later, '... had it been possible to effect an entrance to the submarine during the afternoon [2 June], the list of survivors would have been greater'.

As far as Nicholson was concerned, it was a case of raise the stern and/or be damned. The tugs and the *Vigilant* secured for another tow, this time against the tide to help give more lift. Hart was adamant, 'I told him that I disapproved of it and would not agree to it, but if he insisted I would carry out his desire to the best of my ability, but that he must definitely assume all responsibility, as I considered that the chances were 100 to one against success, and I considered the same thing would happen as happened in the first operation, and that it might cause serious damage and lose what chance of success we had at low water'.

Nicholson agreed to take full responsibility. Hart did suggest not using destroyers ahead of the *Vigilant* to help tow up the submarine's stern as Nicholson had ordered, but rather two tugs, they would be more easy to manoeuvre. The *Crosby* and *Storm Cock* were placed ahead of the *Vigilant*, whose wire was still round the *Thetis*'s stern. They eased forward and ever so gradually the submarine's tail lifted higher out of the water. Perhaps it might, just work.

Like a tube balancing on one sharp end she was becoming incredibly unstable with every passing second. Her main ballast tanks were fitted with holes all along their bottoms so that the air could be forced out into the open sea at a moment's notice. Only about eight tons of water were needed to flood into the main tanks for enough buoyancy to be lost. Inevitably as she was pulled up the trapped air bubbled out through her bottom holes as the water rushed in. At first only a few tons of water seeped in, then four, five, six, right up to eight tons or more and the tail took a sharp twist to port. The wire running from the *Vigilant* round the *Thetis* parted, forcing the submarine to smash into the *Vigilant*, as she slipped beneath the waves for the third time in twenty-four hours. Hart formally reported back to Nicholson that now *really* nothing more could be done until the tide slackened at about 18.00 hours.

Those still clinging to life inside the pressure hull were bumped and thrown around the interior for a second time, little able to support or protect themselves from flying debris and striking the myriad steel fixings all over the interior decks and bulkheads. Some would still have had enough focus to know that all the previous night's efforts to raise the stern, for what they thought would be a quick escape through the mere ⅝ inch thick pressure hull, were now gone in a few minutes. Nicholson later insisted, 'The thing we had to consider in the first place was the desperate situation as it appeared to us, and it struck me and others that whatever action we took was justified.' It may well have been justified, but after finding the *Thetis* seven hours earlier such a bold move was well and truly too little to late.

It was now 15.10 hours. Twenty-four hours and thirty minutes had elapsed since the *Thetis* first went down. At about the same time McKenzie was back out at the *Derfflinger* site aboard the salvage vessel *Bertha*. Two of his key divers were on the bottom when the Boom Defence drifter *Brine* came alongside the *Bertha* and the drifter's captain, Lieutenant Groves handed McKenzie two signals. One was from Cammell Laird, which read:

THETIS POSITION IS DESPERATE. THERE IS AEROPLANE WAITING AT LONGHOPE TO TAKE MR MCKENZIE AND PERSONNEL AT LIVERPOOL – THREE OR FOUR DIVERS – CHANGING AT INVERNESS TO BE AT SPEKE AERODROME (LIVERPOOL) AT 16.00 HRS.

The other signal was from the Admiralty:

GRATEFUL FOR YOUR ASSISTANCE. REQUEST YOU START IMMEDIATELY TO SUBMARINE IN POSITION 53° 34′ NORTH, 3° 52′ WEST. SUBMARINE LYING FORE PART FLOODED AND AGROUND AND TAIL JUST ABOVE WATER.

'I called my divers up from twenty-three fathoms by emergency signal', said McKenzie. 'That is a signal, which is only supposed to be given when they are in danger'. Diver Sinclair 'Sinc' Mackenzie later put it succinctly, 'When you receive an emergency signal you must come up if possible; it is a thing you do not question'. From about 140 feet the men opened the inlet valves on their dive suits and shot straight to the surface without decompressing. They were hauled into the *Bertha* where McKenzie told them what was really happening. Still in full diving dress along with two attendants, McKenzie and another salvage officer, left in the *Bertha* at full speed while the divers stripped off their gear en route, arriving ashore at about 15.30 hours.

The Kings Harbour Master had a car waiting for them at Lyness on the Orkney island of Hoy for the short run to Longhope, nine miles further south. The only available plane was designed to carry seven people. With two salvage officers, two attendants, three divers and the pilot, there were eight men crammed into the tiny machine. The pilot took off from the makeshift grass runway and headed out across the Pentland Firth south to Inverness. Upon their arrival an hour later the Admiralty had chartered another plane from the airline Scottish Airways. McKenzie added, 'At 17.30 hours we arrived at Inverness and changed to a faster plane, which had been chartered by the Admiralty. The pilot of the plane was just about to leave with a full complement of passengers, but they were all ordered to disembark so as to leave the plane free for us'. By 17.33 hours they were on their way to Speke Aerodrome.

While McKenzie's team was making a cross country and water dash, Hart had not given up hope of finding the tail. Luckily the submarine's indicator buoy was still attached to her and was still clearly visible to all the ships impotently bobbing around doing nothing. The burning gear was transferred from the *Crosby* to the *Vigilant* and later that evening at low tide the *Vigilant* managed to pass a small wire under the stern and up to a camel to hopefully raise the tail. The wire bit tight against the smooth, steel hull of the submarine as, yet again, she slowly left the seabed. Hart was finally retaking control of events. The more the tail rose, the more strain went on the wire until it parted with a loud crack as the *Thetis* plummeted back to the seabed, ripping off her marker buoy along the way. She was now well and truly lost.

The *Thetis*'s violent slewing and final loss may not have been entirely due to the botched salvage efforts. At some point, long after all life was supposed to be extinct two men, Stoker William Matthews and one other managed to crawl into the escape chamber. Another crew-member forced his concentration to close and then lock the door slowly remembering and executing each monumental command. The two men flooded the escape hatch and, like the two times before, they waited for the pressure to equalize. The door again had sprung open – and, again, jammed at about the 3 inches up from its recess. This time no loud hammering was heard.

They signalled to have the door opened back into the steering compartment. Somebody heaved their racked body up to the door and went through the agonizing process of opening it to let Matthews and his colleague back in to the hell they hoped they would not see again. Unfortunately, a combination of being dazed, disorientated and struggling to focus against the mental and physical pain, someone forgot to close the seawater inlet. As the hatch door opened a wall of water poured into the steering compartment at a rate of about three quarters of a ton per second. Those on the engine room side of the escape chamber still had the presence of mind to close the bulkhead door to protect themselves from the water pouring into the steering compartment.

All ninety-nine men had congregated in the engine room and steering compartment sometime before their end where many, but not all, were wearing their DSEA sets. For those in the steering compartment the inbound wave pressurized the carbon dioxide. With no way for the gas to vent the levels soared, bringing on a rapid and agonizing end for those still alive. Eyes bulging, gagging like dying fish out of water, some bit down into their tongues, others retched or simply hugged each other for a little human comfort until a welcome death enveloped their horror and ended their suffering.

Many had no DSEA sets on, and oddly a lot of unused sets lay scattered around the two compartments with no attempt being made to use them. Lieutenants Chapman and Jamison were among those wearing them, although strangely they only breathed ¾ of their available air supply before succumbing. Hambrook's oxygen bottle was full, having breathed nothing from his cylinder at all. Lieutenant Commander Bolus was also wearing a set. He breathed it to the end, knowing that once his last breath was exhaled there was nothing left but poisoned air to fill his lungs. After an instinctive, though futile struggle he, like his ninety-eight comrades, became another victim of the disaster.

Chapter 8

'The Admiralty Regrets . . .'

During the 400-mile journey from Scapa Flow to Liverpool Bay, McKenzie had plenty of time to think over what he was about to face. On 19 January 1917 the 1,980-ton K Class submarine HMS *K-13* was, like the *Thetis*, on her sea trials in Gareloch with her fifty-three-man crew along with thirty-seven assorted shipbuilding employees, civilian contractors and Admiralty officials. The 'K' boats were revolutionary in the field of submarine warfare. They were big, fast and steam-driven, meaning they needed funnels to aid their propulsion: a sort of dreadnought of the deep. Being steam-driven meant that their funnels had to be lowered into special deck recesses before diving, where hatches then closed over them before leaving the surface.

But the K boats were not very lucky. They sank no enemy shipping throughout the whole First World War, while at the same time being responsible for killing many of their own crews in one accident or another. Eventually 'K' came to stand for 'Killer' within the Service after more than half the Class ended up being rammed, sunk after uncontrollable dives or lost on their trials. The *K-13* was among those losses. She had in fact just completed her standard two-hour dive trial and been accepted by the Royal Navy, but the Admiralty wanted another test, just to ensure that the funnel hatches and engine room ventilators were, indeed, watertight. They were not.

Her funnels were lowered into their recesses just prior to the dive. The bridge was cleared and the hatch sealed before she flooded main tanks and started to go down. Eye witnesses could see her running with the conning tower above the water, which would usually look quite normal, but they could also see her stern disappearing before her bow, which most certainly was not. Inside the *K-13*, water was pouring in through four open engine room vents and one funnel hatch that was not quite closed properly, flooding the engine room and after torpedo room. The after section was sealed, killing thirty-three men trapped inside. Her captain ordered main tanks blown to get her to the surface as quickly as possible, but she continued to descend with water now surging into the control room through the speaking pipes, shorting fuses and threatening to kill many more of the men now fighting for their lives.

Her ten-ton drop keel was released to instantly lighten her but, like aboard the *Thetis*, this action made no difference and the *K-13* plunged to the seabed. Leaking oil led rescue craft straight to the scene and the following day an air hose was successfully connected, blowing high-pressure air into her ballast tanks. The *K-13*'s bow surfaced, supported by a wire strung between two barges, firmly securing the bow 10 feet above the surface. A hole was cut through the pressure hull using oxy-acetylene equipment and the final survivor climbed out fifty-seven hours after the initial accident. The hull breach was only inches above the water line, but in light of the desperate situation, it was still considered well worth the risk. The next evening the bollards were ripped off the attending salvage vessel and the bow crashed back to the seabed.

McKenzie had every reason to want to duplicate the same plan for the *Thetis*. While working as a salvage officer for the Liverpool & Glasgow Salvage Association he was heavily involved in the *K-13* rescue, making him the only person above and beyond Nicholson, Macintyre, Hart and everyone else involved in the *Thetis* operation to actually *know* what he was talking about. On the flight down to Speke he did formulate a similar plan for the *Thetis*. Granted, the *K-13* went down in only 55 feet and was in very sheltered waters only a mile from land, but weather conditions in Liverpool Bay were more than favourable, the *Thetis*'s stern was securely held above the water, and oxy-acetylene cutting gear must be there. Regarding duplicating the *K-13* rescue, McKenzie later said, 'I certainly considered it on the way down, but the stern was down before I got there'.

Two fast cars and a three-ton lorry were waiting for McKenzie and his team when they arrived at Speke. The cars then sped them to Princes Landing Stage to meet HMS *Matabele* for the final leg out to the wreck site. It was almost dark by the time they arrived, but the many bright lights around the *Thetis* came into view over the horizon long before they arrived at about 22.15 hours. Altogether the Scapa divers had gone from being at the bottom of Scapa Flow to arriving at the *Thetis* in only seven-and-a-half hours, which would be remarkable today, let alone in 1939. Upon his arrival McKenzie attended yet another of the day's many conferences aboard the *Matabele*, this time attended by Rear Admiral Watson, Macintyre, Nicholson, Robert Johnson from Cammell Laird and Hart to review all the proceedings to date. Quite clearly he was too late to do anything effective.

During the conference the question of the action taken which resulted in the sinking of the stern the first time on the previous day was reviewed. Hart recalled, 'I was asked my opinion as to the desirability of the action taken on the responsibility of Captain D [Nicholson]. I informed C-in-C Plymouth [Nasmith] that as we had definitely been assured that the crew of the submarine could not possibly last out for a further five hours until low water, that the action taken which had been described to the Captain D as a "hundred to one chance" against success, was obviously under those circumstances, justified'. Neither the Admiralty Inquiry, nor McKenzie, the only experienced submarine rescue person there, could agree.

Although it is highly unlikely Nicholson ever knew that the Naval Board considered him negligent, he did answer publicly, eventually, for his actions in trying to raise the tail unnecessarily higher against such tremendous odds. On being asked to explain himself, Nicholson replied, 'I discussed every matter with him [Hart] on every occasion, and took no decisions without his concurrence. I mean, he was the salvage expert'. Hart, however, was not qualified to recover such a wreck as the *Thetis*. He had never raised a submarine and the area around Great Ormes Head, although within the Lighterage jurisdiction of the Mersey Docks & Harbour Board, it was more than thirty miles beyond the waterway in which he was licensed to salvage.

In effect it was deep sea, where there were others close to hand, who were far more experienced in making the life and death decisions on a regular basis more frequently than fell to Hart in the normal course of his working life. Being a friend of Admiral Nasmith seems to be the only reason, or qualification, that he was there in the first place. George Critchley, of the Liverpool & Glasgow Salvage Association, was the man for the job.

Once all events had been reviewed it was decided that no further hope of life existed. Both Watson, who had arrived at 19.25 hours to become the sixth overall commander, and Robert Johnson gave their authority for Hart to continue salvaging the *Thetis* as a wreck only. None of this helped the current situation with respect to saving life and the first news McKenzie got was that, for all the many rescue vessels and men around the stricken submarine, she still had not been located since going back down earlier that afternoon.

Although the general consensus of opinion among the senior Naval staff was that all life must now be lost, McKenzie was not about to take a consensus as fact. It was as if all those present had been struck by paralysis. McKenzie, being the only person present to make a proactive decision, later said, 'We had a conference on board the *Somali*, and I suggested that as there had been no communication with the submarine from the time she sank until then, I should get more divers down at once, to see if there was any sign of life. This was at once agreed'. Agreed or not, McKenzie then went to the *Vigilant, Salvor* and *Ranger* in a launch and had to scrounge together enough diving equipment to get a man down to the wreck. The salvage vessel *Salvor* was placed right above the wreck to supply air to the diver. Sinclair 'Sinc' Mackenzie was the first of the Scapa Flow team to make a descent. The tide was ebbing with a force of about 3 knots, not ideal for a diver more than 130 feet down, feeling his way through total darkness. A surface speed of 3 knots is very little, but on the seabed it is equal to a gale. It was now 00.55 hours on 3 June. Medically speaking, all life must now be extinct.

The whites, reds and greens from the myriad navigation spot, flood and searchlights soon faded as Sinc Mackenzie disappeared deeper into the ink-black sea, carrying a 4 lb lump hammer. Soon he touched something solid and round. He then gave a sharp tug on his lifeline to say that he was on the vessel. Having no experience of submarines, he could not say where he was, but on later describing it on the surface, Mackenzie was told that he was on her wireless mast. He followed the mast down until about 140 feet from the surface, unable to see his hand if it was pressed up against his viewing glass and did not venture from the mast for fear of losing his way. 'My feet touched something', he later recalled, 'so it must have been the superstructure. I tapped on whatever I had hold of, I heard faint tappings; it was some distance away'. Somebody was still alive. For Mackenzie it was a simple case of lifting the hammer and striking the hull. For the trapped man, cold, hungry and beyond mere exhaustion, he had to focus all his depleted mental abilities just to lift the metal object in his hands, his lungs hacking, muscles cramping, his eyes watering, and nothing but poisoned air to replenish his racked body.

By now it was pitch black inside the *Thetis* as well as out. Whoever it was, had managed to seal himself off in the engine room from the inrushing water about eight hours earlier. Surrounded by his dead comrades, knowing there was no way out of the escape hatch, all he wanted to do was let Mackenzie know that against all scientific and medical theory he was still alive, and more importantly, still wanted to live. Sinc Mackenzie had no idea where the tapping was coming from because sound travels so clearly under water, especially if the hull is not fully flooded. Without a doubt, hearing the banging must have unsettled the diver, knowing it was probably the fading, last-ditch attempt of dying men trying in vain to cling on to life and crying out for him to help. It was impossible to tell forward from aft, but Mackenzie continued to strike the steel plating several more times, getting faint replies right up the time he left. The ebb tide was increasing constantly until he had great difficulty holding his position in the gale-like run of the tide. It was time to leave the *Thetis*, and her thin thread of fading life.

Mackenzie was later questioned about the so-called signals he heard, especially when all those aboard should have succumbed several hours earlier. He remained adamant. 'I certainly got a response to the knocking that I gave, but whether it was a definite signal they were giving to me, I could not say because I was unable to hold myself in one position for any length of time so that I could concentrate on what I was hearing. The tide was too strong and the eddy of the tide coming over the superstructure was rather much. The tide was increasing all the time, getting far stronger with every passing minute'. He was below for only seventeen minutes, but it was long enough to confirm that there was still life aboard and thus it was still a rescue, and not a purely salvage, operation.

At 03.00 hours the Admiralty experimental deep diving vessel HMS *Tedworth* finally arrived and was able to lend much better equipment to replace the harbour gear the Scapa divers were using. Although Thomas McKenzie's other two divers, Taylor and Thomson, were soon fully suited and ready to go, they had to wait until the tide slackened at about 06.00 hours on 3 June. At about 06.30 hours the two men were ready to make a relatively safe descent. McKenzie instructed them to make contact with the *Thetis* by also knocking on the deck. They put on their heavy bronze dive helmets and gave the thumbs-up signal to say that they were ready to step off the dive-boat ladder and into the sea. Unlike Sinc Mackenzie some six hours earlier, they had the benefit of daylight and, upon reaching the bottom, both men had a good view of the massive grey submarine level fore and aft, but listing about 20° to starboard.

Within a matter of minutes the divers were walking on the submarine's deck casing. They moved about 70 feet aft of the conning tower both hammering on the deck as they went. The sharp, metallic echoes inside the pressure hull must been very loud indeed, if not painful on the ears. Then Taylor and Thomson continued their walk forward of the conning tower, again striking the casing, again every few feet. Thomas McKenzie explained. 'I had instructed them to tap on the hull immediately they got down to ascertain whether there was still any sign of life and to report to me at once by pre-arranged signal.

'About five minutes later they signalled "no sign of life".'

Whoever it was trying to signal Mackenzie some seven hours earlier had finally succumbed. After securing a 2.5 inch wire for another indicator buoy, Taylor and Thomson had to surface as they were now diving past the prescribed time for that depth. The tide was now flooding, stopping any more diving until about midday on 3 June. Thomas McKenzie thought that just because there were no 'signs' of life that did not mean all were dead. After all, Woods had specifically asked for the hull to be tapped early on the day before when, despite getting no response, nearly everyone was still alive. McKenzie again went from vessel to vessel, this time scrounging all the necessary parts to prepare the equipment needed for drilling air holes into the pressure hull. All that morning the Scapa divers were kept busy, preparing adaptors and air pipes necessary to work at that depth and finally feed sweet, fresh air into the foul pressure hull.

'At about 12.20 hours the tide was about high water slack and my divers were ready to descend with submersible drills operated by pneumatic power', McKenzie said. 'At this time, however, Mersey Docks & Harbour Board Salvage Officer on the *Salvor* [Hart] reported to the S.N.O. [Senior Naval Officer, Watson] that he had the 4.5 inch wire fast and expected to have the stern of the *Thetis* up in a few minutes. I was therefore requested, I think by the salvage officer, to suspend our operations in the meantime'. Predictably lifting the tail failed and no further attempt was made to pump air into the pressure hull. Valuable time had been lost and the tide was now running too fast to connect the airline.

McKenzie did later clarify his opinions and how, had his offer of help to both Cammell Laird and the Admiralty been accepted early on the morning of 2 June, the outcome might have been somewhat different. 'I should have been very insistent on getting craft alongside each side, and when Captain Oram's information was given that the

88

condition of the men was poor, I should have treated it as a matter of extreme urgency to get a hole cut into the ship and made an attempt to rescue the men. In the case of the *Thetis*, the stern had positive buoyancy. In any other submarine it might be quite different. There are rarely two salvage jobs alike'. This was just the start of recriminations and blame that would haunt the *Thetis* disaster right up to today.

Late in the afternoon on 3 June the last conference was held between Hart, Brock, Nicholson, Watson, McKenzie and other relevant members of the rescue operation. They had to admit finally that all their rescue efforts had failed. Watson composed a signal, informing the Admiralty in Whitehall that no one else had escaped. Whitehall in turn announced to the waiting world that it was all over for those trapped aboard. Sombre in its brevity, the press, public and loved ones were finally told officially, 'The Admiralty regrets that all life aboard must now be con-sidered lost. It is now a matter of salvage'. Cammell Laird, as owners, were to undertake salvage. As the Mersey Docks equipment was on the spot, they agreed to leave it there, for the time being at least.

It will never be known at what stage each man finally died. Unlike the loss of the Russian submarine *Kursk* in 2000, no man aboard the *Thetis* left behind any personal notes to their loved ones. This clearly indicates that right up until each man strained to suck in his terminal breath, he truly believed that rescue was on the way. There were scenes of complete and utter despair outside Cammell Laird's gates, all exacerbated when the families were informed when a copy of the Admiralty telegram was pasted on to one of Laird's office windows. Its clipped announcement confirmed that all ninety-nine husbands, lovers, fathers, sons and brothers aboard were never coming home. Lieutenant Commander Bolus's wife, Sybil, was among those who had been waiting for some, any, information. Knowing her husband was dead, she was still seen to be perfectly calm, showing more concern for others, doing all she could to comfort the shocked, crying or sobbing loved ones of those who had perished under her husband's command.

Sybil's words and embraces of comfort were stoically and genuinely given in what must have been the greatest crisis of her life. Before too long some of the bereaved she was helping ensured she would be answering for her husband's alleged incompetence in a bitter legal fight lasting many years. An incensed media began asking difficult questions. Banner headlines demanded to know why it took so long to find the *Thetis*, especially after those aboard had so skillfully managed to get her stern a good 18 feet above sea level. Then, once found, why no action was taken to cut into the submarine to get those trapped aboard out.

Criticism of how the Admiralty handled the rescue soon gathered momentum. The first person to speak out in greater detail was McKenzie, who quite clearly defined what should have been done as soon as the tail was seen. Firstly he would have secured the stern between two vessels (like with the *K-13*) instead of one, as Hart had done. More than one wire running between the two, ensuring that they were forward of the aft hydroplanes and propellers, would also have been much better. With two barges, or camels, or tugboats and wires she could have been held securely in that position until a hole could be cut into the pressure hull. It was a certainty. The hole would have been well above the water line, then another through 146 bulkhead and into the steering compartment. It was that simple.

McKenzie said, 'My own view was that towing was a mistake although no doubt it was regarded by those present as the best thing to do in the circumstances'. He knew that the *Thetis* disappeared finally at about half ebb tide, meaning that if they had held on to her another 10 feet of the tail would have been above the waterline for several hours until the evening flood began. When the flood made, the supporting vessels could have lifted the wires under the tail, bringing her still more out of the water. It was a similar approach to that suggested at the confidential Naval Inquiry about a month later. Until the day he died of cancer in 1954, McKenzie felt disgust at the way the whole *Thetis* operation was handled. In February 2008, McKenzie's grandson, Ian Murray Taylor, spoke frankly on how his grandfather's views were known within the family. 'It wasn't what he said, it was what was obviously left unsaid that was still burning inside that I think is a good description'. Murray Taylor revealed, 'He was very frustrated. He knew the loss of life was needless. If his offer of help had been taken up when he gave it and he was got down there in time he could have organized any deficiencies in the equipment and put the right stuff forward. The outcome would have been different and the delay was almost criminal'.

Murray Taylor added, 'It was one of these subjects I did not get enough opportunity to talk to him about because I was away at boarding school and he was working and I did not know at that time that there was a death sentence on him'. More could have been said, but in 1954 terminal cancer sufferers were not necessarily told how severe their condition was, or how long they had to live. Thus Murray Taylor lost the chance to talk more to his grandfather about his involvement in the *Thetis* rescue operation, his experiences with both the public tribunal and confidential Admiralty inquiry or his personal thoughts regarding culpability.

Within a month of the disaster McKenzie was summoned to appear at the *Thetis* Public Tribunal to explain his way to save the men as well as his criticism of those who failed. He made it quite clear that competent salvage men were not present, especially after some eighteen ships or more, hundreds of men and an Admiralty chain of command failed to rescue those trapped. Regarding the events in Liverpool Bay, Lawyer E. W. Brightman acting on behalf of the Mersey Docks & Harbour Board, and thus Hart's Counsel, wanted McKenzie to qualify his assertions regarding salvage competence, or lack of it. 'You told us that there are rarely two salvage jobs which are alike', said Brightman.

'Quite' replied McKenzie.

'In those circumstances', retorted Brightman, 'would you think that all other things being equal, the men on the spot were in a better position to judge what it was best to do than anybody who was not there?'

'I think I would say it depends on the men.'

'Presuming they are men of equal experience?'

'Men of equal experience I would have every faith in, if they had actual experience with that class of work'. Brightman tried to soften the blow by telling McKenzie that the weather conditions at the time made the job much worse, especially with a 3 knot tide running'.

'I have considered that', replied McKenzie.

'And with a swell'.

'The weather was almost flat calm'.

'You were not there, and those who were there tell us there was a swell.

'I rather think the urgency of the case would justify the risk. The risk would be probably of damaging the tug or salvage steamer rather than the submarine, because they would have been up against the hydroplanes. I do not think it would cause any serious damage to either, under the weather conditions that prevailed that day.'

McKenzie was also certain that, again as with the *K-13*, a small air hole could have been cut into the *Thetis* to remove the bad air and fill the pressure hull with a fresh, breathable atmosphere. Each hole only needed to be ¾ inch in diameter. If pneumatic equipment was not available, a hand ratchet could have been used in a very short time, even below water. 'My point regarding the two air pipes', continued McKenzie, 'is that if you can get fresh air into the ship, you can keep men alive for a considerable period, and the condition, according to Captain Oram's report, was that it was only a question of hours, perhaps, twelve to twenty-four hours before the men would be dead in any case.'

McKenzie was also critical of the task Orton was given when he failed to locate the gun recuperator to carry out Oram's plan, saying that the diver could have cut an air hole anywhere around the conning tower area. This was not in line with Oram's salvage plan, but at least the men would have got air to breath, and thus buy more time for the plan. 'He ought to have done it in an hour easily', said McKenzie. There was about an hour and a quarter left of Orton's dive when Hart called him back in. The other hole could have been cut into 146 bulkhead near Z tank without even the use of a diver, as it was still well above water at this time. Even if Orton could not have cut the hole, two could have been drilled side by side into the bulkhead near Z tank without anyone even getting wet, and ensure enough fresh air could have been forced in there as well, or instead of near the conning tower.

Finally McKenzie's comments on actually cutting a hole big enough to get the men out carried a force of experience that somewhat shocked the Court. 'Each hole would take about five to seven minutes to cut, quite big enough to get the men out. There is no question about the speed of the cutting. I have seen it done many times before.'

Mr Justice Bucknill presiding over the Inquiry replied, 'When you say five to seven minutes, are you thinking of your own special and probably powerful gear, or any ordinary oxy-acetylene gear.

'No, replied McKenzie confidently, 'any ordinary oxy-acetylene gear with an expert cutter'. Bucknill asked him if the necessary oxy-acetylene equipment was on site. 'I know there was oxy-acetylene there; whether the full apparatus was there or not, I am not certain. I rather think there was some time before we arrived'.

'Have you any doubt at all that a contrivance of this nature can be found at Cammell Laird's, said Bucknill.

'You mean oxy-acetylene apparatus, replied McKenzie, 'I am certain of it; they must have'.

Hart was quick to retaliate against an accusation alleging his incompetence. In an angry letter through his lawyers he stormed, 'Mr McKenzie states that had he been able to arrive while the stern of the *Thetis* was still above water his immediate endeavour would have been to get two salvage or other craft [such as camels] alongside the stern on either side and pass wires under the vessel forward of the hydroplanes or propellers to prevent slipping and thus support her until such time as a hole could have been cut. For some hours after my arrival at the submarine we were specifically told to hang off from the submarine pending the escape of the crew by means of the Davis gear, so as not to jeopardize the chance of the submarine's crew safely escaping'.

Hart also attacked McKenzie's notion that more wires should have been used to support the stern. One wire of 3.5 inches was, in Hart's opinion, sufficient enough to give *any* support that might be necessary, so long as the stern was buoyant. He added, 'When the submarine for some unexplained reason lost her buoyancy the 3.5 inches wire carried away and this would also have occurred to wires on camels as suggested by Mr McKenzie. If so many or such strong wires had been passed between the camels that the submarine was still supported with buoyancy lost, the submarine would have been strained, or broken'. No one else in authority agreed. Perhaps the *Thetis* would have been damaged, but ninety-nine men trapped inside did not really care. They just wanted to get out and live their lives. Hart also emphasized that the decision to tow was not his, and that he was strongly against it. When it came to cutting into the pressure hull, Hart simply did not see how. 'At no time when merely supported would it have been possible to cut a hole in the submarine sufficiently low to allow of the escape of the crew through it, and the only way in which this could be done was (1) by heaving the submarine into a more upright position – which was done, or (2) by heaving the submarine bodily upwards – which was impossible'. McKenzie, the experienced submarine rescue man, knew differently.

McKenzie and his men had rushed to Liverpool Bay with every intention of utilizing their expertise and experience to save life. Every chance to exploit both were rendered impossible long before they even got there. On Sunday 4 June McKenzie saw no further reason to stay. 'After everybody had definitely agreed there was no further hope of saving life I informed Captain Hart that I wished to withdraw my men because I had very important work waiting at Scapa'.

Chapter 9

The Final Death

Two days after all life was declared lost, Parliamentary Secretary Albert Victor Alexander asked Prime Minister Neville Chamberlain whether he planned to make a statement regarding the disaster. After giving a lengthy account on what was known to have happened the Premier said that, in view of the magnitude of the disaster, a full public inquiry would be held after the *Thetis* had been salvaged. Alexander rose and asked Chamberlain bluntly, 'Can the Right Honourable Gentleman say that a public inquiry will take place almost immediately, or does he anticipate that the salvage of the ship, which he puts as preliminary to the inquiry, will take a considerable time? Would it not be better to satisfy the public mind and the relatives by having the inquiry opened as early as possible?'

Chamberlain replied, 'I should have thought that it was quite impossible for the inquiry to be brought to any satisfactory conclusion until the submarine had been salvaged and conditions inside the vessel had been ascertained. I am afraid that I am not in a position to give the House an estimate as to how long it will take before the submarine can be raised to the surface'.

While Chamberlain was answering questions in the Commons, the salvage operation had already begun and there was every expectation that she would be raised in a few days. Cammell Laird had already resumed responsibility for their wreck and after Captain Hart had agreed to leave the Mersey Dock's salvage plant on site there was no need for Laird to delay getting their submarine back. In fact, within twenty-four hours of the rescue mission being cancelled, the salvage was under way. Then, just as quickly, the calm weather that had prevailed throughout the rescue attempt suddenly changed for the worse.

Later that week Chamberlain had to go back to the House and tell the Government what had happened. 'The camels were secured to the submarine and all the lifting wires were in position under the submarine. Unfortunately, the weather deteriorated as the tide rose and early this morning a heavy northwesterly swell threw a heavy strain on the wires. The wires on the after camel parted and the wires on the foremost camel had to be slipped'. The *Thetis* then crashed to the sea-bed for the fourth time in about a week. The whole salvage attempt was abandoned and the following morning all the equipment was recalled when it was realized that a great deal more plant, and expertise, were going to be needed if the *Thetis* was to once again see the light of day. McKenzie's theory that the escaping air meant considerable water was flooding the pressure hull was right. Had she only been flooded in the front two compartments, the submarine would have come up, but she had now gained more than 600 tons, possibly a great deal more, meaning that a whole new salvage approach was needed.

The media had a different view on whether the *Thetis* should be salved. The *Liverpool Echo* claimed that the relatives, having already held a very moving memorial service over the wreck, would rather their loved ones stayed at the bottom, with their fellow shipmates. Bringing back the dead would, the paper told its readers, reopen the wound and for no good reason it would create further unnecessary sorrow. Such sentiments eventually reached the House of Commons, putting Chamberlain back under the microscope to answer some difficult questions. The Labour MP for Leigh in Lancashire, John Joseph Tinker, wanted an assurance that whatever happened the salvage would not be abandoned. 'It will be a sad reflection on our engineering if we cannot raise a vessel at that depth', he told Chamberlain. 'There would be only one inference to be drawn from it, and that is that there was something to hide. Whatever else happens, I hope the submarine can be brought to the surface so that a full examination can take place'.

'First of all let me say that no one is more anxious than the Government to see this vessel raised', asserted Chamberlain, 'for reasons that have been put forward. While the vessel is at the bottom of the sea there may still always be doubts as to what happened, and those doubts might be cleared away if the vessel were raised. I cannot go any further than to express the hope and the expectation that success will be achieved. I have no reason to think that they will fail to bring the vessel up. The Government expect the vessel to be raised'. Chamberlain then U-turned on waiting until the *Thetis* was salved before opening the inquiry and both ran concurrently throughout the rest of that year. Little did the Prime Minister know, when he told the House that the Government expected to see the *Thetis* raised, that the salvage operation had already been undermined, not through any political, technical or sentimental trouble, but money.

Within days of the disaster Cammell Laird's insurance brokers Robert Bradford & Co. of London urged Robert Johnson to abandon Laird's interests in the *Thetis*. Bradford told the Managing Director that under such circumstances it was customary to do so, but it was ultimately his decision. Bradford's were right to be concerned. Should Johnson wish to maintain his interests in the wreck, they stood to be the main losers. The insurers were already facing a massive claim for the entire loss of the submarine amounting to about £350,000, or in today's monetary value about £10.5m. If further attempts were made to raise her, under the terms of the insurance contract, they could face an even bigger payout with every chance of no submarine to show for a costly and protracted salvage operation.

Once the submarine was raised, and all evidence gathered, there was a chance she could be refitted and put back in service. But one of Bradford's advisers, a Mr Mackinnon of Messrs Hogg, Lindley & Co. said, 'I cannot believe it is possible that the *Thetis* can be either reconditioned or reconstructed to the satisfaction of the Admiralty and if that be so, anything salved will be of scrap value only'. Bradford's sought to distance themselves even further after Mackinnon stressed, '. . . In view of the conflicting interests in the vessel it would be as well at this stage to mark the distinction between the Underwriters' material interests in the vessel and the Admiralty's interest in satisfying public demand for raising of the vessel for investigation purposes'. That is, from a cost-effective point of view, leave her where she lay. If the Admiralty wanted to recover the dead and find evidence for her loss, then that was their business.

Johnson knew that once he gave notice of abandonment he would relinquish all ownership in the submarine, which could still be a very valuable asset. He openly stated that he wanted the dead, many of whom were his employees, to receive a Christian burial. On the same day that Johnson refused to abandon the *Thetis* to the brokers, he held a meeting at his offices in Birkenhead to look more deeply into whether she could be raised or not. Altogether sixteen men, including Third Sea Lord Vice Admiral Bruce Austin Fraser, Captain Hart and Senior Salvage Officer George Critchley of the Liverpool & Glasgow Salvage Association were there. Captain Hart was reluctant to continue salvaging the *Thetis*, not on practical, but rather legal grounds. Only being licensed to undertake salvage operations within about five miles of the River Mersey put his firm at a serious legal disadvantage. Although this was overlooked while attempts were being made to save life, for a commercial or forensic enterprise he was not allowed to take part.

At the meeting Vice Admiral Fraser reiterated Chamberlain's comments in the House, that both the Admiralty and the Government had decided that the *Thetis* must be raised. With Hart refusing the job, the only other person capable of leading such a difficult and costly operation was Critchley, particularly if they could get access to the Port of London's heavy-lift salvage equipment, including two camels of a larger size, capable of lifting 1,500 tons each, and they were self-propelled. To augment the Association's salvage vessels *Ranger* and *Salver*, Fraser guaranteed that the Admiralty would supply HMS *Tedworth* with Navy divers Dick Oliver, Petty Officer 'Soapy' Watson, Dick Harknett and Petty Officer Henry Otho Perdue. They were all highly skilled divers who, with McKenzie's men at Scapa Flow, were among the best.

Admiral Fraser then asked Captain Hart what the best method would be to lift the *Thetis*. Hart explained that either air or wires could be used, but not both. He also thought it would take ten tides from the first lift to get her into shallow water, meaning that eight days fair weather were necessary for putting the wires under the hulk and lifting and towing her to shallow water, getting between one and two miles each tide. This meant adopting one of the oldest salvage methods known, called a 'tidal lift'. The tidal lift method dates back to medieval Venice and was used to recover sunken gondolas from within the city. During a spring low tide, ropes were passed from one gondola on the surface, under a sunken hulk, and back up to another on the other side of the wreck. Then, as the tide rose, the hulk left the seabed a few feet at a time. The same routine was repeated on successive tides until the gondola was far enough inshore for repairs above the low tide mark.

Gondola or submarine, the technique should still work. Critchley agreed, generally, except that he thought compressed air could be used. By pumping it into the forward chamber through the torpedo tube, which was known to be open, and thus force out the water through the same tube, just as the crew had tried to do without success. The danger remained that if air was pumped into the compartments the bow might raise too fast and become unpredictable. Admiral Fraser was left with the final decision on which method to adopt – compressed air, or tidal lift. 'I think it is clear', he decided, 'that the non-air method should at all events be adopted first'.

With all in agreement, the next stage was to approach the Port of London for the use of their self-propelled camels. Critchley, along with one of his chief salvage officers, Mr H. Thomas, left for the Capital immediately to visit Port of London Harbour Master Commander E. C. Shankland, inspect the camels, agree terms, and ensure that they could be dispatched without delay. Upon arriving in London Critchley and Thomas met Shankland. The Harbour Master did not have good news. The camels were not self-propelled, as Critchley had been led to believe. 'Nevertheless', said Critchley optimistically, 'we considered that if in other respects the camels were suitable for this case we should give very careful consideration to their employment'

The camels were moored at Tilbury Docks in Essex, about thirty miles down the Thames from London. While Critchley stayed at Shankland's office to negotiate hire terms, Thomas went to Tilbury for a more thorough examination of the craft. When he returned, Critchley later remembered that Thomas, 'Reported to me in the presence of Commander Shankland that the camels were not fitted with any modern appliances for heaving in, securing and releasing the wires'. They were useless.

In desperation Critchley telephoned the Mersey Docks & Harbour Board to try to convince them to part with four of their camels. The Harbour Board held an internal meeting, but would only release three due to their legal requirement to keep the Mersey open to traffic at all times, and the fact that they were being used outside of the Board's legal boundary. One wonders whether the Board only allowed three, knowing this would not work, and thus they could be seen to have at least tried to help. Whatever the true reason, with the Government, the Admiralty and public opinion demanding that the *Thetis* be raised, Critchley was again at a dead end.

In anticipation of the Mersey Docks & Harbour Board failing to supply all, or any, of their camels, Critchley wondered whether a conventional cargo ship could be adapted to do the same job. Could the *Thetis* be literally suspended beneath a steamer and taken ashore on successive tides? It was radical, but he had used one cargo ship to lift another sunken vessel in a similar way before. So, he thought, what works for a sunken ship should work for a submarine. Liverpool & Glasgow Salvage Officer Thomas and Admiralty Surveyor, Doctor A. M. Robb surveyed many ships in Cardiff to look for just the right one. The salvage operation now wholly depended on a vessel of about 2,500 tons with enough free space on deck for specialized conversion. She also needed the structural integrity to carry an evenly distributed load in excess of 1,500 tons beneath her keel.

Thomas and Robb left for Cardiff on the night of 2 July to inspect what might well be a suitable vessel. She was the collier SS *Zelo*, a merchant ship belonging to the Newcastle-based Pelton Steamship Company. At 308 feet long and 43 feet wide, with a deadweight capacity of 3,350 tons, she was just what Critchley was looking for. She was a tough, sturdy, well-ballasted ship with good winches and derricks. The *Zelo* was also in better condition than the other ships that were available, she was ready immediately and, best of all, she was already under Admiralty charter.

Changing from one Admiralty charter to another contract still allowed the Pelton Steamship Company a large degree of latitude during the new negotiations. Admiral Fraser's appointment of Naval Officer Captain Fitzroy to observe the salvage operations now paid off. Fitzroy, along with Critchley, spent four hours finalizing the deal. Critchley later recalled how tough Pelton's really were, knowing how badly the Admiralty needed their ship, 'The owners demanded a rate of £2,000 per month and he [Fitzroy] got them down to £1,600 for the first month and £1,550 for the rest.' Overall it was a good deal. The hire of Mersey Docks & Harbour Board camels would be £35 per day per camel to which would be added the cost of insurance and the wages and maintenance of the crew. Each camel would also require the attendance of a tug. At Liverpool rates this would be £52 per tide per tug, at a time when the buying power of £10 was worth about £500.

After taking on about 450 tons of fuel and fresh water the *Zelo* sailed from Cardiff for Cammell Laird's Wet Basin to be refitted as a salvage vessel. Firstly 12 inch^2 wooden beams were fixed fore and aft along the main deck, covering the hatches and tanks. Upon these were placed struts, and 12 inch^2 wooden beams were fixed across the wooden structure from port to starboard. These were made up into groups of four 12 inch^2 beams to become 2 feet^2 solid, wooden arms. The final structure looked something like a large, thick ladder of beams with those running across the main deck, protruding about 3 feet over the end of the ship like small jibs down each side. These beams also had a green heart to allow for flexibility.

The overhangs were further enforced like large bobbins into which the wires could bite. Altogether there were nine 2 feet^2 cross beams to take a wire on each outboard end, thus giving a secure point for eighteen ends of wire with the *Thetis* suspended between them under the *Zelo* in her own steel cradle. For added strength the underside of the main deck was bolstered with myriad wooden beams to ensure it did not buckle under the weight of a T Class submarine suspended below. When she was ready, the newly converted *Zelo* was securely moored over the *Thetis*. To ensure she did not drift off the site, either through bad weather or strong tidal conditions, six sets of anchors from her bow, stern and quarters were trailed from specially adapted mooring points along her decks down to the seabed some considerable distance away. The effect was to ensure that if she was pushed in any direction, the thick wires would counter each other and hold her firmly in position.

When she was securely in place, the job of passing wires under the *Thetis* could begin. This was going to be one of the hardest stages of the operation, but Critchley had a simple method. He proposed to lift the bow first using a 4.5 inch wire. While the *Thetis* was suspended in mid-water two 9 inch and one 7 inch wire would be placed under the keel along the fore end before she was lowered back to the seabed. Then the same procedure would be adopted along the after end and thus all the wires would be positioned equally distributed without divers having to literally gouge out the seabed to pass the wires through.

After so many mishaps since Laird first attempted to lift the submarine, hauling the *Thetis* to the surface was finally looking like a reality. So much so that Critchley announced, 'We are confident that given a few days of reasonably calm weather the first lift can be made and the present intention is to [secure] at each successive low water after the first lift, so as to carry the vessel without delay into shallower and more sheltered water'. The next day a strong southwesterly gale blew up, causing the *Zelo* to drag her moorings. She then broadsided to the gale, putting incredible strain on the wires and the ship – ripping two bollards right out of her deck.

She had to return to Laird for repairs, causing even more delay. All the bollards were removed and replaced with a much stronger and heavier type, and surrounding deck areas were strengthened to ensure it did not happen again. Her mooring lines were also increased from six to ten, five being placed on her stern and stern quarters alone. Divers Harknett and 'Soapy' Watson did the first half-hour under-water stint trying to get the moorings in place. All the time Harknett's diving helmet was leaking, but he still managed to complete his shift and get safely back aboard the *Tedworth*.

If the salvage crew were not held up by the constant bad weather, the anticipation of it was still enough. Early in the operation the Air Ministry sent a weather warning of strong northerly winds up to Force 7. While all the salvage personnel took shelter or stood around doing nothing, the weather remained more than calm enough to carry on with the job. Thomas was becoming exasperated. Critchley later recalled after Thomas had told him how bad things were, 'It is apparent from the tenor of our officer's message that he is finding the delay due to weather conditions rather trying, especially as we know he was restrained from commencing to moor *Zelo* on last night's tide by a morning forecast that did not materialize.'

Finally all the wires were passed underneath the *Thetis* and back up to the other side of the *Zelo*. This was not without a great deal of frustration for Thomas. Due to the sub-surface current, an angle of as much as 70° could run from the seabed to the top, causing the wires to bend in every direction except under the submarine and back up to the ship. Thomas realized that such a divergence between surface and bottom currents could cause the *Thetis* to swing violently while in suspension. He said, 'Although we do not anticipate this will result in uncontrollability, it is nevertheless a fact that there is no such experience of this condition at that depth as will enable us to forecast definitely its effect upon the behaviour of the surface craft'. Other variables constantly dogged the operation. Wires wrapped around the *Thetis* just before being winched up. Sometimes hours of work compiling detailed surveys of the clay and sandy seabed around the submarine were wiped out in one tide. All this while the divers were working in a depth of water at the maximum limit that late 1930s divers could endure.

Regardless of any doubt, untried science and bad weather, eventually the *Thetis* was ready to lift. On Friday, 22 July the weather was still and calm. Low water was at 21.40 hours Thomas started to wind in the slack on the wires at 19.15 hours on the ebb tide. When low water was reached all the wires were perfectly tight. Thomas examined them, altering the strain on some, so that the load, as far as could be judged, was evenly distributed. Should some wires be bearing more than others one could part, adding the extra load across the rest and causing a ripple effect of parting wires and the loss of the *Thetis*, yet again.

Thomas explained that adjustment to the wires particularly applied to Numbers One, Six, and Seven. These were rendered approximately up to 18 inches before the other wires took any load. At that stage, which was about an hour after low water, they held on to everything, and he thought that they had got a good pin down, that is, with the wires held tight in place. Under bright floodlights the wires groaned and stretched as the *Zelo* slowly edged up on the rising tide. As the *Thetis* went into ascent, no one aboard the *Zelo* noticed that the groaning of Number Five wire was not as much as on Numbers Six and Seven. Suddenly the crossbeams facing over the *Zelo*'s side on Numbers Six and Seven wires gave out a loud crack like a gunshot as the massive beam began to twist violently, their green hearts bursting through the outer wooden layer.

All Thomas could do was to continuously release the wires in a bid to spend all the trapped energy and try to save the other beams. 'The wires rendered around the drum ends of the baulks [beams] in a series of very severe jerks', he said. 'It was not safe for men to try any further regulation of the load, and at that stage the tackles holding the ends of wires carried away. The series of jerks and rendering continued, and the full range of the tide passed without the forward end of the submarine rising very far from the bottom'. Yet another salvage attempt had failed.

Underwater the submarine's stern had risen some considerable way while the bow stayed firmly on the bottom, causing the jerks and the stress on Numbers Six and Seven wires. Sudden mechanical failure had wiped out more than two months of hard and frustrating work. 'I can see no means', concluded Thomas, 'during any further attempts to lift the submarine, of retaining the lifting wires in their allotted positions, having regard to the strength of the tides and the impossibility of sending divers down to check the positions of the wires in the limited time available'. There was no alternative but to replace the existing wooden structure with steel girders capable of resisting torque due to the concentrated loading.

Now, after fighting so hard to ensure the *Thetis* was raised, even Robert Johnson felt it was time to give up on his submarine and declare a total loss. 'The *Thetis*', he despaired, 'should lie where it is and the bodies be left in peace'. But the operation did continue. The *Zelo* was soon back at Cammell Laird where they ripped out all the elaborate wooden lifting structure and replaced it with steel. Admiralty surveyor A. M. Robb calculated that to spread 1,000 tons equally under these new conditions required each wire to be 188 feet apart. To achieve this the *Thetis* would have to be stressed beyond her structural limits. Robb was confident that her stress figures were higher than would be acceptable for ordinary working conditions, but he did not consider them so high as to cause any real structural failure. 'It must be borne in mind', he said, 'When considering the figures that the pressure hull is constructed of high tensile steel, and also that the assumptions are possibly more severe than the actual conditions. Hence it is believed that the method of slinging is feasible'.

Before the *Zelo* was on site, divers Perdue and Harknett were ordered to descend and survey the submarine's stern and propeller shafts prior to the lift. Perdue dived first and when on the seabed he asked for Harknett to follow. The survey was completed within the allotted thirty-minute shift and the two divers signalled that they were coming up. Harknett left the seabed first, but just as Perdue was leaving he became snagged on a grapnel. Harknett went to his aid and very shortly they were both on their way to the surface.

Standing on the after end of the *Tedworth* waiting for the divers was Petty Officer Jack Dymond. Somehow Perdue's suit became over inflated and was now as rigid as a board, leaving the diver powerless to move against the pressure. Perdue's dive helmet broke the surface first. No sooner was he on the surface when Dymond saw him flip up so that his feet, not his head, were now visible. It was a simple error that could have happened to any diver. Dymond hauled Perdue in and released the pressure through a valve before unscrewing Perdue's faceplate and having a chat about what had happened down below. But, as Dymond removed the glass, he saw a man in excruciating pain, claiming to have a severe bend. But there was something rather odd about his symptoms.

Perdue was helped into the *Tedworth*'s decompression chamber along with Dymond to act as his nurse. As soon as they were in the chamber Perdue collapsed. Taking the pressure back down to about 150 feet to the seabed put a pressure on the men to about six times that at sea level. Once the decompression chamber reached the same pressure, Perdue began to breath more easily, but was still unconscious. The *Tedworth*'s doctor needed to further examine the diver, but when the pressure was brought back to surface levels for him to enter Perdue relapsed. Ten minutes later his heart stopped and the young, fit Navy diver with eight years experience was dead. Although Perdue claimed to have had the bends a post mortem discovered the real cause of his death. He had had an undiagnosed case of tuberculosis at some time in his life that had eaten away more than twenty per cent of both his lungs.

While the inquest was being held the *Zelo* was back in place above the *Thetis*. In the early hours of Monday, 28 August, she was ready for another attempt. This time Thomas did not raise her slightly to pass the wires underneath, nor send divers down. Altogether the tugs swept them under the submarine: two under the keel forward of the conning tower, two forward of the keel, two under the keel after of the conning tower and two more aft of that. This time the plan worked and the *Thetis* was on her way back to the surface. Nine lifts were needed during seven days to get her above the low tide mark in Moelfre Bay, Anglesey. Neville Chamberlain's wish, and thus the British Government's and the Admiralty's, that the *Thetis* would be salvaged, was now, finally about to become a reality. On the afternoon of the sixth day 2 September she was only 36 feet below low water after the eighth lift was made. The final lift was made successfully on the afternoon of the following day, Sunday, 3 September 1939. The event went unnoticed within the Tory Cabinet when, at about the same time, the Prime Minister who brought Great Britain 'peace in our time' was being forced to declare war on Germany.

Chapter 10

Raising the Dead

Although Cammell Laird received several letters from funeral directors offering their services for the burial arrangements, many more enquiries came from people wanting to enter the submarine and help remove the dead. Either through some morbid interest or genuine, though naïve, offer of help, these started arriving long before she was even raised. In fact, the first letter arrived only two days after all hope of saving life was abandoned.

Albert Tucker was an ex-sick berth steward, now working as a clerk in the Admiralty's Devonport Dockyard. 'Experience has shown me that this type of work requires a great deal of tact and initiative', he told Laird's directors, 'also it is a task which a good many would care not to undertake hence my reason for offering my services for this delicate task'. Albert certainly felt that should Laird need him, as he already worked for the Admiralty, he, 'No doubt should have no difficulty in obtaining special leave of absence'.

Mr J. Westcott of Fleetwood in Lancashire said, 'I am writing to ask you if you want anyone to help to get the men out of the *Thetis*. I am willing to go down in the sub to get the men out. I have bean [sic] on slimber [sic] jobs were [sic] we had to put the men in bags to get them out. I am a rigger by trade'.

Former stretcher-bearer and ambulance driver Owen Lewis Jones from North Wales seemed a more genuine offer. Owen claimed to have dealt with every type of battlefield casualty and was more than 'willing to help'. Hospital worker Richard Jones wondered, 'If you have the influence to suggest the point, I would like to volunteer to enter the *Thetis* with Stoker Arnold. I wrote to you last week. Please put it to Stoker Arnold. Yours Richard Jones'.

On 27 June 1939 J. H. Aldred told Laird, 'I beg to offer my services on the recovery of the bodies in the submarine *Thetis* when it has been salved'. Somebody at Laird thought it prudent to underline in thick,

107

red crayon the first eleven words. The forty-year-old Aldred went on to explain his qualifications for the job. 'During the last war when the Royal Naval Barracks at Chatham was bombed, I was in charge of the party which [removed] the numerous dead. Waiting on you at your convenience'.

After Mr A. Nixon of Stockport offered his services, Laird replied, 'We thank you for your letter of the tenth instant and will bear your name in mind should we require any work done of the nature referred to'. All the offers received this same more or less standard reply, rather like a publisher's or a potential lover's rejection. Although they do not say yes, they never quite say no, but between the lines they always mean never. No member of the public would set foot even near the salvaged wreck, let alone have access to her dead. It was highly specialized work, for which even the Admiralty had to seek instruction. But before that phase of the operation could be put into effect, the *Thetis* had to come further up the beach, which was not achieved without further misfortune.

As the tide dropped The *Thetis*'s crumpled bridge and conning tower broke the surface three months and five days after her prescribed two-hour dive time had passed. Although the *Tedworth* had left the scene, three of her divers, Dymond W. Linton and Petty Officer Nelson Victor Keys from Chatham Dockyard stayed behind to help the Liverpool & Glasgow Salvage Association's own divers complete the final salvage phase.

If all her hatches except the stern could be sealed with strongbacks as well as other outlets blocked, she could be blown with compressed air and after the crew's two previous failed attempts the water could be forced out. The plan called for the stern to again break surface, this time to allow surplus water to drain out of the open torpedo tube. Finally strongbacks were fitted across the deck hatches, The stern hatch was left untouched to allow a direct line into the pressure hull where a special custom-made plate was constructed to cover the entry point through which the necessary piping could pass. This required opening the engine room hatch, which led to a diver almost losing his life, not through any mechanical or human intervention, but shock on a grotesque scale.

Nelson Keys had lied about his age when he joined the Navy at the start of the First World War at only fourteen years old. He saw action at the Battle of Jutland before leaving the Navy in 1918. He later re-enlisted in 1937 as a diver based at Chatham. His son, David Keys, who is now retired and living in Spain, still vividly remembers his father telling him how the Chatham divers were ordered to attend the *Thetis* disaster. David said, 'My father and the other divers were shipped up from Chatham to dive on the *Thetis* and he told me it happened very, very quickly. One minute they were living ashore and the next thing they were bundled into lorries and they were on their way north with their diving equipment'. By the time they arrived the job was clearly one of salvage rather than rescue, and they became part of that operation.

Once the *Thetis* was ready for the final move, Keyes and his two colleagues were helping seal the hatches and prepare the engine room hatch for the piping to go into the submarine. All British divers in those days worked with bare hands to help complete their job by touch alone. As the hatch was opening one diver put his hand in the coaming to help ease it up. As the divers' fingertips swept across the cold steel, sending the subtle information to his brain, the diver had a complete mental picture of what he was doing. Suddenly his fingers traced from the hard cold steel to something much softer.

David explained, 'My father said it was pretty murky down there, they were doing everything by feel, the other diver put his hand on the face of a body that had suddenly appeared'. The body was that of Torpedo Gunner's Mate Ernest Mitchell who had tried to close the watertight door in Number Twenty-five bulkhead with Lieutenant Woods to prepare them for pumping out. The diver's air demand accelerated rapidly, as he reeled back in panic. Then the hatch opened fully and Mitchell's well-preserved body shot out and hit the surface a few seconds later. David continued, 'They hauled the diver to the surface because they had lost contact by telephone, and my father said his hair had turned white and he had lost his mind. It had affected him so much that he ended up in a Naval hospital for many months afterwards'.

Another two days passed before the hatch was removed to prepare the open hole for its new use. Until the piping arrangement could be delivered a wire mesh had to be placed over the open hole, just in case any more bodies drifted out into Moelfre Bay. This final salvage phase took another two months to complete, as a strong northwesterly gale blew continuously, and further obstacles had to be overcome within the pressure hull. The divers had to enter through the engine room hatch and walk the full length of the submarine to ensure all the watertight doors were open and any necessary valves were shut. All of this had to be achieved while risking constantly snagging any part of their delicate equipment on the pipes, controls and bulkhead fittings along the way. They were ordered to stop at Number Forty bulkhead as the rest of the submarine needed intensive investigation for possible evidence. That was the plan, but straight away their entry into the submarine from beyond the engine room was well and truly blocked.

When the weather conditions allowed, the wire mesh was removed and the divers slowly descended into the pitch black wreck. As the clanking and scraping of their heavy boots grated over each ladder rung, the claustrophobic engine room enveloped the men the deeper they went. Upon striking the bottom plates it was time to switch on their torches and take a good look around. Everywhere the white glow fell it reflected off more than sixty pallid corpses. Many were twisted and knotted together, some were frozen in their last staring death throws. Others looked as if they were only asleep. Put it all together and the scene looked more like some grisly Madame Tussauds' nightmare. The sight looked somewhat more macabre because, for no apparent reason, many men were virtually naked, or their clothing was in tatters. What was once a state-of-the-art T Class machine space was now a steel-lined mass coffin tightly packed with bodies, blocking the divers' entry any further than the ladder, let alone into the rest of the submarine.

The original government plan stated that once salvaged the *Thetis* would be towed to Cammell Laird's yard where she would be opened up under strict Royal Navy control and the bodies removed there. Once they were removed a lying in state would take place at Liverpool Cathedral, but Johnson was emphatic that the dead would not be removed from the submarine in his yard under any circumstances. On 31 August 1939 the Admiralty issued a notice, stating that all bodies were to be removed from the *Thetis* once she was in dry dock at Holyhead instead. However, if her salvage was to be continued this order very quickly needed to be revoked and many had to be removed at once if the submarine was going to get to Holyhead. But no one was quite sure what state the dead would be in after long-term exposure to seawater.

On 1 September 1939, exactly three months to the day since the *Thetis* was lost, Surgeon Commander S. G. Rainsford advised the Admiralty on what they could expect to find. Rainsford explained how the United States Navy reported the state of bodies aboard the submarine USS *S-4*, which sank after being rammed by the United States Coast Guard cutter *Paulding* in December 1927. The *S-4* had been

110

The launch of T Class submarine HMS *Thetis* into the River Mersey on 29 June 1938. She promised to be a cutting edge war weapon, but was dogged with bad luck from her early trials until her final loss, as HMS *Thunderbolt*, in 1943. (*Courtesy of the Royal Navy Submarine Museum*)

HMS *Thetis*'s official badge showing Thetis, mother of Achilles, rising from the sea. (*Barrow-in-Furness Branch of the Submariners Association*)

A rare image of the *Thetis* on her aborted trials in Gareloch. After several mechanical failures had occurred, the trials were abandoned when her forward hydroplanes jammed, rendering her useless as a submarine. (*Courtesy of the Royal Navy Submarine Museum*)

Diagram of the bow of a T Class submarine showing the torpedo compartment in relation to the stowage compartment. (*Cross section in watercolour of a submerged T Class submarine, painted by William McDowell in 1946, on display at the Royal Navy Submarine Museum*)

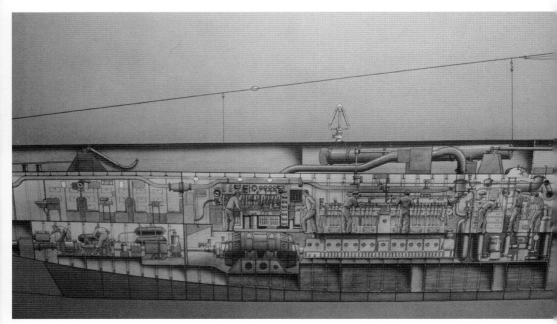

Diagram showing the engine room and the steering compartment/stokers' mess, where ninety-nine trapped men congregated towards the end. Taking the scale of the men in the diagram, there must have been very little space for each person. (*Cross section in watercolour of a submerged T Class submarine, painted by William McDowell in 1946, on display at the Royal Navy Submarine Museum*)

This diagram was used at the Public Inquiry to show the torpedo tubes in relation to the bow cap control levers and the mechanical indicators, which run down the middle of the six tubes. Number Five torpedo tube is bottom right.
(*National Archives, Kew*)

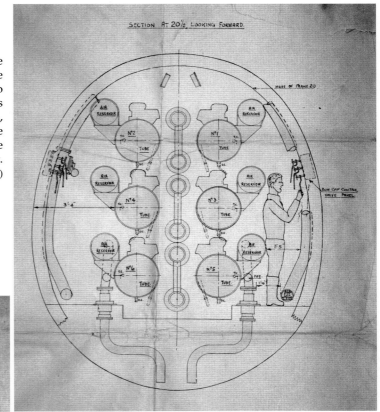

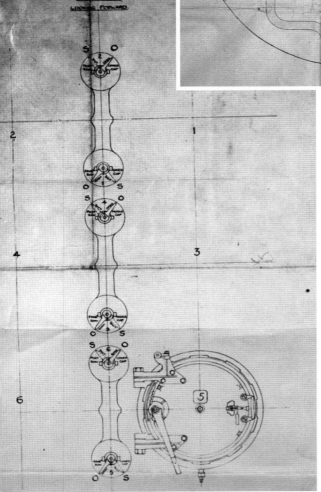

A close-up of the bow cap indicators, in relation to Number Five torpedo tube. The indicators run in groups, from top to bottom as 'Two, One'; 'Four, Three' and 'Six, Five'. The layout has been heavily criticized for perhaps causing confusion as to whether a bow cap was open or not, but the crew were highly trained and not likely to make such a basic error.
(*National Archives, Kew*)

First Lieutenant Harold 'Bert' Chapman as a midshipman. He was a very competent First Officer, but made a drastic error of judgement in allowing four men into an escape chamber, which led to all their deaths. (*Courtesy of the Royal Navy Submarine Museum*)

'To Kitty with Love'. This well worn and faded photograph is of Leading Stoker Thomas Kenney who was one of the four men who drowned, kicking and fighting, in the escape chamber after Chapman's plan went drastically wrong. Kitty was Kenny's wife of many years. (*Courtesy of the Royal Navy Submarine Museum*)

TO KITTY WITH LOVE

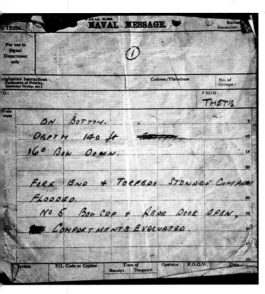

This is the first of five pages taken to the surface strapped to Captain Oram's arm, prepared by Commissioned Engineer Roy Glenn with other senior personnel, to show how to get air into the submarine, and what had happened therein. (*National Archives, Kew*)

Glenn explains how to blow enough compressed air into the fore end, from the outside, in a bid to remove the water from the two flooded compartments. (*National Archives, Kew*)

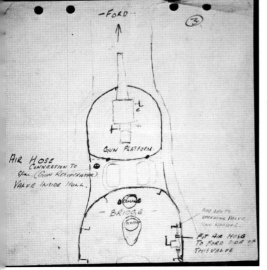

To avoid any confusion, Glenn drew this rough sketch, showing exactly where the two best inlet points were, being the gun recuperator valve and the whistle, but a diver was still unable to locate them. (*National Archives, Kew*)

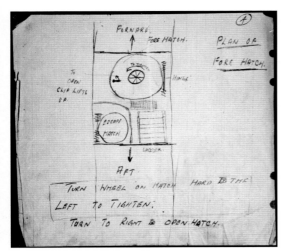

The drawing on page four describes how to secure the fore hatch, essential to the success of the plan. (*National Archives, Kew*)

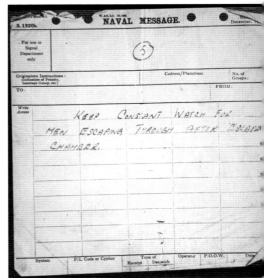

The message on the last page delayed the rescu of the trapped men; no one realized that there was not enough air left in the *Thetis*. (*National Archives, Kew*)

So near, yet so far. An aerial view of the Mersey Docks & Harbour Board salvage vessel *Vigilant* almost touching the *Thetis*'s raised stern. The trapped men are literally feet away from help that never came. (*ITN Stills*)

Mersey Docks & Harbour Board Wreck Master, Charles Brock, is seen here trying to remove a plate to gain access into Z Tank. Shortly after this photograph was taken he had to jump off the stern as it slewed to port and sank within minutes. *(Courtesy of the Royal Navy Submarine Museum)*

Sybil Bolus, wife of the Captain of HMS *Thetis*, with children at the gates of Cammell Laird after the incorrect news that all the trapped men were safe. *(Mirrorpix)*

Going ... An attempt to secure the stern has made it cant over to one side and lose precious buoyancy.
(*National Archives, Kew*)

Going ... Air trapped in tanks is now spilling out. Those inside know what is about to happen.
(*National Archives, Kew*)

Gone ... Water is now flooding into the *Thetis*, pressurizing the carbon dioxide, and killing many, but not all, those inside.
(*National Archives, Kew*)

Photograph taken from one of the two tugs ordered to tow the salvage vessel *Vigilant* higher out of the sea. The plan failed with disastrous consequences. (*National Archives, Kew*)

Parents, children, wives and sweethearts wait outside the gates of Cammell Laird for any news of their loved ones. By now many were already dying or dead. (*From 'SOS* Thetis'*, Hans Müller Verlag, Dresden, 1943*)

After the *Thetis* sank, for the second time, preparations were made to place a heavy steel cable round her stern to keep it above water. (*Courtesy of the Royal Navy Submarine Museum*)

The cable parted. It carried away the marker buoy and the *Thetis* was lost for nearly eight hours. (*Courtesy of the Royal Navy Submarine Museum*)

Thomas McKenzie, the Scapa Flow salvage expert, whose offer of help was accepted too late to save lives. He told the Tribunal that he could have got the men out in under fifteen minutes. (*Ian Murray Taylor*)

One of the four *Thetis* survivors, Fifth Flotilla Commander, Captain Harry Percy Kendall Oram, photographed with his wife on his way to the Tribunal in London. (*From 'SOS Thetis', Hans Müller Verlag, Dresden, 1943*)

Leading Stoker Walter Arnold and Cammell Laird's Fitter Frank Shaw, both survivors, on their way to the Tribunal into the loss of the *Thetis*. (*Courtesy of the Royal Navy Submarine Museum*)

The Pelton Steamship Company's 3,350-ton cargo vessel SS *Zelo* seen here in later life. She was pivotal in ensuring the *Thetis* was successfully raised after the submarine was stropped beneath her for the slow passage to shallow waters. (*Michael Helm*)

Once the *Thetis* was beached, it was clear to see Number Five bow cap open to the sea (circled). (*National Archives, Kew*)

Passers-by brave the pouring rain to stop and look at the *Thetis* in which the remains of ninety-nine men are still entombed. (*Courtesy of the Royal Navy Submarine Museum*)

Another view of the beached *Thetis*, showing her forward hydroplanes still at a dive angle. Lieutenant Commander Bolus had given the order to surface once he knew the *Thetis* was sinking. The reason why they are still at a dive angle has never been explained. (*Courtesy of the Royal Navy Submarine Museum*)

Looking towards Number Twenty-five bulkhead, leading into the torpedo tube space. The door on the left is where Woods, Hambrook, Mitchell, Howell and Crombleholme fought to escape through and secure to prevent further flooding. At top, right of the door can be seen the only butterfly bolt out of eighteen that was successfully closed. (*National Archives, Kew*)

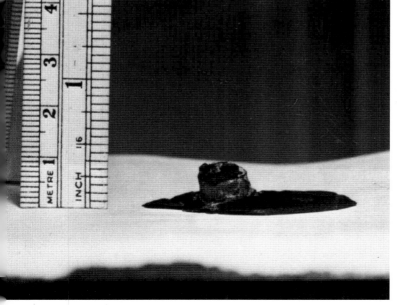

This is the tiny piece of enamel that blocked an inspection port, leading Lieutenant Woods to believe that the Number Five torpedo tube was not flooded. (*National Archives, Kew*)

Minister of War Sir John Anderson. Several years after the loss of the *Thetis*, German author Count Michael Alexander claimed that Anderson was involved in an insurance scam to protect Cammell Laird from bankruptcy. (*From 'SOS* Thetis', *Hans Müller Verlag, Dresden, 1943*)

Secretary of War Lord Quintin McGarel Hogg Hailsham whom Count Alexander claimed masterminded a credit agreement between Cammell Laird and American bankers J. P. Morgan. (*From 'SOS* Thetis', *Hans Müller Verlag, Dresden, 1943*)

Removing the dead was a specialized operation. The Admiralty used employees from several West Midlands-based mine rescue organizations seen here fully prepared for their gruesome job. (*Courtesy of the Royal Navy Submarine Museum*)

Only seven bodies were buried in Holyhead with full military honours. Afterwards there were too many bodies for such a luxury. (*Courtesy of the Royal Navy Submarine Museum*)

The funeral service taking place in Holyhead's Maes Hyfryd Cemetery. The coffins had to be more than twice the normal size and zinc-lined due to the rapid decomposition of the bodies once they were exposed to ambient air temperature. (*Courtesy of the Royal Navy Submarine Museum*)

Temporary gravesite in Holyhead set aside for the dead. (*Courtesy of the Royal Navy Submarine Museum*)

Eight years after the *Thetis* disaster this more permanent monument was placed over the site. Each man's name, age and profession are carved into four Welsh slate slabs. (*Author photograph*)

on diving trials off Provincetown, Massachusetts when she was lost. Rainsford wrote that the bodies, 'Had lain in the USS *S-4* for five months, were not putrefied to any great extent when first seen, a fact attributed by the pickling effect of cold sea water. It would appear possible that such a condition of affairs may well exist in HMS *Thetis*'.

He felt sure that the men aboard the *Thetis* would be just as well preserved, so determining the cause of death would be a relatively easy job. He was concerned that should the bodies be out of water for too long, not only will post mortem examination be impossible, but, 'Should these bodies be allowed to lie in the submarine for any length of time while exposed to air at atmospheric temperature that they may become so swollen and putrefied that it would be impossible to remove them through the submarine's hatches'.

Before any further salvage work could be attempted the dead had to be removed, all that is, except those in the steering compartment, aft of the direction the divers had to go. Although they tried several times to open the door through the escape hatch something, or somebody, was jamming its progress and the area was left. Nearly three weeks were needed to complete the grim task. Each body was separated, wrapped in canvas, hauled out of the engine room hatch, and up to the surface. A tug flying the Red Ensign at half-mast placed the dead in canvas coffins and conveyed them directly from the scene to Holyhead, to await identification. Two Naval ratings transferred from the *Thetis* shortly before the dive trial volunteered to help Arnold identify each man before relatives could receive final confirmation of their worst fears. The Admiralty needed every piece of help it could to put a name to each body.

Once they were exposed to the fresh sea air, Rainsford's biggest fear was realized. Decomposition was rapid, as if what would have taken several weeks or months to happen, actually took a matter of hours. Anglesey police superintendent W. E. Jones along with one sergeant and seven constables were tasked with trying to help identify the dead through personal effects. With physical features all but gone, they only had things like clothing, personal papers and jewellery, but even this proved to be unreliable after many men were found to be wearing the clothing, watches and keys of others. Relatives were asked to supply identifying characteristics, but all too often this, too, proved unreliable as mistakes were made, or they could not give enough information to be of help.

111

On 7 September, Anglesey coroner Doctor E. R. Hughes arrived at Stanley Hospital, an imposing Victorian building in Holyhead, to conduct an autopsy on Ernest Mitchell. Although he was in a well-preserved state when recovered from the sea, within hours this was no longer the case. Hughes wrote in the clipped style of a professional attending an everyday job of how this man died and under what conditions the autopsy had to be carried out, 'The swelling was rapid, especially around the head, scrotum and thighs. Blood stained frothy fluid was coming out of the mouth, with swollen tongue where indentations of teeth were clearly visible. Eyeballs were also bulging and red. Slight post mortem discolouration of face, chest, back, varying from deep red to yellowish green. Deep green discolouration of lower abdomen, scrotum and thighs, and bright green discolouration of soles of both feet, and deaquation [excessive loss of water] of skin of whole body. Nails absent from fingers'. 'Both lungs had collapsed and lying at back of cavity'. The description of Mitchell's tongue, bulging eyes and collapsed lungs reveals how rapid his end finally was.

Hughes did what he could, but by the time Royal Navy Surgeon Commander Rainsford and Royal Navy Consulting pathologist W. W. Woods arrived the next day there was very little left to autopsy. As Rainsford put it, 'This body was then in an extremely advanced state of post mortem decomposition, and as we had been informed that further bodies were to be removed from the submarine on 9 September, we decided that a complete post mortem examination of this body would serve no useful purpose'.

On the morning of 9 September four more bodies were available, which had only been exposed to the late summer warmth for two hours. The full autopsy with Hughes in attendance took a further four hours while every minute the body decayed a little more, then much more until the skin and hair started to slip off and bloating worked faster than the Surgeon's scalpel. 'Gloving would start on the hands whereby the entire skin from the wrists to the fingertips would drop off and the body would start to turn greenish black. 'Only one of the four was selected for complete necropsy. Rainsford explained why, 'We judged it to be the least decomposed of the four, although in this respect there was little difference between them'.

He was a tall, fully dressed well-developed man who was still wearing his DSEA set. Apart from tattoos on his right leg and both forearms, positive identification could not be made from his physical appearance alone. 'Skin macerated and peeling all over, with red, and a few green, areas of discolouration, especially on the abdomen. Skin of right hand shed completely as a glove. Absence of skin and muscles over large areas of face owing to post mortem liquefaction [literally rotting into a liquid form]; exposing bare bone of upper and lower jaws and forehead. Hair of scalp mostly absent. The absence of water in the trachea and bronchi and its almost complete absence in the stomach suggest that death was not due to drowning'.

Although there was no shortage of corpses on which to autopsy, Rainsford asserted, 'In view of the fact that this body was examined only two hours after its removal from seawater and that any further bodies will have been exposed to atmospheric air for a longer period before they can be examined, with resultant increase in post mortem decomposition, we submit that post mortem examination of more bodies would serve no useful purpose'. Although further autopsies were not possible, two key facts had been established. The absence of water in the lungs, and the fact that one body had collapsed lungs and bulging eyes meant that death was not due to drowning. The cause of death was recorded officially as asphyxiation through carbon dioxide poisoning, which was then applied to all the dead.

Once the dead were identified their relatives were informed by telegram as soon as possible, and they were given two free third-class rail vouchers to make the trip to attend a funeral at Holyhead. If the relatives wanted a private funeral, their loved ones were sent in a coffin to their home railway station after the inquest. In all cases specially made zinc-lined coffins were needed to fit the bloated corpses and prevent any liquid seeping out prior to burial. In light of Johnson's refusal to allow the bodies to be removed in Birkenhead, the Liverpool & Glasgow Salvage Association offered to oversee the task of removing the dead, which involved deciding the coffin size. Costing on average £10 each, they recommended that half the coffins should be 6 feet long and the rest to be 6 feet 3 inches. Their width was to vary between 2 feet and 2 feet 6 inches, and their depth to be 2 feet. This was more than twice the size of a normal coffin.

Relatives were deterred whenever possible from viewing their dead, but at times some still wanted to see them, and could not be forced away. Putting aside the state of each corpse, perhaps to know for sure that the man held dear really was never coming home was more important. Such was the state of the post mortem decay that one wife positively identified her husband, only to find that she had made a mistake some considerable time later. Leading Stoker Arnold and the two ex-*Thetis* crewmen did what they could, as well as two Cammell Laird's staff and an Admiralty official. Once recovered, all their tattered clothing was removed and burnt while the naked bodies were transferred to a makeshift mortuary for Arnold and the others to see. All other items where handed over to the Anglesey police, including money and valuables, which were passed back to the relatives through their local police station. Some relatives complained that certain items were missing from their dead loved ones.

County Durham resident Alfred Mortimer lost his son, telegraphist Thomas William Mortimer, in the disaster. Alfred wanted some of his son's personal effects that he knew his son had with him on the day of the trial dive, especially a wristwatch and strap. Alfred wrote to Captain Oram to try to discover if the watch had been found. Oram advised him to contact Cammell Laird direct, as they were tasked with cleaning out the submarine after the Liverpool & Glasgow Salvage Association had removed the dead. This request was made after Alfred had found the strength to formally identify his son's gruesome remains in the makeshift mortuary. All Alfred really wanted was his son's watch. He described to Laird how he knew the watch was not on his son's body, 'I was at Holyhead when his body was recovered on Sunday, 12 November 1939,' he wrote 'and received what there was at the time except his wrist watch and strap which was not on him then, on account of his left hand being off by the wrist, which I saw for myself when identifying the body'.

Alfred was informed that the watch would be returned once Laird had found it. 'I have let enough time elapse', added Alfred, '...There will also be his cap and maybe somethings [sic] with his name on, so I would like information from you regarding my enquiries, as I know for certain that he wore his wrist watch in the day of the disaster. Hoping to have an early reply'. One note scrawled on the bottom of the letter says, 'Regret unable to find personal belongings'. A formal letter to Alfred confirmed that the watch and any other personal effects known to have been with his son could not be found. Those relatives who went to the mass funerals were all accommodated in a local guest-house called The Sailor's Rest. Its owner, Mrs West, not only gave the bereaved bed and breakfast, but also cared for them before each funeral took place. The Admiralty wrote in a confidential report, 'Owing to her assistance the naval authorities were spared this responsibility'.

The dead removed from the engine room first began to be buried in Maes Hyfryd Cemetery, meaning in Welsh 'beautiful ground', which in relation to a cemetery would make an odd yet perfect description. The *Thetis* monument today holds a prime location in this particularly peaceful cemetery overlooking Holyhead and the Irish Sea towards where she was lost. Only family members and invited guests were allowed to attend when the first seven victims were interred with full military honours on 14 September. They were conveyed on four lorries headed by a naval firing party as it passed through Holyhead to the cemetery, each man's coffin draped in a Union Jack and smothered with wreaths. Behind the lorries were many private cars for the relatives. Every business along the way shut and the route was thronged with people as the heartbreaking cortège passed on its way.

On two subsequent burials that month there were too many bodies to lead to the cemetery in such a grand style. The Admiralty arranged for all the coffins to be delivered throughout the morning where a naval guard was posted around them until the funeral could take place in the afternoon. In some ways this was better for the relatives because they were able to lay their own wreaths on the coffins before their men folk were finally placed beneath the earth. During the second funeral on 27 September, as with the first, ministers from all denominations conducted services at the graveside. Afterwards a Naval party fired three volleys over the grave and buglers sounded the Last Post and Reveille. One of the dead, twenty-two-year-old Stoker William Orrock was found wearing Lieutenant Commander Bolus's captain's monkey jacket. Orrock only had his trousers and vest to keep out the cold and Bolus, who was found in his shirtsleeves, had given up his jacket to the young stoker, to help keep him warm.

At the same time that the funeral was taking place a large number of people gathered along the harbour to see the Holyhead pilot boat tow a fishing vessel out to sea. Aboard were two Union Jack-draped coffins surrounded by six Naval ratings. One coffin held Lieutenant Commander Bolus, the other Cammell Laird's engineer manager Arthur Stanley Watkinson. Leading stoker Arnold was also aboard to see his captain safely on his final voyage. Aboard the pilot boat were Watkinson's widow, Marjorie, without their two sons Richard, aged fourteen, and John, aged seventeen. Bolus's sister represented his family. Sybil did not attend. Once the two boats reached a spot five miles from Holyhead the flags were removed and wreaths were lightly tied to the coffins before they were slowly lowered over the side and into the Irish Sea without any religious ceremony. As the coffins slipped beneath the waves and glided to the bottom the wreaths became detached and drifted slowly back to the surface, bobbing on the light swell.

The *Thetis*, along with the thirty or so men still trapped in the steering compartment needed to be towed around to Holyhead as soon as possible before being towed to Birkenhead. And, of course, the remainder of her dead had to be removed. The last two bodies placed partly below the engine room plating were also still there. They were two who died in the failed four-man escape attempt, and were packed tightly into a confined part of the engine room, so as not be seen by the living. A lasting reminder of a tragic failure that could, and did, befall the others.

Before she could be moved from Moelfre Bay a survey there took several weeks to complete, only to be further delayed after some leaks were found in a rather odd way. While the divers were working in the control room, their air bubbles were escaping through the damaged periscope, which had been bent over and later broken off during the salvage. The periscope's optical box, through which Bolus viewed the outside world, was removed and an expandable wooden plug fitted to take the pressure of the compressed air blow needed to remove the last of the water. Another leak through the port engine exhaust was stopped, simply by closing an exhaust valve that was found to be partly open.

On 21 October blowing recommenced throughout the day and continued on the next. Shortly after noon on the 22nd the bow slowly climbed to the surface, for about four minutes, only to lose buoyancy and sink back to the seabed. It was essential that the stern surfaced first, so the water could pour out through Number Five torpedo tube. Had the bow ascended beforehand, all the trapped water would run to the stern and not escape. The best way to lower her back down was to vent some of the forward ballast tanks, which worked very well. When the stern still could not be raised, divers drilled a hole through the lower part of the pressure hull in the after crews' quarters to permit removal of the water trapped below the level of the door to the engine room.

The drastic action helped tremendously. On 23 October she was finally ready to be fully blown. Some effort was needed to break her stern out of the mud, as well as the extra weight of the thirty-three bodies still trapped in the steering compartment. Just after lunch the stern surfaced followed half an hour later by the bow. She was afloat. Eventually, floating on an even keel, she was towed round to the L.M.S.

dry dock in Holyhead where she docked on 10 November. Before they could enter the submarine, the remaining bodies in the steering compartment were removed, and the whole submarine deodorized to make conditions as pleasant as possible for common entry and inspection for the Tribunal.

There was no need for the divers to remove the dead this time. After all, they had done more than their fair share clearing the engine room and the *Thetis* was no longer submerged. Instead the job went to Hedensford Mines Rescue Station in Cannock, Shropshire. The first mines rescue station was opened at Tankersley near Barnsley, South Yorkshire in 1902. The concept did not become fully established across the country until after the 1911 Coal Mines Act made their establishment compulsory to lessen the national toll of miners who were killed or seriously injured. Hedensford came into being in 1914. At its height the rescue station gave emergency cover to more than forty pits in the Staffordshire and Shropshire areas, covering such incidents as explosions, underground fires and cave-ins.

The Admiralty contacted Hedensford superintendent fireman Joshua 'Josh' Payton to see if he could mount such an operation to remove the final trapped bodies. Its success relied on two points, the Hedensford chairman agreeing, and whether the men could use Proto breathing apparatus. Better known as just 'Proto' this apparatus was fully self-contained and gave the wearer at least two hours breathing time while undertaking hard physical work. The principal was that the wearer repeatedly breathed the same air, but every time he breathed out the carbon dioxide was purified through a form of soda lime and a small amount of oxygen was injected back into the mix. The system was perfect for working prolonged hours in the close confines of a submarine as well as a coal mine. Payton readily agreed, as long as one man could be sent from each colliery in the Hedensford area, meaning six altogether.

Upon arriving at Holyhead the team converted a disused barn into a make-shift work station, including baths, tables for equipment and large storage facilities for specialized equipment as well as much needed heating and lighting as the cold and darkness of winter 1939 began to bite. They started removing the bodies on 11 November. The rescue team tried to enter the *Thetis* through the engine room bulkhead door, but had to abandon the idea for the same reason as the Admiralty divers, being that the door was blocked. Instead they gained access two

117

at a time through the Davis escape chamber directly into the steering compartment.

The escape chamber door squeaked open and the first man ducked as low as he could to slide through the tiny door and into the steering compartment. He looked around the mass of steel pipes, deck plates and equipment, all of which showed signs of rust and decay. Climbing into the cramped steel chamber, wearing heavy breathing apparatus was extremely difficult. Once inside they were faced with just as gruesome sight as the divers two months earlier, but this time the decay of the dead was much worse due to exposure to the air over a longer period. After 163 days sealed within the pressure hull one man was still sitting grasping his attaché case. A few were lying down, as if asleep. The Mines Rescue Service's own account of the operation reads, 'It was very hot and the stench was very, very bad'.

Looking across at the bulkhead door into the engine room it soon became apparent why the Admiralty divers could not gain access. Bodies were, indeed, piled up against the door. Before removal each man was enclosed in a grey canvas bag and a Naval type, green envelope. Ironically they were then hoisted up through the very same escape chamber they had tried in vain so hard to achieve while still in life. A crane had to hoist them out and up on to the quay, due to the greatly increased weight of the bodies. Payton added, 'On Sunday morning at 06.00 hours the Chase team were down at the harbour ready to continue. Everyone was as keen as mustard, and at 12.40 hours after six hours continuous work, the last of the remaining nineteen bodies was out, during which time the men had worn three sets of apparatus without a break, and not a single hitch. After a good hot bath, they were ready for a good dinner, and none the worse for their gruesome task'.

Chapter 11

'We Find as Follows . . .'

After the final body had been removed, and the submarine fully deodorized, temporary electric lighting was strung up from the engine room right up to Number Forty bulkhead. A four-man team, representing the Admiralty and other interested parties went into the submarine to inspect the first two compartments before walking back through the vessel in November 1939. The stench of death was still everywhere. Eventually they reached Number Forty bulkhead and carefully opened the escape hatch doors and climbed over the broken furniture and other debris that nearly stopped Woods from making his escape. Soon they were facing Number Twenty-five bulkhead door at the other end of the compartment.

Climbing over the coaming down into the torpedo compartment the inspectors looked up at the six rear doors. All were securely shut, except Number Five, which was clipped firmly back in its safety recess to prevent it slamming around in rough weather. Photographs were taken of everything, especially the state of all the bow cap operating levers. Now they could all see the most startling piece of evidence yet gathered since the *Thetis* was lost. Number Five indicator was at 'open' and *not*, 'Shut' as Woods had so convincingly stated under oath. And all the bow cap operating levers were at 'neutral', not 'shut'. But this came too late for the confidential Admiralty inquiry, that opened and closed about four months earlier.

Commander-in-Chief Portsmouth Admiral Sir William M. James had only been in office for three days when he ordered Fort Blockhouse to conduct a confidential in-house full and detailed investigation into how the *Thetis* was lost. On 6 June 1939 Vice Admiral Robert Henry Taunton Raikes chaired the three-man committee appointed to get those answers. With his in-depth knowledge of submarine procedure as Flag Officer (Submarines) at HMS *Dolphin*, he was well suited to the job. The two other members were Captain Claud Barrington

Barry, commander of the submarine depot ship HMS *Medway*, and Rear Admiral William Frederick Wake-Walker, Senior Officers' War Course tutor at HMS *President*, the Royal Navy war college in Greenwich, Kent.

During the next three weeks fifty men, ranging from Navy experts, Cammell Laird's employees, McKenzie of Metal Industries, as well as the four survivors, were summoned to Fort Blockhouse to give evidence. The investigation's full title was the 'Finding of the Board of Inquiry into the Loss of HMS *Thetis*' and by the time Committee completed its task, their evidence showed serious flaws in Admiralty submarine design, training and the conduct of its senior officers involved at all levels of the search and rescue operation. On 29 June 1939, exactly one year to the day since the *Thetis* was launched, Raikes' confidential forty-nine-page report was ready for James to read.

The three-man committee, or Naval Board, summarized the main events, starting with Woods opening the rear door of Number Five torpedo tube, before looking more closely at how it was possible for the bow cap to be open at the same time as the rear door. Woods' emphatic assertion that all indicators showed that the bow caps were shut at the time the power was put through to the bow cap operating panel was of key importance. If the Lieutenant was to be believed, the report stated that this situation should have resulted in the bow caps shutting when power was on if they were not shut already. The Board thought it improbable that so many highly trained and competent submariners missed such an obvious point, as an open bow cap, but something went wrong somewhere and now a submarine was lost and ninety-nine men were dead.

Perhaps there was another reason for such a drastic error. Consideration was given to the bad positioning of the bow cap indicators. They could not all be seen at the same time, and the shut position was different for each tube. 'Although the evidence is that these indicators were inspected from close to', Raikes confirmed, 'it is thought, however, that this would have involved a remarkable combination of errors and unlikely in the circumstances that a mistake should have been made both in the case of the bow cap operating levers, and the bow cap indicators'.

The Board drew the conclusion that the most likely reason for the bow cap being open can only have been for one of two reasons. Something jamming it could have caused it to be partly open, or 'Failure in the gearing between the telemotor ram and the bow cap due to a break or link becoming disconnected'. As an added safety measure each degree of movement of the bow cap was magnified three-fold on the indicator, so the slightest jam should have been clearly exaggerated in the torpedo space for all to see. But it was not. 'To sum up, there must have been either a mechanical failure by which the bow cap indicator showed "shut" when in fact, the bow cap was open or else the position of this indicator was misread by Lieutenant Woods'.

Then Woods' opening the rear door was considered. He was asked if he used the rimer to clear the inspection hole, to which he said he had not, but further investigation proved that this oversight was not the Lieutenant's fault. A rimer was a narrow pencil-like wire inserted into the inspection hole to clear any debris blocking it, and thus preventing the tell-tale spurt of water from escaping. 'There is no evidence to show that this instruction was given when Lieutenant Woods passed through the training class and he states he was not instructed as to the use of the rimer at all. Generally, from the evidence of members of the Torpedo Equipment Trial Party, Lieutenant Woods and Lieutenant Coltart, we consider that sufficient importance is not attached to the presence and use of the rimer as part of the safety arrangements of the tubes'.

On this point Woods was not held to blame, but rather Royal Navy training which, although a small detail in a submariner's instruction, would have saved the *Thetis* and all those aboard her had it been used. The Board absolved Woods of not taking further steps before opening the tubes, such as checking the automatic inboard vents, or AIVs. These allow the torpedo tube to flood up immediately a torpedo is fired to ensure the submarine did not shoot up once the weight of the torpedo was gone. These would show in an instant whether water was in the tube, stating quite clearly, 'The inboard vents of the tubes were not tried before the rear doors were opened, but the test cocks should be sufficient indication of the state and are fitted for that purpose'.

The Board drew a controversial conclusion that was not made known to the Public Tribunal, although there was every reason that it should have been. There was never normally any danger attached to opening the rear doors during work on torpedoes under war conditions where speed was everything, especially when re-loading. On this particular occasion, though, the *Thetis* was on her dive trials. There were no torpedoes on board and the rear doors became part of the normal safety fittings of the submarine, such as the lower conning tower hatch, which Bolus would expect to be closed before diving.

Raikes and his colleagues informed Admiral Sir William James, 'We consider that in these circumstances there was no adequate reason for Lieutenant Woods opening the rear doors and he was not justified in doing so without instructions'.

Once the rear door was open, the Board found further criticism of the crew's actions, especially while trying to close the door in Number Twenty-five bulkhead. The delay was acknowledged as being due to the lower clips hanging down and jamming in between the door and the coaming. 'These clips should have been secured and held clear in the spring holders which evidence shows are provided on the doors. Those stationed in the compartment should have seen that these were correctly in the holders'. Woods was adamant that had they not been hanging down, then the compartment could have been shut much sooner and thus the submarine saved, but a late Admiralty design change was more directly responsible rather than crew error when the quick-closing door was changed for one with eighteen clips. Completely abandoning the torpedo stowage compartment at Number Forty bulkhead was also criticized. 'If one or two men had stayed behind to make further efforts to close the door in Number Twenty-five bulkhead,' continued the report, 'and had been shut in the compartment, it is probable that they would have been able to join the remainder of the crew later through the forward escape chamber'.

Attempts to enter the flooded compartments to shut the rear door of Number Five tube and prepare the compartments for removing the water was seen as a gallant and worthwhile action, even though it failed through Jamison, Chapman and Smithers suffering severe effects of pressure. But had they succeeded, simply blowing the air out of the flooded compartments was never going to be enough to restore buoyancy. According to the Board, it was not known whether Bolus, Oram and Laird's men fully appreciated just how unstable the *Thetis* would then become. A complex action of flooding some tanks and not others would also be needed, or the stern could take a much steeper angle while the bow could shoot upwards or sideways with no knowledge of how or where it would settle.

Barely eight hours after the *Thetis* went down there was a way of getting oxy-acetylene burning equipment on its way to the scene. The report stated, 'The Admiralty report that at 23.00 hours they had communicated by telephone with the Liverpool & Glasgow Salvage Association after some difficulty and informed them that their services would probably be required. Mr Critchley, Joint Manager of the

Liverpool & Glasgow Salvage Association, states that this message was not received and the misunderstanding has not yet been explained. Mr Critchley states that had this message reached the firm the salvage vessel *Ranger* would have been sent out at once and oxy-acetylene cutting gear would have been available from the first.'

Critchley did more than just state that he could have got the essential burning gear in place much earlier than it finally was. In a private correspondence to Laird's Managing Director Robert Johnson, and the Admiralty, he confirmed getting a call much later on 2 June, but emphatically denied ever receiving the telephone call at about 23.00 hours on 1 June. Had such a call been made, he asserted, it would have been answered, and acted upon at once. After all, they were a professional salvage organization, the biggest in the United Kingdom, on call twenty-four hours a day. Why would such an important call, from one of their best clients, be missed? Privately Critchley, like McKenzie, was angered at how the Admiralty handled the disaster, so much so that he refused to take part in any post disaster investigations.

The conduct of Captain Hart and Captain Nicholson, one of their own senior naval officers, was next put under scrutiny. They considered that the decision to tow the stern to pull it upwards was wrong. From the moment that a horizontal pull was introduced, a slew of the submarine and consequent loss of lift was inevitable once the tow got out of the direct line of the submarine. 'The decision to tow was taken on the initiative of Captain Hart, but Captain Nicholson should have become aware of it and was actually on board *Vigilant* while it was in progress before it had caused a slew and took no action. Any attempt at towing the submarine under these conditions must inevitably result in slewing the submarine rather than lifting the tail unless the pull could be kept directly in line with her and we consider that reason, backed by earlier experience, should have shown that a direct vertical lift was the only operation that has any real chance of success'.

Hart's and Nicholson's view that the submarine was being kept under by the force of the tide and that it would re-appear about 18.00 hours at slack water was also wrong. Then the 60° angle on the stern, added to the 12° list, as she began to roll over, received special mention. 'This large angle must have had considerable effect on men inside already weakened, though with what definite effect it is not possible to say'.

Lieutenant 'Bert' Chapman was also criticized for putting four men in the escape chamber at the same time. 'We consider that the action taken to put four men in the escape chamber after Captain Oram and Lieutenant Woods had gone up was extremely hazardous and most unlikely to be successful, and it can only be assumed that this was attempted as it was thought that time was an essential factor if all were to be saved, and this justified the risk. We are of the opinion that this decision was wrong and in the result caused considerable delay and the failure may have affected the morale of the remainder'. Arnold reported that morale was very much affected by Chapman's action. The drains from the escape chambers were found to be a faulty design, which would require a complete overhaul to correct. 'Escape chambers are at present fitted with open drains. This is dangerous as the loose water may well fall on electric machinery and cause an electric fire'. Which was exactly what happened.

Raikes' findings went on to be even more critical of, at times, the Admiralty's own salvage and rescue operations. This was especially so after the disaster escalated into one of abstract chaos when Nicholson finally realized, far too late, just how 'desperate' the situation really was. 'We cannot find anyone directing the operation at this time who had any clear idea with what object they were employing this rather drastic method of lifting the stern. There was a general impression that a hole was to be cut, but where exactly it was to be cut was not decided, and the burning gear had not then arrived. After the wire parted it appears to have been again thought that the tail of the submarine was being kept under by the force of the tide and that it would re-appear about 18.00 hours at slack water. There was little justification for this view since the tail had not been kept down by the tide under similar conditions during the forenoon before lifting operations began'.

During the lifting operations the submarine must have lost considerable buoyancy, which cannot be accounted for entirely by escaping air from her ballast tanks alone when she was raised to such a steep angle. In the light of after events an additional buoyage of the submarine would have been a wise precaution, so if she carried away, there would be no problem finding her again. The basic salvage precaution Thomas McKenzie was to explain to the Public Inquiry about three weeks later. The Committee concluded, 'We consider that the decision that desperate measures were necessary was correct, but that to try and tow the tail up was unsound and certain to fail and the alternative of a vertical lift should have been tried'.

Lieutenant Commander Bolus was next in the firing line. Once he realized that a major accident had taken place, his blowing of Numbers

One, Two, Four, and A tanks, 'Should have brought the stern above water even when the two foremost compartments were completely flooded'. For some reason, Bolus did not order the blowing of Numbers Five and Six main tanks, or they were not completely emptied. Had he blown these extra tanks there was every chance that the *Thetis* could have been found a good three hours sooner – and there would have been no need for Laird's men to change the internal piping. 'A costly exercise that used up a great deal of breathable air'.

Perhaps Bolus did not want to risk using too much air because further expenditure might have been needed to keep the stern up at a later time. Or perhaps he felt that it would take more than simply blowing these tanks to get the tail out of the water. But as Raikes pointed out, 'A relatively small quantity of air would give a considerable amount of buoyancy and positive movement. It is difficult to understand why, if full, they were not used to bring the stern of the submarine up earlier.' There was supposed to be enough air still available in the air bottle groups to get the stern up. With all the evidence at hand, as well as knowing that Bolus's training told him this was possible, the Board could not understand why he failed to execute this basic submarine operation.

Supposing Bolus was waiting for a better moment to empty them, had he ordered the blowing of the tanks when the *Thetis* sank for the last time at about 15.00 hours on 2 June, he could have kept the stern up long enough to allow air to be piped in, or the rescue of the crew. This unsolved mystery runs through a large part of Raikes' investigation. But the Board could only speculate, 'It is probable that by this time, owing to the exhaustion of the crew, and perhaps to some extent the disturbance resulting from the large angles put on previously by the towing operation, they were incapable of taking any further action'.

The Chief of Staff to Rear Admiral (S), Captain Ian Macintyre was later criticized for not ensuring that an experienced submarine officer and a technical expert were appointed by him to oversee the situation until the *Winchelsea* arrived at about 16.15 hours on 2 June. As overall commander (at the time) Macintyre was criticized for taking a ship to Liverpool and arriving quite late, as he perhaps should have flown. He thought that, under the circumstances, going by ship was the best way forward. Air Marshal Sir Frederick William Bowhill, Air Officer Commander-in-Chief, Coastal Command, Lee-on-Solent, ordered an aircraft from Number One Coast Artillery Co-operation Unit, Gosport, to be ready and at Macintyre's disposal, should he want it. Macintyre refused, saying that to receive signals and direct the operation in a plane was not possible, but it was.

Macintyre later testified before the Public Inquiry, 'I did not consider that under the circumstances in my particular case time was the most important factor as representing the Rear Admiral of Submarines. I considered that it was more important to remain in touch with everybody concerned, so that I could make the necessary suggestions or give the necessary instructions in the absence of the Rear Admiral of Submarines. In considering this before I left Fort Blockhouse, it seemed to me that there would be possibly two experienced submarine captains at Birkenhead who could proceed to the spot'.

He did, or at least thought he did, have two experienced officers very near to the spot. Lieutenant Commander Garnet of the *Taku* and Lloyd of the *Trident* should have been found quickly enough to render assistance. Macintyre said that he did check with Cammell Laird to make sure that the two officers were not aboard the *Thetis* when she went down, and was informed that they certainly were not. All attempts to locate the much-needed men failed – until the terrible truth finally dawned. The Admiralty Board ruled, 'In this connection it is noted that is was not known at this time that the Commanding Officers [Garnet and Lloyd] of the other submarines building at Messrs. Cammell Laird were also on the *Thetis*'.

The Public Tribunal would later make much of trying to decide if too many people were on board for her dive trials. There were not so many men aboard for the first attempted trials in Gareloch in April 1939, but it was quite rightly pointed out, the trials in Liverpool Bay were further out from the mainland than before, and on this occasion there was a legal requirement to carry more personnel to ensure a full three-watch rotation was maintained. But this was not the full story. Although the Tribunal inquiry evidence that the number on board could not have been reduced under any circumstances, and did not pursue this line of questioning, Raikes' confidential investigation certainly did.

A submarine on her diving trials was considered to be at a minimum risk, especially with the number of highly trained naval and engineering personnel aboard, and the fact that the first dive is carried out in slow time. The Admiralty wholly supported this approach because out of all the submarines that had been built for them during the previous forty years or so, only one had been lost on contractor's trials prior to the *Thetis*. Raikes explained how this rule applied to the *Thetis*, 'On this occasion, a diesel electric trial was to have been carried out on completion of the diving trials and the firm had provided means, by the presence of the *Grebe Cock*, whereby any personnel not required for the diving trials could be disembarked. But though opportunity was given, no one elected to avail themselves of it, neither were they instructed to do so'.

It had always been the custom for officers from other submarines of a similar class building at the same contractors to gain experience on her diving trials. That was why Lieutenant Commanders Lloyd and Garnet were there, along with engineering officers. There was no better way for an officer to see first hand how his own submarine was likely to perform. The *Thetis* dive trials were no exception and the Board saw no objection to this practice. However, 'The numbers in *Thetis* during her diving trial were more than normally is the case. Had the numbers been cut down to only those required for the diving trial, a marked reduction could have been made amongst the Admiralty representatives'.

Going even further in their criticism of numbers, the Board stated, 'It is considered that the following could have been temporarily disembarked for the diving trial: The two representatives of Rear Admiral (Submarines), the representative of Engineer-in-Chief, probably three Admiralty Overseers. With regard to the officers from other submarines, we consider that the number on board was excessive and not more than two should have been there. Captain Oram was the Commanding Officer of the Flotilla to which *Thetis* was destined and the reasons he gave for being there we consider adequate.

'With regard to the personnel of the firm, the Board do not feel in a position to lay down exactly who was required for the diving trial, but feel sure that a number could have been temporarily disembarked without interfering with the effectiveness of the diving trial.' Robert Johnson publicly admitted that a good six men could have left, but were there for the ride, including Pilot Norman Wilcox whose decision to take the joy ride eventually cost him his life. The key is in Bolus's message to Godfrey when the tug captain asked if any were leaving. Bolus shouted through his megaphone, 'All are accompanying us on board for the dive. My diving course is 310°'. The use of the word 'accompany' under such conditions as a submarine's first dive is a little odd. The five dictionary definitions of the word are variations of 'to be close to' or 'with something or someone'. Bolus was a highly educated man and as a commanding officer, he knew the importance of clear and concise communication. Had all aboard been necessary for the dive he would have said something to the effect of, 'none are leaving', or 'All are needed aboard', or 'all are staying aboard'. But not, 'accompanying us on board'.

There was no air purification system on the *Thetis*, as it was thought that a submarine could always surface during the hours of darkness to refresh the air supply. With a normal crew of fifty-three men, each person would have about 400 feet^2 of air. Then about 0.7 feet^2 of carbon dioxide would be released per hour, rising to 0.18 feet^2 per hour. That would give, under normal operational conditions, a safe dive time of 16.5 hours before the internal atmosphere reached three per cent carbon dioxide saturation. Above that, the safe operational efficiently of the vessel would be compromised.

When she sailed there was twice the number on board, cutting their available air to about 200 feet^2 per man. That meant that the carbon dioxide rise was now 0.36 feet^2 per hour. After the *Thetis* went down, with two compartments flooded, their available air space shrank to only 160 feet^2 per man, with each person breathing about 11 feet^2 per hour. Altogether the Board thought that there were about five men too many. Add to this Johnson's view that there were six more men that should have disembarked, gives a conservative estimate of eleven men that should not have been there.

Altogether, taking into consideration space filled with machinery and men, there was about 16,640 feet^2 of available air. Although it will never be known exactly how fast the air deteriorated, or the individual endurance of each man, had these eleven men been absent there would have been about 1,760 feet^2 available. Taking into consideration that four men escaped, and a great deal of air was used up while changing the piping to re-ballast the stern, the remaining ninety-nine men would, roughly, have had another two hours of life, let alone an extended ability to focus on survival.

In light of Admiralty policy and the evidence gathered from expert salvage officers the Admiralty remained entrenched in their unbending view that 'We consider that experience in this case again shows that salvage operations of any kind undertaken with the object of raising a submarine, partly flooded, which is unable to come to the surface by her own efforts, and thereby rescuing her crew are most unlikely to be successful in time to save life'.

With the introduction of the DSEA escape apparatus, and its limited success on one submarine disaster six years earlier, that was all a submariner had. The *Thetis* disaster showed that perhaps there was room for a salvage element, especially when Oram, the commander of the Fifth Submarine Flotilla and a man who knew well Admiralty policy on such matters, saw it as the only way to save the men and the ship. The Board made eighteen recommendations to change submarine rescue procedure, one of these concerned the rear doors of torpedo tubes in all submarines. 'These have been clearly shown to be a source of danger as except for the test cock, which should indicate when the tube is full, there is nothing to prevent the rear door being opened when the bow cap is open. It would be possible to fit an interlock between the bow cap and the rear door, but no interlock is entirely reliable, and so this is not recommended.'

'We recommend that the present quick-opening type be retained and a clip fitted against which the door will bear directly it is free, then if no water comes out the clip can be taken off and the door swung open. It must be impossible for the clip to be taken off until the door is free'. The clip did eventually become integral to British submarine design from the Second World War right up to today, and is known generally as a '*Thetis* clip' This point and many others from the Board's findings formed the basis of a much larger formal report compiled by Admiral Nasmith to look much more deeply into how the Admiralty addressed matters of safety aboard its submarines.

Taking away the sheer bad luck that befell the *Thetis* from the time she was conceived right up to her slow death, the Raikes report is a damning indictment, not only of costly errors made during the search and rescue operation, but also by illuminating ingrained Naval incompetence with individual officers and Admiralty procedure. Four days after the report landed on Admiral Sir William M. James's desk, the Public Inquiry began under authority of Prime Minister Neville Chamberlain. Its findings would often be diametrically opposed to those of the Admiralty and would form the cornerstone of public perception of what happened to this day. But while it became the basis, albeit strained at times, of mainstream public acceptance, Raikes' findings remained confidential for many years and are still not widely known to exist. But for one man's decision, this never had to be the case.

Chapter 12

'A Sea of Trouble'

After Chamberlain announced that the *Thetis* Tribunal would begin before the submarine was raised, its planning and execution could now go ahead. Leaning on the despatch box, he looked around his own Party members and across to the Labour Opposition. 'Of course, the Government will give the Tribunal all the assistance in its power', he said 'and as a considerable amount of preliminary work will be necessary before the Inquiry can be opened, the Treasury Solicitor has been instructed to place his services at the disposal of the Tribunal for the purpose of collecting all the evidence and other material which the Tribunal may require to have submitted to them'. Its full title was 'The Tribunal of Inquiry into the circumstances attending the loss of His Majesty's Submarine *Thetis* and the subsequent attempts to save the lives of those in the ship' but it was, and still is, more commonly known as the '*Thetis* Tribunal' or the '*Thetis* Inquiry'.

Throughout the month of June Treasury Solicitor Sir Thomas James Barnes collected evidence from more than fifty expert witnesses in a similar way to Raikes' investigation, often calling on the same men. Some volunteered their evidence, others involved in the construction, sea trials, rescue and recovery were summoned. Each one had to give a full written statement before being required to answer questions on their recollections.

The Right Honourable Sir Alfred Townsend Bucknill presided over the Tribunal, which opened at 10.30 hours on Monday, 3 July 1939 at Admiralty Court III in the Strand, London. Altogether eight legal representatives were present to examine, and at times to cross-examine, the witnesses. Acting for the Government were Attorney General the Right Honourable Sir Donald B. Somerville OBE, KC, MP, Mr H. U. Willink, KC and Mr Cyril Miller. Laird's Liverpool-based legal firm Messrs Laces & Company instructed Mr A. T. Miller KC to represent their

131

clients. Other King's Counsels and legal representatives appeared for the dependents of seventeen men who perished aboard the submarine.

The first business that Monday morning was for each legal representative to be sworn-in before Bucknill. Attorney General Somerville then informed him of what order he thought the witness's should be heard. Somerville told Bucknill that he thought it would assist Bucknill if he, Somerville, outlined the facts that would be proved by the witnesses. 'Naturally', he added, 'I am not proposing, at this stage, to suggest hypotheses. I then propose to put before you in as concise a form as possible the sequence of events, and then to proceed to call the witnesses'. Bucknill agreed with everything Somerville said, then began the gathering of more than 2,000 pages of evidence in a bid to get to the truth of what happened and why. However, the Tribunal, or Bucknill, under instruction from those who appointed him, already had fixed ideas of how the Tribunal was to work.

Many people, including the represented dependents, were hoping that in some way over the coming weeks the evidence would shed some light on who was to blame for the disaster. Then legal action could be taken through the civil, or at worst criminal, justice system to gain compensation for the seventy widows and ninety orphans left behind to cope in the wake of the whole fiasco. Bucknill, however, refused flatly to hear any hint of Government or Admiralty responsibility, especially about whether the *Thetis* was actually seaworthy on the day, or how the fifty-hour rescue operation failed to save the men. He stated clearly, 'This Tribunal is not sitting to allocate possible blame in this matter. It is appointed to find out what happened, why, and, possibly, what can be done to prevent it happening again'.

Throughout the Tribunal, evidence was heard (and never followed up) that could well apportion blame, a matter that frequently caused friction between the various legal Councels, especially from those representing the deceased relatives' families. Mr R. T. Paget along with Mr A. M. Lyons KC was representing the relatives of eighteen-year-old electrical apprentice William H. Smith, the youngest person to die aboard the *Thetis*. Paget was, without a doubt, the most aggressive lawyer present, often being told to curb his questioning techniques, as well as being quick to criticize Bucknill and the general court procedure. Barely had the proceedings begun when he complained of how some Counsels were being treated. 'It would be an enormous help to us', said Paget, 'and a saving of time, if we could be supplied with such documents as are going to be used, and are not of a secret nature because then, before the witness comes, we should know something from the documents, and be able to frame our questions, and perhaps not ask a great many'.

'On the other hand', replied Bucknill, 'you might ask a lot more.'

'As your Lordship says, but this is working under very great difficulties'.

One important document was a copy of the chart showing every location of each ship involved in the search and rescue operation and at what time, which the Government's Counsel often referred to when questioning witnesses. Willink tried to explain to Paget that it would be impossible to produce every scrap of paper from every witness along the way, but, if Paget insisted, he would get a copy of the chart and Paget could mark all the various shipping positions throughout the rescue operations himself. Paget replied somewhat acidly, 'As we have not the signals and we do not know what they are, that would be difficult'.

The four surviving personnel, Oram, Woods, Arnold and Shaw were the first to give evidence, covering events before, during the dive trials and finally up to the time each man escaped. Then followed evidence from those involved in the search and rescue, both at the scene and from as far away as the Admiralty in Whitehall. This included both civilian and military experts in submarine construction, procedure, air quality and dozens of other facets that surround a submarine from design to deployment. A great deal of information was discovered that helped to build a picture of what happened. But there was always an undercurrent of not probing too far, in case perhaps inescapable proof was discovered that official procedure had failed, either at best through accident, or at worst through design.

Later in the proceedings Lyons touched on the subject of what more could have been done to save the men, only, like Paget before him, to face Bucknill's wrath. When Lyons was questioning Mersey Docks salvage officer Captain Hart, his questioning became aggressive when it came to why so many ships in the area could not have done more to secure the tail of the submarine, or get the men out. Lyons asked Hart, 'Do you say that nothing could have been done and nothing could have been brought to bear at any time? With all the shipping there was, and must be, at the disposal of the Mersey Docks & Harbour Board, nothing could have been done to raise that submarine?'

'I still say, looking back, and generally looking back one discovers flaws in what one has done', replied Hart. 'I cannot see that anything further could have been done than the putting into operation of the plan with regard to supplying air to the gun recuperator'. Lyons went on to question Hart regarding the ready availability of all the salvage equipment such as camels, boats with cutting gear, compressors and air hoses for a trial dive. Had it been more readily available, perhaps all 103 men would still be alive instead of only four 'I see no objection,' replied Hart, 'except on the score of expense'.

'Does that matter?'

'I suppose expense enters into everything, yes'.

Lyons replied with not so much a further question, but rather a curt statement. 'Expense cannot be an objection when you are safeguarding human lives in the pursuit of duty'.

Bucknill predictably leaped to Hart's defence, 'Is that really a reasonable proposition, Mr Lyons?'

Lyons shot back, 'I should have thought so, with respect – have everything ready'.

Then followed one of the most heated debates of the whole Tribunal, with Lyons refusing to back down on a valid point, and Bucknill applying a rather odd analogy to prove the King's Counsel wrong. Bucknill explained with a controlled hint of sarcasm, 'Let us think for a moment. A submarine which has been built with the greatest care and tested in many ways should go out on a perfectly fine, clear day, accompanied by tugs and divers and camels in case somebody opens a door of a torpedo tube and unfortunately that is open to the sea, and this disaster should happen?'

'With great respect', Lyons retorted, 'at the time when it is going for a diving trial in a fresh area with a bad tide, and 101 [sic] people on board. In those circumstances I would have respectfully suggested that nothing is too much trouble, or too much expense, which will operate as a safeguard'.

'I quite agree, nothing is too much trouble and too much expense to save life. One might well say that a doctor and nurse should stand by every gun before it is fired in case there should be an explosion in the breach, which does occasionally happen when a big gun is fired, with most disastrous results, but you do not expect it to happen, and you make reasonable precautions. It is not reasonable to have a doctor and nurse standing by every time a gun is fired'.

Picking up the doctor/nurse analogy, Lyons was having none of it, 'Every time, no; but there might be occasions when a gun is being fired in an area where a gun has never been fired, where people are very sensitive to noise, and there might well be occasions when it would be an ordinary reasonable safeguard to have medical assistance at hand in case something untoward happened'.

An exasperated Bucknill closed the debate affirming his pre-set ideas on culpability, 'I do not want to stop anybody from criticizing anyone in this case, and if their criticism is that something amounts to negligence, that does not stop them in any way whatever. All I say is that I do not think that I should attribute blame in my report'. And he certainly did not.

Only two witnesses challenged the conduct of the salvage and rescue operation, and the conduct of the Admiralty during the whole *Thetis* shambles. They were both civilians and were among the country's very few true salvage experts. Thomas McKenzie was one: the other was his former employer at Scapa Flow, Ernest Frank Guelph Cox. About fifteen years earlier Cox initiated, against all odds, the salvaging of the scuttled German Imperial High Seas Fleet after the Admiralty claimed it could never be done. McKenzie gained a great deal of his salvage experience under his former employer.

Cox did not know until Saturday morning, 3 June that the *Thetis* was down. He immediately telephoned Cammell Laird to offer his assistance. No one was available to clarify if he was needed and, as with McKenzie's initial offer, Cox's help was never accepted. Feeling such a strong conviction that he could have helped, Cox wrote to Bucknill on 4 July to offer his views to the Tribunal on what could have been done, and what might help avoid such a disaster happening again.

He felt that the Admiralty should employ experienced salvage men, to save both life and the ship, who could be called upon to take command and control in such a disaster. During the First World War the Admiralty did employ full-time salvage officers, but after the Admiralty Salvage Department was mostly dissolved, by about 1921, salvage expertise was, and still is today, largely co-opted from the private sector.

Bucknill agreed to hear him, but not before Admiralty Director of Naval Contracts (DNC) Sir Stanley Goodhall went through Cox's six-page letter, word for word, to show that perhaps Cox did not quite know what he was talking about. Some of his ideas were not practical, but others, such as compressed-air usage and flawed submarine design struck to the core of bad Naval planning. Two major submarine disasters forged Admiralty thinking into believing that salvage to save life was not an option, and the best a submariner could hope for was to escape using his DSEA set.

On 26 January 1932 the M Class submarine, HMS *M-2*, sailed from Portland for an exercise in West Bay off the Dorset coast. Her captain signalled their depot ship, HMS *Titania*, confirming that the *M-2* would dive at 10.30 hours. Several hours later a coaster returned to port where her captain described how he saw a submarine go down stern first. Nearly two weeks passed before the *M-2* was found. Her revolutionary aircraft hangar was wide open with the plane still neatly folded inside.

Two theories for her loss were put forward. The *M-2* was designed to surface with her decks still awash then compressors would kick in to blow out the rest of the ballast tanks, a procedure that could take several minutes. If the hangar was opened too soon, with the deck still awash, she was doomed. The other theory was that because the *M-2*'s hydroplanes held her on the surface while the ballast tanks were fully emptied there was a possibility that the after hydroplanes failed. This would cause the submarine to topple off her seaborne perch and crash to the bottom. More than ten months were spent trying to raise her, including 1,500 dives and heavy cost. Cox acted as a consultant for the operation. After a great deal of friction between the Navy and himself, the *M-2* was a mere 18 feet from the surface when bad weather caused her to plummet back to the seabed where she still lies today.

Had Cox delved into the *M-2* salvage failure before the Tribunal, the Admiralty had prepared a list of twelve questions covering how three attempts under Cox's direction failed to lift the submarine, such as his recommendation to use wires attached to pontoons. This was adopted, but they parted on four occasions. Or how he refused to read the salvage report on a similar accident to the United States Navy submarine *S-4*, which showed how wires would work. This was seen as some kind of arrogant affront, but Cox did exactly the same back in 1924 when he was offered the Admiralty salvage reports on the scuttled fleet at Scapa Flow. The Admiralty stated, 'Where they rest, they will rust. There can be no question of raising them'. Cox promptly refused to read their in-house salvage report and went on to answer their question by raising more than 200,000 tons of scuttled shipping over the next eight years.

When Cox came to give his evidence, the need to apply such damning techniques were not necessary. He told the Court in great detail how it was essential to get drilling and cutting gear out to the *Thetis* as soon as possible, had it been available. In much stronger terms than McKenzie had done, he said, 'That is one of the contentions I am striving to press upon persons, that there was no real organization really [a point made quite clear by Raikes in his confidential Naval inquiry]. No salvage man would have gone out without burning gear'. He then got down to telling the Court, based on his own experience of raising sunken warships, how compressed air could have been used to blow out the *Thetis* and raise her easily, with or without trapped men aboard.

It was a simple case of drilling a hole through Z tank, and into 146 bulkhead if necessary, to blow air in to revive the men, and blow out the water, just as McKenzie had said. Cox was adamant that all bulkheads in all seaborne vessels leaked, regardless of whether they were built into a battleship or a submarine. Attorney General Sir Donald Somerville said, 'Have you ever tried a submarine bulkhead?'

'No, I have not', replied Cox.

'You know that they are tested to 150 lb, whereas I think the ordinary battleship bulkhead is tested to 25 lb. Would you tell me whether you knew that?'

'I was aware of that.'

'Then the experience you have had with bulkheads tested to 25 lb may not help very much when you are dealing with a bulkhead tested to 150 lb?'

With the voice of hard-learned experience Cox answered, 'You can have a bulkhead tested to 150 lb of pressure, but after a short period of use there are various pipes going through that compartment; there are various electric wires, or various rods, and every one of those has got glands, and we have found in every case that the air goes through them'. Expert opinion did not agree with Cox, nor did he with them, and there was evidence to show that he was right. But how and where the air hole was to be drilled were to have far reaching consequences.

Somerville told Cox, 'I am advised that if this action which you suggest had been taken, about putting compressed air – assuming you have got it – into the body of the submarine, it would have lifted the hatches?

'Not if the men inside had been alive, definitely no, because there are clips on them'. Cox was speaking from memory after having broken up several obsolete submarines as a scrap dealer.

Bucknill suddenly cut in to Somerville's examination. Turning to Cox, he said, 'I am told you are wrong. I am told you could not screw them down to more than 5 lb or 10 lb at the outside.

'Then I wish to stress that more than ever; it is a very, very wrong design and it does not give the men a fair chance, and that is one of the things that should be rectified'.

Bucknill told Cox that he must deal with the *Thetis* as she was. Cox snapped back, 'If it is the fact that the forward hatch had no clips then the whole of my evidence is of no use. My plan of salving the *Thetis* would have been a washout, in view of this terrible disclosure'.

Somerville replied angrily, 'You have not the slightest right to make an observation of that sort'.

'I am entitled to have my views. I would like to give a little more evidence concerning the hole because it is my opinion that could not have been done—'

Bucknill cut Cox in mid-sentence. 'I do not think your evidence now is of any value because, so far as you are giving expert evidence, I do not think you ought to come here and take advantage of your position in the witness box to condemn the boat.' Cox could see no point in continuing with his evidence and stood down, but his observation on the hatch having no way of being fastened tightly from inside the submarine was already being closely investigated with regard to reverting back to a simple clip system.

The whole thrust of Cox's plan was to salvage the submarine to save life, something Oram had been trying to do since the night of 1 June. Ironically, and unbeknown to Cox, the Admiralty had decided in 1934 that salvaging a submarine to save life was not viable. It could be said that such unbending thinking defied the basic fundamental law of salvage, as McKenzie had said previously that no two operations are the same and should never be treated as such. Still, an internal Admiralty memo clarified their policy, saying, 'A submarine is designed as a warship and whilst due consideration is given to the question of saving life in the event of an accident, it must be secondary'.

Although the Admiralty was confident that Cox was wrong on some key points, the memo concluded, 'Mr Cox's arguments will be very plausibly expressed and the danger is that his scheme would be sound if all the hatches remained tight, or reasonably so, against an internal pressure of $50\,lb^2$. They leak at $3\,lb^2$ unless strongbacks are in place [or internal clips]. Even with them it is probable that leakage will occur at $20\,lb^2$, becoming serious at $50\,lb^2$'.

Bucknill's 105-page published report made up only one twentieth of the evidence gathered. It was divided into six parts. The first part explains the structure and appliances of the *Thetis* in laymen's terms, enough to understand the wealth of technical evidence covering work carried out prior to her trial and what happened during and after she dived. The next part is dedicated solely to the testimonies of the four survivors. The third part sets out events that occurred outside the *Thetis* regarding attempts to find the submarine and rescue her trapped personnel. The last two parts cover the state of the submarine after she was salved and deals with the causes of the loss.

Bucknill listed six facts, leading to the disaster, which he called 'A Sea of Trouble'. They were: 1. The precise moment when the bow opened is the critical and most obscure point in the case. 2. The failure of those aboard the *Thetis* to effectively close the port watertight door between the torpedo tube and the torpedo stowage, compartment. 3. The failure of those in the *Thetis* to expel the water from the two flooded compartments. 4. The failure of those outside the *Thetis* to render effective assistance. 5. The failure of those aboard the *Thetis* to escape by Davis Escape Apparatus.

But 'failure' does automatically reflect culpability or negligence, especially when each event is put in its true context. The precise moment the bow cap opened was not the crucial point, nor even who opened it, but rather the culture aboard that led to the event. The failure to close the watertight door in Number Twenty-five bulkhead was due to poor design, not professional incompetence, a flaw corrected in later T Class submarines. The failure of the crew to remove the water from the front two compartments would never have worked because the submarine's pumps were not capable of removing the water as fast as it came in. The failure of those aboard to escape was due to poor setting of the escape apparatus induced by severe carbon dioxide poisoning and all its impeding mental and physical effects. The failure of the Royal Navy-led rescue operation could, if the law prescribed, amount to blame for incompetence.

The sixth event contributing to the loss was, 'The complete blocking of the test cock in the rear door of Number Five torpedo tube with bitumastic enamel'. This could just as easily, and more accurately read, 'The failure of the Admiralty Overseer, Edward Grundy, to discover in the course of his daily professional duties that the inspection hole was blocked'. Choosing his words very carefully Bucknill did say that if Grundy had examined the interior of the doors he would have noticed that the test cock was, indeed, blocked. It was the duty of the Admiralty Overseer to examine it, and, if satisfied, to pass it.

He said, 'By some perverse mishap, the enameller did not take sufficient care to see that the test cock hole was kept clear of bitumastic, and the Admiralty Overseer did not use the rimer, Lieutenant Woods did not use it, nor any one else from 15 May to 1 June'. Although an experienced Overseer, this was the first time in Grundy's career that he had been tasked to check torpedo tubes. The Overseer *was* an Admiralty employee, and it *was* solely his responsibility to ensure the test cock was clear, the line of defence, so to speak, to ensure that the *Thetis* was fully seaworthy. He even admitted under oath that he 'forgot' to check the holes, another key point that never made Bucknill's final report, which simply says that the test cock was completely blocked. To further deflect the heat from Grundy, and thus the Admiralty, Bucknill emphasized that Laird's charge-hand painter Taylor should have been more thorough in carrying out the painting of the tubes.

Mr A. T. Miller KC on behalf of Cammell Laird thus represented Taylor. The original Court transcripts show how he pounced on Bucknill's claim that his client should have been more thorough. Miller insisted that the Court was now being asked to assume that it was Taylor's job to carry out an inspection of the test cock and not Grundy's. Taylor's job was to merely see that the bitumastic, 'Was in a condition in which it was reasonably proper to call in the Admiralty Overseer to pass and approve'. Like Paget and Lyons, Miller was becoming exasperated with the Court's determination to deflect any blame from the Admiralty. He concluded rather bitterly, 'The responsibility in the matter rests not with [Taylor], or with Cammell Laird, but with Mr Grundy and Mr Grundy's employers, the Admiralty. However, that is a matter which your Lordship is not, I understand, concerned to find'.

On 31 January 1940 Bucknill finished his report, which Treasury Solicitor Sir Thomas Barnes, who later published the report, called 'a plain, straightforward statement, and is on the whole, I think, quite satisfactory.' In fact, after so much evidence and investigation had been accumulated, Bucknill's six 'in sequence' findings were very close to those Chamberlain put before the House of Commons two days after the tragedy six months earlier. For example, Bucknill's first finding reads, 'The precise moment when the bow opened is the critical and most obscure point in the case'. Chamberlain said, 'So far as can be ascertained, sinking of the *Thetis* was caused by the flooding of the two forward torpedo compartments through one of the bow torpedo tubes'.

On 5 June Chamberlain told the House, 'The men in escaping from the compartment were unable in the time available to close the first watertight door behind them, but the flooding was restricted to the second compartment.' Bucknill concluded, 'The failure of those aboard the *Thetis* to effectively close the port watertight door between the torpedo tube and the torpedo stowage compartment'. The list goes on. Chamberlain said, 'All possible measures were taken by the crew to lighten the submarine ...'. Bucknill said, 'The failure of those in the *Thetis* to expel the water from the two flooded compartments'. Bucknill's conclusion that, 'The failure of those outside the *Thetis* to render effective assistance', was integral to her loss. Chamberlain went on to list all the efforts made to rescue the men and how each was thwarted in one way or another. Chamberlain already knew, 'No further escapes had been made by Davis life-saving apparatus'. Bucknill's final finding was, 'The failure of those on board the *Thetis* to escape by Davis Escape Apparatus'. The words might be different, but the meaning is the same.

Within a couple of weeks the Admiralty had carefully examined in great detail what Bucknill had to say. Apart from a few minor and valid deletions on the grounds of national security, such as showing the location of where submarine test adjust compasses, a known time of weakness as the submarine has to stop and thus became more vulnerable to enemy attack. The only real change was made at the top of page ninety-two. The bottom of page ninety-one states, 'The unscrewing and removal of these two manhole doors in Z tank and the bulkhead would have enabled those in the *Thetis* to speak to the men outside—'. Overleaf the last six lines of the paragraph have been scraped off the page and a thick, black line runs through each deleted word to further hamper any attempt to decipher what was there. In further copies of the Tribunal that are known to exist the gap is closed up, making a shorter paragraph. So what was said in the deleted words is now lost forever.

The internal memo to outline the publication continues, 'I should add that, for the Prime Minister's information, that the lessons to be learned from the *Thetis* disaster have been taken into account by the Admiralty. As regards blame, the Tribunal points out the omissions for which Lieutenant Woods and Mr Grundy, the Admiralty Overseer, were responsible, but the actions of these two men only formed part of a series of what the Judge himself called "perverse mishaps". However, in certain very important matters it has not been found possible to establish the whole facts. We have come to the conclusion that it is desirable to put on record that the Admiralty will not hold Lieutenant Woods or Mr Grundy to blame for the disaster, and that in this respect the matter is to be regarded as closed'.

When Chamberlain first announced that the full Public Inquiry was about to proceed he assured the House, and Bucknill, 'The report of the Naval Inquiry and the evidence given will be made available to the Public Inquiry'. This could well have made Bucknill's findings read a completely different way. Towards the end of the Tribunal's investigations, Lyons prompted Bucknill to see if the Justice would take advantage of Chamberlain's offer to scrutinize the Naval Board confidential report. Bucknill replied, 'I can tell you, Mr Lyons, that I have not seen the report of the Inquiry to which you refer, and speaking for myself, I would rather arrive at my independent conclusions quite unfettered by any conclusion that anybody else has arrived at. I have seen the witnesses and heard the evidence and I believe that nothing has been kept back from this Tribunal which appeared before that Tribunal'.

Chapter 13

The Paisley Slug

Regardless of Bucknill not apportioning blame, the Admiralty memo ended rather chillingly, 'I have to report that nineteen writs have been issued on behalf of the personal representatives and dependants of certain civilian officials and workmen who lost their lives in the disaster, claiming damages against Lieutenant Woods, the personal representatives of the late Lieutenant Commander Bolus, that is his wife Sybil, and Leading Seaman Hambrook, and Messrs. Cammell Laird & Co. Ltd'. The dependents were going to, at least, try to get compensation for the loss of their loved ones in what would become one of the most complex, dramatic and bitterly fought civil cases in British legal history.

In early August 1939 Messrs Evill & Coleman advised all the dependants, whose loved ones were members of the Amalgamated Engineering Union, to commence proceedings for negligence. By now there were twenty-five writs issued on behalf of members of the Union and a further five were on behalf of members of the Electrical Trades Union. Both unions were prepared to cover the legal costs of their former members, while the remaining six cases were to be privately brought and funded. Laird's Engineer's Fitter Archibald Craven's widow, Mabel, and Rose Duncan, widow of Brown Brothers' steering gear fitter, David Norman Duncan formed a consolidated test case of the original nineteen writs seeking claims for negligence. Evill & Coleman believed that the two had a very strong case. After all, regardless of not placing blame, Bucknill's report put Hambrook and Woods in the tube space at the time of the accident, the former near the lever while the latter was in charge of the torpedo space. Lieutenant Commander Bolus was in overall command. Wailes Dove had blocked the test cock and Cammell Laird was contractually bound to ensure that the *Thetis* was safe for the open sea, and senior Laird and Naval personnel had signed to the effect that she was safe. However, almost immediately, within the highest levels of government, plans were being made to have the actions withdrawn.

First Lord of the Admiralty Albert Victor Alexander, Solicitor General Sir William Jowett and Treasury Solicitor Sir Thomas Barnes, the latter being two of the country's leading lawyers, set out to derail the case. With the agreement of Attorney General Sir Donald Somerville they planned to convince Trades Union Congress (TUC) General Secretary Sir Walter McLennan Citrine that it was in everyone's interest if he persuaded his union leaders to withdraw their members' actions. Alexander, Barnes and Somerville were unanimous in their belief that the actions ought never to have been brought and that an effort must be made to dispose of them. Then, it was hoped, the remaining private actions would collapse once the weight of the unions was out of the equation. The evidence for this comes from several either undated or unsigned letters and memos that both clearly show the Government's and especially the Admiralty's views on the subject, and their offhand attitudes towards the deaths of their own officers and ratings.

Their reasoning for killing the actions was quite simple. One memo addressed to the Law Officers department, dated 6 November 1940, and signed 'D. B. S.' says that this was a case he thought anyone could or would express a confident opinion one way or the other as to the result. But he adds, 'There is a possibility envisaged by the Bucknill report that the real cause of the disaster may have been an unwitting interference with the levers by someone unknown'. Bucknill did say this, as it could never be proved how the levers were opened. But the memo continues, 'On the other hand, I think myself that a finding that Lieutenant Woods and Able Seaman Hambrook were negligent is a possible result and perhaps a not unlikely one. They were jointly engaged in opening the rear door and in fact one bow cap was open and the levers were in the neutral and not the shut position. When an accident happens in circumstances such as this, however fortuitous the group of circumstances which led to the disaster, the court rarely, if ever, find it was accidental'. Even if there was intervention by another person who tampered with the levers, D. B. S. goes on to say, 'This would not necessarily negative [sic] negligence by Woods and Hambrook'. So even at this early stage the Admiralty thought the decision might go against Woods and Hambrook, and thus against Their Lordships.

Treasury Solicitor Barnes gave three main reasons why the Admiralty should try to make the unions back down. Firstly, 'There are difficulties in fighting the case and it is by no means certain that the plaintiffs would not succeed'. Secondly, 'In the present circumstances it would be very difficult to fight the case because many of our essential witnesses are otherwise engaged and some of them have already lost their lives'. And thirdly, 'It is obviously undesirable in the public interest that questions relating to construction of submarines should be discussed in open court and, while the Admiralty could claim privilege in respect of many matters involved, there might well be some feeling of injustice to the particular claimants if, by reason of a claim to privilege, they were debarred from pursuing what would otherwise be a good claim'.

The preferred option to halt the proceedings was for First Lord Alexander to approach the union leaders informally to persuade their plaintiffs to back down. In return the Admiralty would cover all legal fees to date, and make a substantial donation to the Lord Mayor's *Thetis* fund, which had already collected more than £115,000 within the first ten days or, in today's monetary value, more than £5m. But the Admiralty added the proviso that this latter approach was not to be made before trying to convince the union leaders to give up on the grounds of public policy first. In a letter to First Lord signed 'R. H. H.' the sender adds, 'I particularly dislike this second suggested payment, which seems to me to amount to an admission of Admiralty liability'.

First Lord Alexander held a meeting with Solicitor General Jowett on the subject. Jowett said that it would take time for him to get in contact with Sir Walter Citrine, and that all that could be done for now would be to go slow with all these cases to gain time. If anyone could sway the union leaders Citrine was the only man for the job. Get him on board and there was every chance that the Admiralty and the Government could kill the actions and everyone was off the hook. During the meeting the two also agreed that it would be better if Solicitor General Jowett took Alexander's place in the negotiations.

Sir Thomas Barnes wrote to the Permanent Secretary to the Board of Admiralty, Sir Henry V. Markham, that before Jowett met with Citrine he wanted to know exactly what terms the Admiralty was prepared to dispose of the actions. That is, should they cover all legal costs, and just how much should they put into the *Thetis* fund. He added, 'The Solicitor General tells me that he thinks that some such payment must be made if we hope to get the actions withdrawn. He expresses the view that a sum of £10,000 [or about £355,000 today] would be an appropriate figure, but I told him that when I had considered the matter in November last, the figure that I had in mind was £5,000.

'I would suggest that approval be asked for an outside figure of £10,000 with an understanding that we should try and settle for a lesser figure. When I get these instructions I shall have to negotiate with Cammell Laird, who are joint defendants, in order to get them to contribute to the costs and to the token payment of the fund'. Ninety-nine men were lying dead at the bottom of Liverpool Bay and the Admiralty's only consideration when offering such a large donation to the *Thetis* fund was to protect their own interests – and the least amount they could get away with the better.

There was always the nagging doubt that even if the Admiralty paid off the unions to ensure all the pending cases were dropped, this did not guarantee that any future cases could be taken care of in the same way. But although the terms were more than a little unpleasant to the Admiralty, Sir Thomas Barnes had a strong argument and, quite honestly, it was the best deal they could hope for, provided Citrine and thus the union leaders agreed. Jowett did convince Citrine to talk to his union leaders, but the final hurdle for the Admiralty to overcome was to get the Treasury's agreement to pay out public money for such a venture.

On 3 April 1941 a confidential letter was sent to Treasury Chairman Sir Bernard Gilbert, putting forward the Admiralty's views and asking his consent for the payments. On 12 April the Treasury agreed, as long as the financial damage could be kept to a minimum. However, squeezed between both these letters is an unsigned confidential memo issued from the Treasury building at Storey's Gate, London SW1 saying, 'I myself do not like very much the idea of paying these people anything, but in the circumstances it may be wiser to make a contribution to the fund for the benefit of all those who have suffered by reason of the disaster than finding ourselves having to meet judgments obtained by these particular plaintiffs. I hope moreover, that we shall be able to get all the actions withdrawn, although I agree that the Trade Unions do not represent all the plaintiffs. The non-Trade Union plaintiffs will not, I think, want to go on if the Trade Union support is withdrawn.'

Regardless of this rather elaborate attempt to get all the cases withdrawn the Union leaders did not back down. The Duncan/Craven test case was going ahead and Evill & Coleman were well prepared for the fight. In Evill & Coleman's opinion, Cammell Laird was negligent. They allowed the submarine to go to sea for her diving trials. They failed to discover the defect by neglecting to provide proper and adequate supervision or inspection of the painting carried out by their sub-contractors. They also failed to provide any person or system to ensure that the submarine was as fit for her trials as reasonable care and skill could make her. Wailes Dove Bitumastic, Ltd. were negligent in that their employee, John Stinson, while painting the rear door managed to block the test cock hole, thus preventing it from functioning properly. This negligence, they asserted, was the direct cause of the accident.

The Solicitors added that Woods was negligent because, as the torpedo officer in charge of the torpedo compartment, he did not exercise proper supervision or care in detecting the true state of the torpedo tube. Then he failed to detect that the bow cap was open before opening the rear door. Hambrook was also negligent. While he was in charge of the levers controlling the bow cap, he either opened it or caused or allowed it to be opened. In the absence of Hambrook, writs were issued against his mother Matilda Ann. Just the kind of accusation the Admiralty was trying to avoid. In the absence of Bolus, the blame fell on his widow, Sybil, who had tried so hard to bring help and comfort to the widows when they learned that all their men were dead. The facts appeared to speak for themselves, or what in Law is called *Res ipsa Loquitur.* Case law on this type of action also spoke for itself and Evill & Coleman were confident that quoting Donoghue v. Stevenson the judge would see it the same way.

On a hot August evening in 1928, shop assistant May Donoghue took a tram from Glasgow out to Paisley where she and a friend sat down in the town's popular Wellmeadow Café. Her friend ordered a drink for herself as well as an ice cream and ginger beer for May. The waiter poured May's cool ginger beer over her ice cream shortly before she tucked into the welcome treat. Then, while they chatted, her friend poured the remainder of the ginger beer over the ice cream while May was savouring the cool ice cream and thirst quenching ginger beer in her mouth. Suddenly, as May's friend tipped up the bottle, the sticky remains of a rotting slug plopped on to the half eaten ice cream. May, by now very distraught, complained of violent stomach pains, which were later confirmed to be gastroenteritis – not to mention emotional distress.

147

May decided to sue the manufacturer for damages. The case collapsed because there had been no contractual obligation between May and the café owner because her friend had made the purchase and it was a gift. But May, who is recorded as being a 'pauper' would not let the matter rest. After twice being refused her claim in the Court of Session, Scotland's supreme civil court, she took the matter to the House of Lords. The judgement read that reasonable care must be taken to avoid acts or omissions, which would be likely to injure those closely and directly affected by such actions. May Donoghue finally won her battle three years later and was awarded £200 compensation, or a little less than £10,000 today. According to Evill & Coleman, whether a putrid slug in a girl's ginger beer, or the loss of a T Class submarine and nearly all those aboard, the principal remained the same. Laird owned the *Thetis*, and between Managing Director Robert Johnson and all those he employed to build the submarine, they owed Mabel's and Rose's loved ones a level of care to prevent their death or serious injury. Donoghue v. Stevenson was, and still is, a classic piece of case law that in theory would give Mabel and Rose what they wanted.

Locking horns with Evill & Coleman in the King's Bench Division of the High Court was Treasury Solicitor Barnes for Woods and Hambrook. For Cammell Laird was Carpenters of London on behalf of Laird's Liverpool-based lawyers, Laces & Co. Radford, Frankland & Mercer of London represented Wailes Dove on behalf of their lawyers, Maugham & Hall, Newcastle-upon-Tyne. The legal battle began on 17 April 1940, which relied not only on case law, but the production of key documents in the possession of several defendants, or their employers.

Among the sixteen documents requested were the contract for the *Thetis*'s hull and machinery, letters written before the disaster relating to the vessel's trim, reports as to the condition of the submarine when she was raised, a large number of plans and specifications relating to various parts of the vessel and the notebook of Cammell Laird's foreman painter, Taylor. This last document was pivotal in establishing whether Laird knew that the rear door of Number Five torpedo tube had been checked or not. Although the plaintiffs' lawyers requested the documents, the Admiralty blocked their release. Crown Privilege was used and thus, in the public interest, the greater good of the entire country was more important than a couple of widows seeking compensation for the deaths of their providers while on Government business.

Evill & Coleman had a strong case for, at least, getting access to some of the withheld documents. They said, 'It was urged before us that whatever the true principals upon which production of the documents should be refused on the ground of public interest, some of these documents could not validly be withheld because they had already been produced before the Tribunal of Inquiry into the loss of the *Thetis*, over which Mr Justice Bucknill presided, and because some reference was made to them in his report'.

The decision rested with Admiralty First Lord Alexander, who had already attempted to undermine the legal actions, and he was having none of it. His decision was passed to Treasury Solicitor Barnes, as lawyers for the Admiralty, to inform the plaintiffs' lawyers that Crown Privilege was claimed, adding that if this was not accepted as sufficient to found a claim for Privilege then Barnes would obtain an affidavit from Alexander making the claim formally. The House of Lords actually recommended this procedure. In law a formal claim strengthened the case for Crown Privilege. Evill & Coleman did not accept the decision, forcing Alexander's hand.

On 29 January 1941 Alexander swore an affidavit referring to the documents, stating, 'All the said documents were considered by me with the assistance of my technical advisors and I formed the opinion, that it would be injurious to the public interest that any of the said documents should be disclosed to any person. I accordingly instructed the Treasury Solicitor to write on behalf of the Lords Commissioners to the Solicitors to the said Defendants not to disclose the documents set out in the said list, their contents to the Plaintiffs or either of them or to anyone on their behalf nor produce them for inspection in this action and to require them to claim privilege for the documents on the ground that it would be injurious to the public interest that the same should be disclosed or produced for inspection'. A long and convoluted way of saying not under any circumstances were these documents going to see the light of day.

Evill & Coleman still refused to back down. After all, it was the corner stone of their action. They took out a summons, which eventually led all through the appeals system to the House of Lords. The Lords were of the opinion that a properly framed, formally made ministerial objection, was conclusive proof that the documents should not be released. The Lords were, however, allowed to at least view the documents to weigh up their relevance to the case in question versus public interest. The Lords never took the opportunity to see them and actually set a new precedent that it was no longer necessary to view any such documents offered under a formal ministerial affidavit.

Throughout the spring and summer of 1943 Mabel's and Rose's test action was placed before Mr Justice Wrottesley. In October he gave his judgement. Referring to the allegation of negligence against Lieutenant Woods and Leading Seaman Hambrook, Wrottesley said, 'In no way were Lieutenant Woods and Hambrook negligent. They were attached to the ship for instruction. Neither of them could have been expected to be on guard against what happened in this case, when the hole [was blocked] in the test cock by being enamelled over before the *Thetis* sailed.

'I have been warned in this case about being wise after the fact. Lieutenant Woods and Leading Seaman Hambrook did not know the state of the test cock and there has not been established to my satisfaction the failure of any kind by them to take responsible care. The man of the Bitumastic Company who did this painting did a slovenly piece of work. Two of these holes were obstructed and a cursory inspection would have shown them to have been blocked'. That cursory inspection should, Wrottesley asserted, not have been made by the Admiralty (Grundy, who was to have the last say on quality control) but Cammell Laird.

He added, 'On behalf of the Wailes Dove Bitumastic Company it was said they were humble painters. This argument was not available to Cammell Laird, who were not humble painters, but shipbuilders and engineers. In fact their master painter inspected the work and should have been in a position to have noticed the blocked hole. Although primarily Cammell Laird's obligation was to carry out their contract with the Admiralty I think it must be accepted that they owed a duty in the circumstances to those who set out aboard the *Thetis* to take reasonable care that the vessel was fit for the trial in question'.

Wrottesley found what he called 'the management' of Laird to be at fault in not arranging for an inspection of the Bitumastic Company's painting of the rear torpedo doors by a competent engineer or qualified person quite irrespective of the Admiralty Overseer. This was between the time the bitumastic was put on and when she sailed two weeks later when further work was being carried out aboard the submarine. He decided that there was nothing in the contract, which absolved Laird from ensuring that the work was done in a proper and workman-like manner. The *Thetis* went to sea with these defects. Cammell Laird was responsible to the Admiralty because until after a successful trial, the vessel remained in their hands.

'In my view each of the plaintiffs succeeds in establishing the liability of Cammell Laird on the loss of their wage earners on the grounds of negligence. They failed to discover the defect in the test cock of Number Five torpedo tube. As against the other defendants the claims against them fail'. Wrottesley formally entered judgement for Mabel and Rose against Cammell Laird, with costs. The legal floodgates were now wide open for the other twenty-three cases pending, and perhaps many more from the dependents of the other seventy-four or so men who died from what has been decided, was all Laird's fault.

Johnson was now facing a multi-million pound lawsuit that could very realistically break his 116-year-old company and then some. Three options were open to him if Laird was to survive. Pay up and be bankrupt, hope that his insurance on the submarine would cover them for such a massive indemnity, or appeal. Two clauses in Laird's insurance policy appeared to give them cover for such a payout. Clause Twenty-two was what is called a Protection and Indemnity or P & I clause. It stated that if Laird became liable to cover a claim arising from loss of life, personal injury or payments made on account of salvage the underwriters would pay the sum. That is, however, with the restriction that the amount recoverable did not exceed the full insurance sum. Restriction also applied if two thirds of the underwriters contested the claim in writing. Furthermore, even if Laird could overcome these two barriers, they might still have to pay fifty per cent of the claim. But all was not lost. Clause Fourteen also covered liability of everyone except Laird's men by covering in full the builder's and repairers' liability to third parties in respect of her management and crew while she was at the builder's or repairers' risk. Not much, but at least a chunk of the liability might be covered.

The complexity of the insurance world added further hope, not so much from Laird's policies, but those of the unions who represented Johnson's employees. Another part of the contract stated that any amounts the insured became liable to pay that were not specified in the contract but might be recoverable from the Liverpool and London Steamship Protection and Indemnity Association Limited and/or North of England Protection and Indemnity Association. Given a cursory glance, if one part of the policy did not cover Laird for the impending payout, perhaps another would, or at the very worst, someone else was

151

legally bound to pick up all or part of the tab. Under deeper legal analysis the situation was never going to be even that black and white.

At once the Liverpool and London and North of England Protection and Indemnity Associations showed why they were not liable to cover their members. Johnson then wrote to the Iron Traders' Association to seek financial support because some of their members were also lost. After meetings to discuss the matter The Iron Traders' Accident Manager wrote to Laird's lawyers, Laces saying, 'I am writing to you personally because of the delicate position in which I find myself in my anxiety to do the right thing by those whom I serve, and our mutual clients. I do not think it can be expected that the underwriters, through this Association, should shoulder a burden for which there has been no insurance. I agree that our interests are inimical, but at the same time there must be a limit to our responsibilities'. With no insurance cover, Laird was now facing the full brunt of whatever Justice Wrottesley decided the liability was going to be, but, regardless of his legal decision, Laird had a different view of who was to blame and why. They reduced the facts to the contributory causes for the disaster – all, of which pinned the blame squarely on the Admiralty, and their systemic breakdown in procedure dating back to at least April 1939.

The first event was the defective hydroplane gear, resulting in postponing the Gareloch trial in early May. Then the absence of definite knowledge regarding her correct trim before she left the Wet Basin for her final diving trial in Liverpool Bay was known to be wrong. She should never have gone to sea with a slight list under any circumstances. The failure of Woods to use the rimer and failure to test by vent cock rather than opening the rear doors was all carried out by Royal Navy personnel. Their failure to test Number Five tube, through using the drain valve, only compounded the disaster.

The Naval list of errors went on. The probable improper use of the bow cap operating panel lever may have occurred. The delay in closing Number Twenty-five bulkhead door caused the torpedo compartment to flood. The inability of the torpedo hatch to take the internal blowing pressure, which, although built by Laird, was made wholly to Admiralty design. The delay of the *Grebe Cock* to confirm the accident was another. Coltart's delay in sending his message, not anchoring a marker buoy, delay in anchoring the tug, leading directly to all search and rescue services being in the wrong place at the right time. Damage to underwater signaling apparatus prevented communication with the Admiralty vessel standing by searching. The delay in Admiralty

152

rescue arrangements. The mistaken policy of salvage authorities under Admiralty direction not to lash the stern to the *Vigilant* was, according to Laird (who never knew of the confidential Admiralty findings) a major error. Finally it was the jamming of the after escape hatch and subsequent flooding of the submarine through the engine room that finally led to the massive loss of life. Laird claimed that all the above points were entirely Admiralty responsibility and they – as builders – were not involved in any of them.

What, however, could be legitimately called errors on the part of Laird? The only items that could be raised against them were whether they were right to allow the *Thetis* to leave their Wet Basin for her final diving trial without being sure that she was properly trimmed for the trial. Apart from any Admiralty inspection were they remiss in not making sure that the vent holes in the rear doors of the tubes were not blocked with bitumastic enamel? Clearly Laces thought these points were not valid. If the Admiralty knew the trim of the ship was wrong, so that she was therefore not suitable to carry out the diving trials, they should have made Laird aware of the situation before leaving the Mersey. One of Laird's legal representatives concluded, 'Were we not entitled to feel that the Admiralty representative was sufficiently versed in his work to take all precautions. Had all precautions been taken the accident would not have happened'. And had Grundy done his job then the blocked hole would have been freed *ergo* no disaster.

Laird then turned their attention more to Woods. He made the statement that the bow cap indicator showed the Number Five bow cap as shut. The statement, Laird quite rightly said, was wrong when it was found open upon investigation in Holyhead several months later. 'The suggestion that any person other than himself and Hambrook touched the levers or interfered in any way with the bow cap is quite impossible as our men would not touch anything. They were only there to take orders from the officers in charge of the ship. Woods was in full charge of the Torpedo Room once the ship was commissioned and it was his duty to see everything was in order as he was supposed to be experienced, with special knowledge of torpedoes.'

According to Laird's legal representative, Sellers, regardless of what Wrottesley dictated, it was Hambrook's and Woods' responsibility to see that everything was in order. They were the experts and knew what to look for. 'We were never informed or warned by the Admiralty that special care had to be taken to keep the hole in the test cock clear. It only came to our knowledge after the tragedy, but Grundy and his assistant and Woods and his assistant knew, or should have known, that the clearing of the test cock was very important and should have seen it'.

The sub-contract with Wailes Dove provided that the work should be done to the satisfaction of the Admiralty – not Laird, so why was the shipbuilder to blame? All Laird's charge-hand painter had to do was see that the job had been completed and notify Grundy, which he definitely did. Not only did Taylor do this, but, upon informing Grundy of the finished tubes, the Overseer was standing by with an employee of Wailes Dove to be on hand should Grundy want work to be re-done. So, according to Laird place in the chain, two men were informed that the tube was ready for inspection *not* ready for sea.

Further questions arose as to whether Wrottesley was correct when stating that the *Thetis* was not seaworthy just because the test cock was blocked. It was a trivial mistake, which could so easily have been corrected had the proper inspection and correction been followed, by the book, so to speak. Sellers felt, 'In any event, no harm would have resulted if the bow cap had not been open. The responsibility for the opening of the rear door when the bow cap was in fact open lay with Lieutenant Woods and Leading Seaman Hambrook and, in my view of the fact, the effective cause of this casualty was the failure of these two to ensure that the bow cap was closed and their conduct amounted to negligence'.

As the *Thetis* was on her sea trials it has always been thought that Cammell Laird still owned her and thus were ultimately responsible until the Admiralty took formal possession. Under Clause Twenty-seven of the First Schedule of the contract it was provided that after the first payment on account of the price, the vessel should vest in and be the absolute property of the Admiralty without prejudice to the right of the Admiralty to reject. Sellers stated quite confidently 'The first payment on account had been paid before the disaster and it seems clear that the ownership of the *Thetis* at the time that she sank was vested in the Lords Commissioners of the Admiralty'. This point is vital to proving culpability and has never before been made widely public.

Based on all these facts in Laird's view it was the Admiralty who were responsible for the loss of the *Thetis*, not them. Sellers felt sure that it was reasonably probable that other judges would not see the case in the same light as Justice Wrottesley. A view he felt could be put with some force. 'I find it difficult to think that anything further was required of Cammell Laird. The sub-contractor had done the work to the satisfaction of their buyer's Overseer [Grundy] – a highly qualified man for the task and Cammell Laird had no reason to suspect that all was not in order. One must not under estimate Mr Justice Wrottesley's emphatic view but I feel that this view should be tested on appeal before a liability of this magnitude is finally imposed on Cammell Laird's. With no insurance cover, faced with saying nothing, paying up and shutting up was not an option. Not only was Cammell Laird one of the oldest and greatest shipbuilders in Great Britain, but more than 10,000 jobs on Merseyside were at stake. Paisley Slug, or no Paisley Slug, Laird was going to fight.

Chapter 14

'Non-negligent Accident'

Cammell Laird was not the only group seeking to reverse Wrottesley's decision. Both Rose Duncan and Mabel Craven felt that Woods was still liable for having opened the rear door of Number Five tube, thus causing the deaths of their men. Under appeal the Master of the Rolls Lord Greene and Lord Justices Goddard and du Parcq, the whole action was again sifted like sand to see if a different verdict was, indeed, possible.

Lord Justice Goddard thought that Woods had misread the mechanical indicator and that the bow cap of Number Five tube was already open. Du Parcq also agreed, basing his conclusion partly on the ground that no order was given to Hambrook to put the levers to shut. Woods just assumed, the Justices decided, that Hambrook had shut them, and thus did not take proper care to ensure that the full safety procedure was adopted. In the eyes of the appeal judges, the facts were speaking for themselves. It was now looking as though Woods was liable under *res ipsa loquitur* after all.

But *res ips*, as it is more commonly known, could only qualify if the following could be proved: The harm would not ordinarily have occurred without someone's negligence. Whatever caused the harm was under the exclusive control of the defendant at the time of the negligent act and finally there must be an absence of a reasonable explanation as to how the harm occurred. A civil law version of a smoking gun so to speak, and it looked to du Parcq, Goddard and Greene that Woods fitted the bill in every category.

The judgment of the Court of Appeal was based on the following passage from the judgment of Lord Greene, both on the principle of *res ipsa loquitur,* and, 'If this were not applicable, then because in my opinion an affirmative case is established, I feel constrained to hold that Lieutenant Woods was guilty of negligence. He failed to give the proper order to Hambrook to put the lever in the closed position and relied in part on the evidence of the test cock which he ought to have known was never intended to be relied on for such a purpose and was in any case wholly unreliable unless the rimer was used'.

Greene added, 'The Court of Appeal have, however, put the blame on Lieutenant Woods for a more general reason. The case against these two defendants (i.e. Lieutenant Woods and Leading Seaman Hambrook), can, I think, be founded upon the doctrine of *res ipsa loquitur* since Lieutenant Woods was the officer in charge of the tube space, he was in sole control and an accident happened which in the ordinary course of things would not have happened if he had used proper care. But where the thing is shown to be under the management of the defendant or his servants and the accident is such as in the ordinary course of things does not happen if those who have the management use proper care, it affords reasonable evidence, in the absence of explanation by the defendants, that the accident arose from want of care.' The case had now turned into the very monster the Admiralty fought so hard to prevent.

This was all well and good, in principal at least, but what is a principal worth if it cannot practically help alleviate the financial strain Mabel and Rose were now facing. Could Woods, as a mere lieutenant, pay the vast sums he was about to be faced with? In theory the Treasury would cover the financial shortfall on behalf of the Crown, if the *Thetis* could be shown to qualify for registration as a British vessel even though she had still not actually been registered.

Such a case would occur if a warship collided with a Merchant vessel and the Royal Navy captain was held liable. The Crown would only stand behind the captain to the extent of what would have been the liability – a maximum of £15 per ton. The same could apply to Woods, as he was the Royal Navy officer in charge of the torpedo room, and the person who opened the rear door to the open sea. If Woods was found to be at fault that would amount to about £15,000 payable from the Treasury. Hardly enough to cover the sums needed to settle this dispute.

Furthermore Goddard, Greene and du Parcq knew that the Crown, being the Crown, could not legally be forced to pay anything. Regardless of the law, such a handout would only ever be at their discretion. Bankrupting Woods was another alternative, but taking such a route would be very costly and result in no recoverable funds whatsoever. Woods' only chance was to appeal to the House of Lords in a bid to reverse the judgement back to Wrottesley's originally ruling, but he was not the only person seeking to push the case to its legal limit.

Now, in a complete reversal of Wrottersely's decision, under the Court of Appeal Cammell Laird was absolved of all liability and Woods, and thus the Admiralty, after all its efforts to have T.U.C. Secretary Sir Walter McLennan Citrine kill the original actions, were to blame. Rose and Mabel now had their man, but he was never going to be able to compensate them for the loss of their husbands. Although a higher court had cleared Laird of negligence Mabel and Rose wanted the shipbuilder and Wailes Dove to be found negligent yet again. Now Hambrook must be shown as an accomplice to Woods. Laird and Wailes Dove must be shown to have made a poor vessel not fit to be on the high seas.

Between 15 October 1945 and 27 February 1946 Viscount John Gilbert Simon of Stackpole, Lord Hugh Pattison Macmillan, Lord Samuel Porter of Longfield (in County Tyrone) and Lord Gavin Turnbull Simonds conducted the third thorough examination of all the evidence so far collated on the *Thetis* disaster – and culpability. When the review began the case looked something like this: Woods was appealing against the Court of Appeal's judgement on him. Rose and Mabel were respondents, but they were also cross appealing Woods. Then Mabel and Rose appealed against the findings on Hambrook's mother, Matilda. Somewhere in between an action against Bolus's wife Sybil was fully absolved. As Viscount Simon said, it was certainly going to be, 'A complicated and difficult appeal'. Now the House of Lords interpretation of the evidence was once again about to revolutionize the interpretation of the facts. And being the last and highest court in the Land, what was about to transpire would be final.

   With an air of *déjà vu*, the legal representatives for all parties stood before the Lords to again plead their cases. Attorney General Sir Donald Somerville, acting for Woods, was certain that the Court of Appeal ruling against his client was flawed. Somerville put forward the argument that his client did everything in his power to ensure the safety of Craven and Duncan, even though he opened the rear door, which eventually sank the submarine. Somerville argued that before he did this, Woods had taken all the proper steps to satisfy himself that the bow cap was shut, 'As it should have been'. Somerville added, 'He could not be expected to act on the basis of the triple negligence which had in fact occurred, the painting over of the hole, the failure of those responsible for the inspection to detect it and the unauthorized opening of the bow cap by some person unknown'.

If Woods had clearly asked Hambrook whether the indicators read 'shut', and got a firm yes, then how could he be negligent for not ensuring it was safe to open the rear door. After all, tubes Two and Four down the port side and tubes One and Three down the starboard side were opened without any problem whatsoever. Failing to use the rimer was not negligence. Again the argument was that its use had never been codified as standard Admiralty practice. Somerville continued, 'He was entitled to assume that the vessel coming from the yard of a skilled maker was in working order, just as a man who buys a Rolls Royce car is entitled to assume that it is in working order. Accordingly he could legitimately assume that the fact that no water came out of the test cock meant that there was no water in the tube. It was impossible for him to act all the time on the assumption that some part of the machinery was out of order'.

Sir Walter Monckton KC led Rose and Mabel's legal team and held different views on Woods culpability and that of Cammell Laird. Woods was still negligent because, as the torpedo officer, he was in ultimate control of the torpedo compartment, and the actions of those under his direct command. Basically, he did not exercise proper supervision of the safety sequence and opened the rear doors – *Res ipsa Loquitur* in a nutshell. Hambrook was also negligent because, being in charge of the bow cap levers, he either caused or opened the rear door himself. Monkton was emphatic, 'Their negligence was the direct cause of the accident and of the deaths of Duncan and Craven'.

Laird was negligent because they allowed the *Thetis* to go to sea 'in an unsafe and dangerous condition' because the test cock was blocked with paint, a clear case of breach of duty. Monckton told the Lords, 'They failed to discover the defect by neglecting to provide proper and adequate supervision or inspection of the painting carried out by their sub-contractors. They also failed to provide any person or system to ensure that the submarine was as fit for her trials as reasonable care and skill could make her'.

Wailes Dove were negligent being ultimately responsible for the actions of one of their employees who failed to do his job when painting the rear torpedo door of Number Five tube. After informing the Lords that this single action was the direct cause of the accident, Monckton continued, 'This may be a case where concurrent causes have combined to bring about the accident but these respondents are bound to recover, since if Woods was wrong in relying on the test cock to inform him as to the condition of the tube, he acted negligently and if he was right then failure was due to the negligence of Cammell Laird and the Bitumastic Company. As regards the case against Woods, the doctrine of *res ipsa loquitur* applies. Not only was the bow cap open but he was in control of the torpedo compartment, and he himself opened the rear door'.

Like an echo from Greene's, du Parcq's and Goddard's appeal verdict, Monkton reiterated, 'He did not give a clear and specific order to Hambrook to close the bow cap and he relied on the test cock without using the rimer. If the test cock was not primarily for showing whether or not the bow cap was open he should have looked at the indicator again. As regards Hambrook, he was standing by the levers and taking his orders from Woods and the most probable inference is that he moved this lever to "open". The bow cap was closed when the submarine sailed and it could not have been opened until power was put on shortly before the rear door was opened'.

Bucknill's Tribunal toyed with the idea that perhaps someone else entered the torpedo room and through some mistake altered the lever, causing the bow cap to open. Not so, according to Monckton. Evidence collected at Bucknill's Tribunal, at least the small amount that made his public report, added that no one other than those qualified to be there for the dive were seen the whole time. Moreover once the power was on the lever became very stiff, due to the hydraulic pressure built up in the line, and knocking one open by mistake without noticing was not possible.

Monckton seemed quite happy to apply Bucknill's published findings to back up his case. What the KC never knew was that Bucknill had already found Hambrook innocent on the grounds that the evidence against him was too circumspect to hold the man guilty for what could amount to manslaughter. But this finding was among the many that never made his published findings. As for Cammell Laird's share of negligence, Monckton insisted that, 'They put into the hands of the Naval personnel a ship which was in fact in such a state as to endanger the lives of those on board by reason of a trap and they are therefore liable for the loss of the lives so endangered. The mere existence of a chance of intermediate examination [Grundy's inspection] is not enough to break the chain rendering Cammell Laird liable'. Wailes Dove would still be liable, even if Laird could be absolved. Monckton wanted to show, that if one defendant was cleared then the other could not.

Cammell Laird, now fighting their corner for the third time, had lost one action and the Paisley Slug episode was about to haunt them again. In this bizarre case the final result could still go either way. Stating Laird's defence before the Lords were two King's Counsels, Sellers and Nelson. Quite rightly the Lords were told that in this case, getting to an acceptable account of what really happened was never going to happen. Sellers pointed out rather profoundly that the more facts that came to light, the more the course of events were shrouded in the dark. 'Accordingly the actions must fail unless this is a case of *res ipsa loquitur*. To Sellers, like Wrottesley, there really was no danger in the blocking of the test cock since its sole use was in the draining process of the torpedo tubes, a wholly different purpose from showing whether the bow cap was open or shut. So, the logic ran, its blocking was not the cause of the loss because the mere fact that the tube was full of water would not have had that effect when it was opened. That would only have let two tons of water into the compartment and the only persons in danger would have been those in the immediate vicinity of it. Even then the danger was minimal.

Nelson and Sellers placed the blame firmly on Woods for not being careful enough in ensuring the tube was dry before opening the rear door. He should have used the rimer, even if it was not part of the drill, but as Sellers stated, 'What is appropriate in action is not necessarily appropriate to the occasion of a [dive] trial, the object of which is to ascertain faults, so that everything should be approached with suspicion and tested. A trial called for the use of the rimer'. If not Woods, the blame fell on Hambrook for not putting the lever in the correct position, but Woods should have given a clear and unequivocal order to ensure the lever was at 'shut', not 'neutral' or 'open'.

Sellers stated, 'If a man pointed a loaded gun at another man's heart and fired it was no excuse to say later that he thought he had been told the weapon was not loaded'. Woods, Sellers claimed, did not use all the means at his disposal to ensure the bow cap was closed before conducting his rather odd action of opening each rear door while at sea. He must have read the indicator wrongly, and if he knew the test cock might be blocked, he should have used the rimer. Had the test cock hole been blocked with something like seaweed or mud he would have been proved negligent, the fact it was a bit of paint made no difference. 'The next link in the chain was Admiralty Overseer Grundy whose job it was to ensure that the tubes were in perfect working order. If Woods was exonerated in this final action, then Grundy must be held to blame for misleading everyone after passing the tubes as safe, and launching a dangerous thing on the world'.

162

After seven years of legal blame and counter blame Viscount Simon, Lord Russell, Lords Macmillan, Porter and Simonds retired to decide once and for all who was accountable for the loss of the *Thetis* and her men, and who was going to, literally, pay for it. On 27 February 1946 the plaintiffs and defendants waited anxiously to learn their different fates. Viscount Simon was the first to give his decision, but before doing so he stated for all those present how best to proceed. 'Each of these decisions', he began, 'has to be considered separately and pronounced upon in turn. The material on which our decision must be based is contained not only in the evidence given before Wrottesley J. in 1943, but also in testimony extending over seventeen days at a tribunal of inquiry into the loss of the *Thetis* which began in July, 1939 and was presided over by Bucknill J'. By some twist of fate the very report, with all its omissions and avoidances of any blame, now formed a key component in the decision-making process of the highest court in the land to decide just that.

Before the proceedings could start Simon asserted that there was no dispute about both Woods and Hambrook owing a duty to all those aboard the *Thetis* to take reasonable care for their safety. But in law, such an assertion can be interpreted in many different ways, which may or may not amount to negligence. 'Even if he [Woods] were wrong in his deductions when no water came out', Simon explained, 'he was completely justified in regarding the bow cap of Number Five tube as shut when the mechanical indicator told him so. And if it had remained shut, the worst that would have happened is that the contents bottled in the tube would have escaped – a result which involved no disaster to the submarine'. Woods' communications with Hambrook were not obscure or misleading, however brief their conversation had been. Analyzed months, now years, after the event one thing was certain – Hambrook *knew* that he was to ensure that the bow caps were shut. In Simon's own words, 'For otherwise he would never have joined in the suicidal act of opening the rear doors'.

Simon felt that, had the hole not been blocked, raising the lever would have produced a gush of water, 'But it seems to me quite unreasonable to hold that, when the indicator had shown that the bow cap was shut, it was negligence in Lieutenant Woods not to use the rimer'. It was not part of common Naval practice to use the rimer on such a regular basis (although since the *Thetis* disaster it became mandatory throughout the submarine fleet). 'The rimer was not in fact provided for the purpose of thrusting out a seal of bituminous paint, but for clearing the hole on proper occasions of fortuitous obstacles such as seaweed or incrustations. He was, I think, entitled to assume that the submarine was, in this as in other respects, in normal working order and that any paint had been properly applied'.

Viscount Simon found that deciding on whether an action for negligence should be reinstated against Cammell Laird was a much more difficult question. He did outline that, before liability could be established, three points had to be proved. That Laird failed to exercise due care, secondly that the care was owed to those men whose wives were currently suing Laird, and finally that any failure on Laird's part was the 'cause' of their injury. On whether Laird failed to exercise due care, Viscount Simon was about to deal the shipbuilder a crushing blow.

'Cammell Laird cannot be excused by pointing to the clause in the sub-contract which bound the Bitumastic Company to do the work to the satisfaction of the Admiralty. Neither is Cammell Laird's responsibility for leaving the holes blocked removed by the failure of Admiralty inspectors to observe this condition. The shipbuilding contract bound Cammell Laird to carry out the building and completion of the submarine "in a proper and workmanlike manner" and facts proving carelessness in carrying out a contract may also amount to negligence in tort'. Did Laird owe a duty of care to Duncan and Craven? If they did, then Mabel and Rose, and – thus all the other dependents – would win.

Cammell Laird was in possession of the submarine when Duncan and Craven were on board. They, along with the other civilian workers, were there, under arrangements which Laird had made, for their expertise during the dive trial under contract agreement at Laird's risk. Viscount Simon explained in laymen's terms, 'A man in his own carriage who invites or permits another to drive does not thereby transfer possession of the vehicle. I hold that Duncan and Craven were not, vis-à-vis Cammell Laird, mere licensees. Cammell Laird owed a duty to them, analogous to the duty owed by an occupier to invitees, to see that the former's negligence in relation to the premises did not cause such injury to them, as might reasonably be contemplated as flowing from the want of care.'

It now looked as if Cammell Laird was about to have the Court of Appeal's reversal quashed, and again be liable for a crippling compensation claim, but looking like and being like were as obscure in this case as they were in the disaster itself, 'The crucial question has to be

164

answered whether Cammell Laird's negligence can be said to be the "cause" of the disaster'. It was not conclusive to say that the blocking of the hole was not the cause of the disaster because nothing would have happened if Lieutenant Woods had not opened the rear door. 'After much reflection I have reached the conclusion that the Court of Appeal is right in saying that blocking the hole with paint is not the cause of the accident and Cammell Laird is therefore discharged from liability. These arguments also apply to the position of the Bitumastic Company ... Its workmen painted badly, but remedies in contract, if any, are nothing to the point. Leaving aside the opportunities for intermediate inspection, the Bitumastic Company had nothing to do with sending the deceased to sea on a diving trial with rear doors in this condition.

'If it be thought remarkable that after so long and elaborate an investigation no one should have been found liable for this loss of life, the answer is that in order to recover damages it is necessary to prove liability against one or other of the parties sued. The key to what is uncertain may have been lost among the ninety-nine who perished in the disaster. I move that Lieutenant Woods' appeal be allowed and that the decision of the Court of Appeal as to the non-liability of the other defendants be affirmed'. One final decision made, four to go.

Lord Russell of Killowen was unable to attend the summing up. Lord Macmillan stood before the Lords in Russell's absence to present his peer's decision. Lord Russell was clearly with Viscount Simon on Hambrook understanding what Woods' question meant when the Lieutenant asked him whether the bow caps were shut, and that Woods was entitled to act on Hambrook's answer. 'I am not prepared to hold that in the circumstances he was negligent in not using the rimer, Russell confirmed. 'Its use formed no part of the drill in regard to the opening of rear doors. He had never in his experience known a test cock to become choked. He was entitled to assume that the test cock was in order when the ship sailed from Liverpool with all the bow caps closed. For the reasons, which I have indicated, I am of opinion that the appeal of Lieutenant Woods should succeed. As regards the cross-appeal against the widow of Hambrook, I can see no evidence on which a case of negligence against Hambrook can be based. That cross-appeal must fail'.

Russell added that, assuming Laird was careless and their negligence caused the accident, the question still remained as to whether they were in breach of a duty to Duncan and Craven. For Russell the

165

answer depended on whether Laird could reasonably be expected to foresee that blocking the test cock might endanger the lives of those on board. In his opinion no such foresight could reasonably be expected. His rationale was that the use of the test cock was to assist in firing operations and had nothing to do with clearing the aperture on a brand new submarine during its preliminary diving trials.

'If this view is right', he explained, 'as I think it is, Cammell Laird is under no liability to the plaintiffs. As to the case against Wailes Dove Bitumastic Limited, if Cammell Laird are under no legal liability, neither can they be subject to any. I will only add this. The fact that no one can be made liable to the plaintiffs for the damages, which flowed from this disaster is, I doubt not, due to the deaths of so many people, among whom might have been found the person capable of solving the mystery of how the bow cap came to open during the inspection of the tubes. To me it remains a mystery, and no good purpose can be served by suggesting possibilities which have no foundation in the available evidence'. Strike two.

Lord Macmillan remained standing to deliver his own summation. Macmillan agreed with Simon and Russell that Woods was not negligent for opening the bow cap. He had taken the required precautions. The incident of the blocked test cock and Lieutenant Woods' acting with regard to it were irrelevant with regard to his so-called negligence. He added that before opening the door Woods received further confirmation from Hambrook, an experienced rating who Woods had served with before, only adding, 'As to Hambrook himself, the case against him finds no support in the evidence'.

Macmillan found that Laird was responsible to the Admiralty for breach of contract, but that was a very different matter to hold them liable for the disaster. 'While this does not relieve the builders of their responsibility for the defect, it is significant on the issue of their negligence. Where the case against them breaks down is in the connection of their failure to observe and remedy this defect with the occurrence of the disaster. The chain of causation, to borrow an apposite phrase, would appear to be composed of missing links. The case against the Bitumastic Company fails even more signally for the same reason. I accordingly agree with the motion proposed by my noble and learned friend on the woolsack'. Now three out of four Lords had quashed Mabel's and Rose's actions.

Lord Porter had made his decision but he, like Lord Russell, was unable to formally address the Lords. In his place Lord Simonds rose

166

to give Porter's interpretation of the events. Porter felt that when a skilled operator read the indicators provided to ascertain the state of the equipment it must, over time, become instinctive, not only to ensure his own safety, but that of his entire crew. 'Even if he might risk the first, he was not likely to endanger the second'. It was not negligent to put the levers at neutral. He, too, agreed that the use of the rimer was not necessary and that Woods' approach to discover whether the bow caps were shut was correct in every sense. Proving negligence against Woods and/or Hambrook in this case was not possible.

'No doubt Naval ratings may be expected to wait for and to obey the orders of their officers but it has to be remembered that they are not the servants of their officers but of the King and a Naval officer cannot be held liable for negligence merely because the ratings under him are negligent without or contrary to his orders. The question, as I see it, is not, does the accident of itself point to his negligence, but is it right on the evidence as a whole to find him guilty of negligence?' In apportioning blame to Hambrook, Porter stated, 'It is true that the opening of the bow cap is difficult to explain without some negligence somewhere, but this is not a justification for concluding that Woods or Hambrook was the guilty party'. It just did not make sense that two experienced submariners would erroneously allow one out of six bow caps to be open under dive trial conditions.

Porter had no doubt that both companies were negligent, the one for failing to inspect the rear door properly after the painting was finished and the other for faulty painting. But they were not accused of bad painting, rather endangering the lives of those on board the *Thetis*. Does this mean they were negligent towards the loss of the vessel and the men? The two companies owed a duty to all the ship's company, both naval ratings and civilians alike, but would only be guilty of negligence for their deaths if the act or omission complained of by Mabel and Rose would reasonably be anticipated as likely to cause their husbands' deaths. It was a very small part of a very big sequence of events.

If the attack upon Cammell Laird failed, that upon the Bitumastic Company might succeed. 'I cannot follow this argument. It is true that the carelessness of the Bitumastic Company lay in commission rather than omission. It was their workman who painted over and blocked the hole, and by his own admission he knew what any man would know, that a hole should not be painted over. But it is not to be attributed to him or to any officer or servant of the company that he ought to have foreseen the consequences of his careless act. Ought the Bitumastic Company reasonably to have foreseen the possibility of those events happening which in fact happened? The answer is "No". Was the intervening act, the opening of the rear door with the bow cap open, an event reasonably foreseeable by them? The answer is "No".'

Put bluntly, in law a defendant cannot be held negligent unless he knew that his actions would lead to a chain of events conspiring to cause a disaster. Woods had no idea that the bow cap was open when he went to check inside Number Five tube. After all, the others he looked at were fine. Neither was he bound to use the rimer. Hambrook was certain the levers were all correct. When Wailes Dove's employee accidentally blocked Number Five test cock, he did not do it knowing such an action would sink a submarine. Cammell Laird had every right to expect the test cock not to be blocked and were not bound by contract to inspect it, only have it ready for inspection.

Lord Porter concluded, 'Then let the standard of care demanded of them be what it may, they owed no duty in respect of their careless act to the plaintiffs and cannot be made liable for it to them. In the result the appeal of Lieutenant Woods should, in my opinion, be allowed and the several appeals or cross-appeals of Mrs. Duncan and Mrs Craven dismissed'. After seven bitter years Rose and Mabel had won twice in their attempt to seek apportioning of blame. Firstly in Wrottesley's, what is called Court of First Instance, where they could have got compensation. Then they lost that on appeal, only to have the blame shifted to Woods who was not able to make any significant financial recompense anyway. Now as their final chance melted away, the two women and all those pinning their hopes on a successful outcome were left with nothing whatsoever in what was now officially recorded as 'a non-negligent accident'.

Chapter 15

'SOS Thetis'

Every writer of non-fiction, whether in book, newspaper or broadcast media loves to find a good conspiracy theory, but more often than not such theories rarely materialize as conspiracy fact. There is no doubting that the existence of political, commercial and military cover-up has and always will be with us, but due to the very nature of distorted public perception and media spin the more controversial events all too often get pushed further into the dark. Conspiracy theories surrounding the *Thetis* are an essential part of any comprehensive work on the subject, but they must be fully explored in minute detail to decipher the fiction from the fact to see what is left.

Seven years of legal infighting showed that no one was to blame for the *Thetis* disaster. All that remained was a great deal of bitterness and resentment among the dependents as well as the country as a whole, especially as it was patently obvious that the whole debacle was riddled with human error. Lord Porter had already stated that the opening of the bow cap was difficult to explain without some negligence somewhere, but no one was being held to blame. There was always that nagging doubt, why did it take so long for the Admiralty to proactively mount a feasible rescue operation with so much time available? Inevitably in the late 1930s, just as today, the public turned to conspiracy theories for their much-needed answers. Some were well known, others were not, yet more were laced with elements of truth. Either way their very presence only managed to fuel national unrest. One of the more realistic sounding theories was never even heard in Great Britain, but in Nazi Germany.

Author and broadcaster Count Michael Alexander narrated an account of the loss of the *Thetis* on German national radio in March 1943. Alexander's six-part series, which today would be called a docudrama, was alleged to be based on a British secret report stating how, although her loss was through incompetence, the death of her crew certainly was not. Each episode was intercepted and fully translated, copies of which reached Bristol West MP Clive Culverwell. Upon seeing the evidence he demanded an Admiralty explanation to ascertain if, indeed, the allegations were true and whether they were based on a so-called secret report or not.

He first wrote to the Admiralty's Financial Secretary, who in turn passed on Culverwell's letter to the Director of Press Division (DPD). The DPD replied, '[Culverwell] would like to know whether the Germans are using a genuine document or whether their effort is purely fraudulent and, according to the reply, how the document got into their hands or what we are doing to counter the German falsehoods. The last question was only implied in his request, but we had better be prepared for it'.

The DPD went on to assure the Financial Secretary that such broadcasts often took place in Germany and were intended to cause mistrust. He added that at best if word got out that the reports had reached Britain and more importantly that there had been a reaction, such a response could encourage Germany to broadcast more stories. At worst the reaction could be twisted to imply that the allegation had some basis of truth, which in fact it did.

On reflection the DPD thought it a little more than just coincidence that another submarine, HMS *Vandal*, disappeared in late February 1943 during her three-day working-up trial, which included a deep dive. He drew the conclusion that the broadcasts and the loss of *Vandal* might be connected because less than a month had elapsed between the two. But regardless of possible links with another submarine, he concluded his reply to the Financial Secretary somewhat alarmingly, 'It is not known if the German broadcasts bear any resemblance to an alleged secret report on the loss of the *Thetis*, and [an] inquiry from DNI [Director of Naval Intelligence] would be necessary to establish this.' Culverwell had every reason to be concerned. If the content of Alexander's series was true, Cammell Laird, the Admiralty and the British Government had conspired to allow the trapped men to die slowly for political and financial gain.

Episode one was intercepted out of Breslau on 15 March at 18.30 hours local time. While the German people were preparing or already eating their evening meals, Alexander's voice hissed and crackled out of radios all across the Fatherland. He began, 'I have here a document of the greatest possible value. It is from England and is of a very recent date. It has reached us in a very roundabout way'. Alexander went on to say that his narration would be augmented with accounts from leading British newspapers.

The broadcast begins explaining how the T Class submarine was the new wonder British war machine and how, since 1939, this had proved to be wrong. Basically, according to Nazi Germany, the T Class was a flawed design that never lived up to Admiralty expectations. Alexander asserted, 'Old hands in the yards have wrung their hands about the experiment in construction which the designer of this new secret weapon has made. The designer of the Patrol Class [another name for the T Class] and consulting engineer to the Admiralty, to which the *Thetis* belongs, is at the same time chief designer for Cammell Laird and consulting engineer to the Admiralty. He has obtained his position because he is the nephew of [Leopold] Amery, former First Lord and Secretary for the Colonies, the all-powerful principal shareholder of Cammell Laird and representative of this firm in the Commons. His name is Mr E. [sic] Bailey'.

Listeners all across Germany now hear a brief outline of how the *Thetis* sent a dive signal to the Admiralty and how the 160-ton escort vessel *Grebe Cock* is watching over the trial dive. Godfrey and Coltart are scanning the sea in case a buoy surfaces, signaling something is wrong. Shortly after diving, Alexander says a buoy surfaced, but its telephone did not work. Then German actors play what was said to be actual dialogue between Godfrey and Cammell Laird.

Godfrey reports to Laird via a radio link with Port Liscard, 'We are drifting on the strong current, we are losing the position of the *Thetis*'.

'Throw out a sound signal buoy', comes Laird's reply, but Godfrey says, quite correctly, that there were none on board.

An exasperated Laird's official shouts into his transmitter, 'Cast anchor'.

Again Godfrey correctly responds, saying that the anchor, 'Does not reach the bottom. We must lengthen the chains, but that will take time.' Both he and Coltart are heard discussing what best to do next when Godfrey calls up Port Liscard for advice.

Liscard replies, 'Wait until you get orders'.

Godfrey is clearly not satisfied, 'But meanwhile the people are suffocating in the submarine. I must give an SOS'.

'You must do nothing of the kind, do you understand?'

'Who says so?'

'The Yard [Laird] Management. We have the firm order. There are special reasons. No SOS, have you understood. If enquiries come you have to answer evasively'.

'But I cannot anchor, our chains are too short. I must send an SOS. We are losing the position. I shall give an SOS'.

'We repeat, there are reasons, there must be no alarm. The Yard is getting in touch with the Admiralty at once. You will hear from us at once'.

At 18.30 hours on 16 March the second episode was intercepted via the Allouis transmission facility in central France. Alexander now begins to unravel the 'special reasons' why Cammell Laird refuse to allow an SOS to be sent. He informs the German people that, because Cammell Laird was nearly bankrupt at the time the *Thetis* was launched, the shipbuilder did not insure the submarine as per the conditions of the Admiralty contract. With only a few days to go before final Admiralty acceptance, why spend some £3,000 for fully comprehensive cover, or about £90,000 today. Because Laird is still the legal owner of the submarine, all their profits are tied up in a wreck at the bottom of the sea – a worthless uninsured hulk, which is about to sink the company and many other interested parties faster than their submarine.

Laird telephones Minister of War Sir John Anderson, First Viscount of Waverly, to tell him what has happened. Anderson is certain that if the news leaks out that she was lost, rather than just in a little difficulty Cammell Laird will be declared bankrupt. The collapse of one of Britain's biggest shipbuilders, only months before the outbreak of war, would cause a crash on the Stock Exchange. Anderson tells Cammell Laird, 'Today is Thursday [1 June, 1939] If we send out the SOS for the *Thetis* today, and if it becomes clear that the *Thetis* is not insured, we will have a second Black Friday tomorrow. What about insuring the *Thetis* now?'

'Against what risks could you insure it?' a Laird's director asks.

I can't tell you that on the telephone', replies Anderson. 'You know that I am really an insurance expert. I shall conclude the insurance contract within the next few hours so that we can tell the Stock Exchange that the *Thetis* is insured. The most important thing is that no SOS must be sent out until the insurance contract is concluded. If the Admiralty gets to know of the catastrophe, the Stock Exchange will get to know too, and what will happen you can imagine yourself'.

'Yes, but can we postpone the SOS? The air in the submarine will only last till Saturday midnight. Who is going to take the responsibility?

'I take full responsibility in the name of the Government', Anderson says. 'No SOS must be sent until the insurance contract has been completed'. Count Alexander goes on to explain what lengths Laird was going to in a bid to grab any financial liquidity to stay in business, even before their only asset hit the bottom of Liverpool Bay. They had, he claims, been negotiating for some time with the American bank J. P. Morgan for a credit loan. The negotiations were supposed to end on the afternoon of 1 June. 'While those in the submarine brood despairingly on their situation and yearn for rescue', Alexander adds, 'the directors of the firm are dining with the American bankers at the Carlton Club'.

Alexander narrates how Laird's directors knew that if J. P. Morgan were made aware that the *Thetis* was lost, rather than having suffered a minor set-back on her trials, they would never sign the credit agreement. Laird would then go the same way as the other thirteen inter-war shipbuilders of which Johnson told those present at the launch of the merchant vessel, *Jonathan Holt*, at Liverpool's Adelphi Hotel back in June 1938. But why would J. P. Morgan not sign the agreement, even if the *Thetis* was lost? Alexander explains, 'If they got wind of the sinking of the *Thetis*, particularly as the most important members of the firm were on board, who was to guarantee the repayment and the carrying out of the construction programme. The SOS was postponed until the credit contract also had been signed.'

The negotiations for the credit agreement were conducted through Under Secretary of War Lord Quintin McGarel Hogg Hailsham of Saint Marylebone, but just before Hailsham is due to complete negotiations the American bank delivers an unexpected sting. As the talks are about to conclude the bank's representative tells Lord Hailsham, 'Mr Morgan believes that he is not making enough in this armament business. You will have to pay us a higher interest'.

Lord Hailsham says, 'The firm cannot possibly pay you more interest than they have offered'.

'Surely you know me, my Lord. You are paying twenty, twenty-five and thirty per cent dividends. Restrict that a bit, then it will work'.

'I stand and fall by this arrangement of high dividends for armament shares, and with me stands and falls the British Government'.

'Nevertheless, Mr Morgan wants to make more in this business; he thinks the risk is too great'.

The German people listened as Alexander's voice beamed into their homes the whole sordid tale of how the *Thetis*'s crew were sold out for financial gain; many background facts are true. The *Grebe Cock* was in the wrong position and the RAF misled the search party after sighting a buoy and a long shadow in the wrong area. But adding that all this was *really* on the orders of Cammell Laird to mislead the rescue craft, thus postponing the SOS long enough to allow J. P. Morgan to sign the credit agreement.

'Due to this wrong information from the aircraft', Alexander hammered out, 'HMS *Brazen* and the First and Sixth Destroyer Flotillas began to search for the *Thetis* from 21.00 hours onwards, throughout the night with searchlights in the wrong place. Seven hours were lost through the contract negotiations. Now the hours of night were being lost. The critical time 02.00 hours, on Saturday, when the men in the submarine must suffocate, drew nearer'.

At 18.30 hours on 17 March, 1943, Alexander's third episode is intercepted out of Frankfurt this time. He tells his listeners how, quite truthfully, the British public was not informed of the loss, until about eight hours after the incident, but that all available craft were rushing to, or had already arrived at the area. 'All England is paralyzed by this wireless announcement', his metallic voice fizzes and pops. 'Had it been surmised that all those warships were misled in order to gain time for the insurance contract, and that these ships had been sent to an entirely wrong spot – the spot where the *Royal Charter* was and not to where the *Thetis* was lying – the horror of the British would presumably have changed to disgust'. The *Royal Charter* was a 2,700-ton steam ship, which foundered exactly eighty years earlier, but her dark shadow was still visible beneath the sea.

After a lengthy and accurate account of how HMS *Brazen* finally found the *Thetis*, Alexander continues, 'The prestige of the British Fleet diminishes as one reads. There is one ray of sunshine, however, in all the muddle, the Stock Exchange received the news calmly, particularly as the morning papers reported that the *Thetis* was insured. There were no landslides in the quotations of the shares of Cammell Laird, particularly as the Directors of the firm and the Government had intervened in the market to avert the much-feared second Black Friday. The bold headlines of the newspapers were typical'. The German listeners then hear the throng of city traffic peppered with the cries of newspaper boys shouting headlines of 'Submarine gone down: value £250,000: eighty men in danger.' With so many men at peril,

174

and the loss of a brand new submarine dominating the news, British national newspapers, such as *The Times*, *Daily Telegraph* and the *Daily Express*, did make quite an issue out of her insurance and monetary value.

On the following day the fourth episode, is intercepted, again out of Frankfurt, and tells the German public how, with about twenty ships in the area, if the men could not be released, at least an airline could have been fed down and into the pressure hull to keep them alive. How there was no air hose available, or any compressor in good working order to get air to the men comes next. The scene then shifts to Laird's gates in Birkenhead. The mothers, wives, children and others are all asking the same kinds of questions. Had their men been saved? Were they in serious danger? Will the *Thetis* be raised? They only really wanted news of their men folk, but Laird had nothing to offer.

By now it is dark in Birkenhead and the crowds outside Cammell Laird are growing by the minute. Alexander says that an argument breaks out when it is discovered that there were not enough DSEA escape sets on board when she sailed. Admiralty rules specified that there had to be enough sets for every man aboard, plus another third as many again. They were placed in the submarine, in sealed wooden lockers and were available for easy and quick access. In the case of the *Thetis*, as was widely publicized at the time, there were nine sets too few aboard when she sailed on 1 June, these being left at a Laird's workshop. From somewhere in the crowd around Laird's gates a woman shouts, 'Why haven't they got them?' Another voice replies, 'The Management did not want to get new ones. The old DSEA sets lying about the dockyard were supposed to be good enough, but they had become unusable through long disuse and were being repaired'.

Expressions of grief and despair rumble through the already highly charged crowd. They decide to enter the yard, although the gate is barred. Security men are trying to push the crowd back; above all the cries, one guard shouts, 'I can let no one through. Move back please'. Knowing they cannot burst through the steel gates, the crowd is even more incendiary. Another loved one shouts, 'Every foreman in this yard knows that the *Thetis* started her trial run with insufficient preparation. Every turner knows it! Every electrician! Every fitter! Every helper! We all know it! We have a right to speak, when the life or death of our blood relatives is at stake!'

Episode Five covers how Thomas McKenzie and the Scapa Flow divers became involved. Although he is told that all aboard the *Thetis* are safe, Alexander's secret report states that the delay in getting the Scapa Flow men down to Liverpool Bay is due to in-fighting between Laird and the Admiralty as to who foots the bill for the flight rather than an urgent need for his expertise. A German actor playing the part of Captain Nicholson shows his annoyance at the petty infighting. He adds, 'When I heard of it, I immediately gave orders to have him [McKenzie] brought here at the Admiralty's expense. A special aircraft was sent and he's probably on his way. All we needed now was panic on board.'

Alexander explains what happens after McKenzie, 'the famous diver' arrives. 'Not a single attempt had been made by any of the warships at the scene of the disaster to save the doomed men. Midnight struck. Flags on all British warships throughout the world went to half-mast. British sailors everywhere had not moved from their radio sets and knew that – according to the shipyard's calculations – the men in the submarine must have suffocated. The only man who refused to believe the experts was McKenzie'.

Alexander says that it was McKenzie who was first to dive on the *Thetis,* although this was Sinclair 'Sinc' Mackenzie and not Thomas. When he surfaces he accuses Cammell Laird's Managing Director Robert Johnson of having wasted the last three precious hours believing those trapped aboard are dead after he heard definite sounds of life while on the sunken submarine. Thomas McKenzie reiterates that had his services been accepted some fourteen hours earlier the men would have had a much greater chance of survival. In his opinion rescue work was stopped a full three hours too soon. Now, although there is definitely life still aboard, it is too late to act.

At the beginning of the sixth and last episode, again intercepted out of Frankfurt, at 18.30 hours on 20 March, this final instalment claims to repeat verbatim extracts from the evidence presented by survivors to Bucknill's Tribunal. Firstly Woods is heard recalling under oath how he and others are trying to enter the two flooded compartments, which is repeated very much like that known to have been given before Bucknill. Other extracts are just a little more controversial, the greatest being those from Chief Stoker Walter Arnold's evidence after the attempts to enter the flooded compartments had to be abandoned.

Alexander shows him telling Bucknill, 'Well sir, towards the evening an auction of rescuing apparatus took place'.

'A what?' replies Bucknill.

'An auction, My Lord. There were only forty-eight apparatuses, and we were 103. The lot was to decide'.

'Why were there only forty-eight?'

'The others were still on shore being overhauled'.

'That is to say, there was hardly half the necessary rescue kit on board'. Bucknill asks rhetorically.

'Yes, but of those forty-eight only four were in order'.

'Who got the others?'

'Captain Oram and Sub Lieutenant Wood [sic]'.

'By lot too?' Arnold does not reply. 'Arnold, you are under oath, adds Bucknill. 'Don't be so rash as to make a misstatement. I ask you again. Did those two officers receive the apparatus really by lot?'

Arnold replies, 'I don't know. I can't really remember very well. There was terrific panic on board!'

Bucknill changes tack and asks Arnold who got the fourth Davis breathing set. 'The sailor Matthews', Arnold answers. 'I am quite certain of that because he stood next to me during the lottery. But during the night he sold it to Shaw.

'Sold it? Since when can Government property be sold?'

'The haggling went on until the early hours of the morning. The others crouched on the floor and sang hymns, or beat SOS with tools against the hull of the ship'.

Arnold then explains how Shaw tries to buy his breathing set, but Arnold refuses. Shaw then tries to buy Matthews' set with a large cheque. On his sailors pay Matthews could not marry his fiancée, but with Shaw's cheque it would make possible the young sailor's dreams. He decides to gamble his life, hoping that rescue would come before death. But, according to Alexander, Glenn jotted down the following events to show that Matthews' nerve gave out before whatever breathable atmosphere was left inside. 'For Matthews has realized that after he accepted Mr Shaw's cheque, his chances of being saved were rapidly dwindling. Matthews' desire for life became a craze after he had a fat cheque in his pocket. He hatches a plan to save himself at the expense of his comrades. Secretly, Matthews lets water run into the diving chamber, and waits, pressed close to the door of this escape chamber until someone would guilelessly open it, thinking that no water was in it'.

Alexander claims that the following events were based on notes jotted down by Chief Constructor Bailey before he died. Those who had been unlucky in the lottery of the rescue apparatus barred the way through to the door of the DSEA escape chamber and opened it. A tremendous flood swept Matthews and all the others in the chamber, back into the submarine, Matthews' belt catching on the doorway, as he was found when the submarine was opened up in Anglesey. Matthews had counted on this bubble to escape to the surface. If he succeeded in picking his way through the escape chamber, and through the trap door, then he would be saved – with his cheque in his pocket. 'He makes desperate attempts to free himself', continues Count Alexander. 'He tears and pulls at the arms preventing his escape'. Alexander finishes his series saying, 'Thus ninety-nine men died as victims of English power and money.'

If this radio series was true it is quite clear why Culverwell was so concerned, and why he demanded an explanation. After a couple of days of hearing no response to his request he again was pressing the Admiralty for answers, by telephone this time. The Director of Press Division noted, 'I assured him that it might take a few days before a letter could be sent to him. On 25 April 1943, the Director of Naval Intelligence informed the DPD that he, too, agreed with not rising to the Nazi bait. However, he added that there was no way Germany could have pinned the radio broadcasts on the recent sinking of the submarine HMS *Vandal* because, quite simply, her loss was not due to enemy action and had not yet been made public. He added, 'The present Flag Officer (Submarines) was a member of the Board of Inquiry into the loss of the *Thetis* and states the German broadcast is their own invention'.

Nearly two weeks after Culverwell first raised his concerns an answer was finally prepared. Firstly he was advised not to counter the German accusations, which would play into the enemy's hands. They are, in the Admiralty's opinion entirely fraudulent, but the Admiralty had no objection to Culverwell telling those of his constituents who originally voiced their concerns what the official view was. A much closer analysis of Count Alexander is needed to separate the fact from the fiction in his radio series. This is especially so, when Dresden publisher Franz Müller Verlag published a much larger book on the same subject in 1944.

Chapter 16

Conspiracy Theory, or Fact?

Altogether six conspiracy theories developed around the *Thetis* disaster. Count Michael Alexander's book and radio series were by far the most damning, made all the more convincing with their many truths, half-truths and well-constructed arguments. Alexander claimed that the *Thetis* was insured in retrospect for the predicted cost of her salvage should she be raised. He added a rather chilling fact that, 'The public was, however, not informed that the *Thetis* was insured for only twenty per cent and was soothed with the laconic sentence: "The *Thetis* was Insured". Only *The Times* reported on Saturday, 3 June, when the danger of a crash in armament shares was avoided at the cost of human life, for the insurance after the event took many hours, which were later not available for the rescue of the men'.

On Saturday, 3 June 1939 page fourteen of *The Times* published a striking aerial photograph of the *Thetis* surrounded by rescue craft. In the next column, just as Alexander claimed, a very small article reads:

THE SUBMARINE INSURED

Insurances are believed to have been placed on the *Thetis* for £350,000 while she was being built and during trials. In addition armament was covered for £75,000. Twenty per cent was quoted in the London markets yesterday to cover the risk of the total loss of the submarine.

Cammell Laird insured the *Thetis* with Robert Bradford & Co. of Old Broad Street, London. On 6 October 1936, as they were legally obliged to do under Clause Thirty of their Admiralty contract, two policies were issued, sequentially numbered 7022 and 7023. The former was for her hull and machinery, amounting to £305,000 and the latter for £60,000 to cover 'Articles'. On 2 October 1939, after Bradford's collected installments from their many brokers the Admiralty, not Laird, received a cheque for £361,350, which was posted to

179

Director of Navy Contracts E. C. Jubb. The full amount was £365,000 or slightly more than £16m today, but Bradford's held back £3,650 or a healthy £162,000 in today's value, as ten per cent 'settling commission'. The Admiralty strongly objected to the fee, but had no power to recover the funds. Quite clearly Alexander's spin on the true state of her insurance, although convincing, was complete fabrication.

Robert Bradford and their brokers did even better out of the settlement. Should the *Thetis* be raised and reconditioned for less than the insurance payout, the Admiralty were bound to pay one third of the claim back. Since she was salvaged, and reconditioned for considerably less than a new T Class submarine, Bradford's and their brokers shared exactly £38,500.17.5d, or more than £1.7m today. Their newly reconditioned submarine, HMS *Thunderbolt*, cost a little under £180,000, almost £8m today. Even when all other costs, such as salvage, which was about £58,000.00, and the expenses of Royal Navy vessels present, the *Thunderbolt*'s full cost was exactly £250,753.17.4d. That is £100,000, or about £4m, less than a new T Class build, and in half the time.

When Cammell Laird's Managing Director Robert Johnson insisted at the launch of the *Jonathan Holt* that British shipbuilding was doomed unless the Government stepped in added fuel to Alexander's claim that Laird could well have been in trouble. Also former First Lord and Secretary for the Colonies Leopold Amery was a principal shareholder in Cammell Laird, which according to Alexander only made £353,907 profit in 1938. Although his account of the *Thetis* disaster is eerily accurate in places, close examination of the firm's original accounts for 1938 show that the Laird net profit was substantially less than even he stated, at exactly £253,907.10s.0d. In 1939 this had dropped to £225,394.9s.10d.

Overall Laird's book value was increasing year on year and they often made vast profits on both commercial and military builds. In 1938 nine vessels were completed, all at a profit, although this varied considerably, depending on the type of ship on the ramps. The *Jonathan Holt* for instance made a profit of slightly more than £15,000, over £2,000 above its quote. The following year the completed contracts were up to fourteen with the *Thetis* earning £5,270.4s.1d profit, or in today's currency value, about £234,188.16d. Two other T Class submarines were finished, both of which earned substantially more, HMS *Trident* at more than £8,000 profit and HMS *Taku* at nearly

£13,000. Multiply all the profits by forty-five for the cost of living since 1938 and a more realistic profit and loss account can be seen.

In fact, out of more than twenty vessels completed in two years only one made a loss. The new Cunard White Star liner RMS *Mauritania* was, at the time, the largest ship ever built in England, weighing in at almost 36,000 tons. Launched on 28 July 1938, almost one month after the *Thetis*, Cammell Laird made a loss of more than £16,000, or about £800,000 today. The loss cut quite a considerable slice into their 1938 profit margins, but not enough to seriously damage the business. There is also no evidence in their accounts to show that Laird needed to take out a substantial credit loan with J. P. Morgan. On the contrary, because Laird was, in fact, acting as a lending house for other organizations. Laird, like other shipbuilders who survived the bleak inter-war years, was in a position to make such good profits out of Government contracts that the Admiralty would eventually cap the amount a shipbuilder could make in a bid to stop private enterprise cashing in on the public purse.

After the *Thetis* was cleared of her dead and made seaworthy she was towed from her dry dock in Anglesey around the top of Wales, past her original dive site back to Birkenhead. The Admiralty first offered the job to recondition her to Cammell Laird on condition that they only make five per cent profit and waive any rights to the insurance monies after the *Thetis* claim was paid in full. Robert Johnson was clearly not happy with such Admiralty strings being attached to the new contract.

'We consider', Johnson told Director of Naval Contracts Jubb, 'that instead of a provisional amount for profit of five per cent, this should be increased to ten per cent and that the rate of charges appertaining to our entire works should apply'. The Admiralty's instruction to waive any rights to the insurance claim confused Johnson and he explained to the Admiralty that Laird were merely agents for the insurance on their behalf and that all the money had already been paid to the Admiralty by the underwriters. Johnson was quick to point out that although the claim had been paid the Admiralty had yet to clear an outstanding invoice on the submarine's hull and machinery of more than £21,000. Ending his letter, Johnson wrote rather sternly, 'We think as you have received this money from the underwriters there is no reason for you to withhold payment and we would like to get it cleared off our books'.

Eventually the agreement was finalized and throughout 1940 HMS *Thetis* was slowly transformed into the *Thunderbolt*. Altogether

Laird was, despite Johnson's pessimistic speech on 2 June 1938, and Alexander's radio play five years later, a very solvent company who remained in business right up to 1993.

Count Michael Alexander did mention that there was a deep reluctance to cut into the hull at Z tank, as this would render the *Thetis* useless against deep diving and/or depth-charge attack. He gleaned this information from a general feeling in and around Merseyside and elsewhere, that the rescue operation was in a constant state of forced delay with the Admiralty expecting the crew to help salvage their ship from the inside, with outside assistance. The official Admiralty line on this accusation was that if the tail lost its buoyancy and the hole sank beneath the surface then, Z tank, and the rest of the *Thetis* would flood rapidly killing everyone in minutes. The reason why it took fifty hours to make any real headway in the rescue was explained as being due to everyone's expectation that the men would surface in pairs using their DSEA equipment. This was despite the fact that simple classroom arithmetic dictated that there was not enough air left aboard to support ninety-nine men leaving in twos every fifteen minutes from early on 2 June until the air became too poisonous to breath.

Finally, regardless of where Alexander said he got his sources there never was a secret report. The whole weeklong radio series, and Alexander's book, were based largely, but not entirely, on Bucknill's 105-page Public Inquiry that was available to any member of the public to buy and read. The rest was made up from newspaper reports, gossip and hearsay and what today would be called urban myths echoing up and down 1930s Great Britain. Indeed, the book, also called *SOS Thetis* tells a more detailed version of what the radio play had to say, but still is nothing more than a cleverly worded document in which truth, lies and spin are extremely well crafted to give a very convincing argument. The book was published in both French, which are extremely rare today, and German, which can still be picked up in secondhand bookshops today.

In fact Count Michael Alexander was not even a real count. He was born in November 1902 as Walther Richard Max Bennecke. During the Second World War he worked for the Gestapo when, based in Paris, he wrote many other books, many with an Anti-Semitic slant. Where *SOS* Thetis sought to undermine the British Government and the Admiralty, another book was published a year later with a chapter called 'Der Teufel von Whitechapel' or 'The Devil of Whitechapel'. It was about Jack the Ripper, but Alexander/Bennecke and later known

182

as Soltikow, showed the German people so-called flaws in the British legal system, 'To assist the German People in a substantial way to understand the workings of our great adversary to reveal to all the shady side of English justice'. In this book, published a year after *SOS Thetis*, he attacks Sir Robert Anderson, this time not so much for shady insurance dealings, but rather to show how the real Ripper was never caught through Anderson's alleged assertion that both the British media and legal system were Jewish controlled. His *Thetis* radio play, but particularly his book, also alleges Jewish conspiracy undermining the rescue attempt, such as New York-based bankers J. P. Morgan trying to squeeze every last penny our of their credit deal at the cost of the trapped men.

As the war turned against Germany, so Soltikow changed tactics, claiming he had been working against the Gestapo the whole time in the counter-espionage department of Admiral Willelm Franz Canaris. He also embarked on a campaign to exonerate the Jews from their alleged conspiracy against National Socialism. Although his reputation was forever damaged, Soltikow went on writing books prolifically for many years, his last being published 1980.

Count Michael Alexander/Bennecke/Soltikow was not the only person to cover a *Thetis* conspiracy theory in book form. Lieutenant William Guy Carr RN wrote a very successful book called *Brass Hats and Bell Bottomed Trousers*, published by Hutchinson, London, in 1939. The book's subject matter involved the daring exploits of the Dover Command and their attempts to prevent enemy shipping, mainly U-boats, from slipping through the Channel and into the North Atlantic during the First World War. Carr was an ex-submarine navigator who stood by on the R Class submarine, *R-11* and took part in the diving trials of her sister ship, *R-12* under Captain Barry RN, in 1918. Both submarines were Cammell Laird builds, which, like the *Thetis* also undertook their dive trials in Liverpool Bay. Another of his books included a chapter called 'Sabotage and Spies' and was dedicated solely to the loss of the *Thetis*. Carr put forward what, to the layman at least, was a very sound reason for an alleged cover-up to hide why she went down. As an ex-Royal Navy officer Carr always sent drafts of his proposed narratives to the Admiralty for comment. This chapter was no exception, but the Admiralty were somewhat aggrieved by what he had to say. In late July 1939 Lieutenant Carr's draft chapter arrived at the Admiralty in Whitehall.

183

The Admiralty knew his comments came from an independent source and decided to send the chapter to Robert Johnson for further comment. Director of Navy Contracts Jubb wrote to Johnson, 'It would appear that Lieutenant Carr seems quite prepared to make dangerous innuendoes such as those given on pages (2) and (3) for which there seems no foundation in fact, and also make capital out of certain small contretemps which he had (may have had) with workmen in Birkenhead and which seem to have left with him sufficient spleen to generalize about the workmen in the whole place. It is immaterial to me what views Lieutenant Carr has about the matter, but I am somewhat surprised than an ex-officer of the British Navy should, for the sake of some small monetary consideration, rake up a few small truths and mix them with a great many innuendoes which are liable to blacken the characters of a group of men in these works who I can personally state are probably the finest body of workmen in the world'.

Carr explained how, just after the *R-12* had completed her measured mile on the surface, her crew prepared to dive. He added, '[The *R-12*] nearly met the same fate, in almost identically the same location, as that which befell the *Thetis*'. Where the *Thetis*'s hydroplanes jammed, those aboard *R-12* were very stiff to operate. She did dive where a submerged measured mile was conducted, and the Admiralty accepted her into the Fourteenth Submarine Flotilla based at Blythe.

Within a couple of days the *R-12* sailed for her war station off the west coast of Ireland, but bad weather swept across Liverpool Bay just as she passed the Bar Light. Carr wrote, 'It was impossible to remain on the conning tower without securing oneself to the periscope standard with what we call "our body and soul lashing". We decided to dive once our batteries were fully charged to get out of the weather'. The *R-12*'s personnel then went to their dive stations and started to flood up the ballast tanks while the engines were ordered to slow ahead. When the right amount of water had entered the tanks, and the *R-12* reached neutral buoyancy, the hydroplanes were put to 'slow dive' – but she refused to go down. Her commander, Captain Barry, then ordered the hydroplanes to 'dive' and still there was no response.

The *R-12*'s crew thought their submarine's refusal to dive was due to the bad weather so they let more water into the ballast tanks. 'We speeded up the motors and put the hydroplanes [to] "hard to dive" hoping this would force her under. Suddenly the indicator on the diving gauge started to tremble and then it steeply began to move 5 ... 10 ... 15 ... 20 feet, once the submarine started to dive nothing

Barry did seemed able to stop her and we started to go down like a stone at a steep angle. Our hydroplanes didn't work right and we seemed powerless to control her downward plunge'.

Due to the *R-12*'s small size, she weighed only about 500 tons, the submarine was able to level out and surface through blowing her main tanks. Like the *Thetis* eleven years later while on her failed trials in Gareloch, Carr said that the *R-12* had suffered a massive hydroplane malfunction, and if 'Sabotage and Spies' is to be believed, these submarines were not the only two. Carr related the account of another submarine, which had just started to crash dive when she plummeted too quickly. Once the water ballast tanks overcame the operation of the hydroplanes the order was given to 'check hard', meaning putting them in the neutral position and then over to 'hard to rise'. What actually happened was that she dived even more steeply and faster than before.

So why was she still plunging to the bottom? Instead of the hydroplanes being at 'hard to rise' as the control room panel showed, they were in fact at 'hard to dive' – the operation gear had been installed in reverse. Barry gave the order 'hard to dive'. '[The] crew had sufficient confidence in him to obey what at that moment must have seemed like the order of a madman', explained Carr, 'but their obedience saved their lives'. Although there is no independent proof of this that had yet come to light, as Warren and Benson claimed, the steering gear in the *Thetis* had been installed in reverse, so perhaps such a bizarre error is not that far-fetched after all.

Carr added one more interesting point. 'The strange thing about the loss of the *Thetis* is the fact that when she was located her hydroplanes were found to be "hard to dive". Why they should have been found in that position is beyond comprehension, unless it had been found impossible to move them once they had been put in the "hard to dive position". The ordinary procedure would call for the hydroplanes to be placed first in their neutral position and then in their "rise" position once the submarine went down. If the hydroplanes were "hard to dive" when he thought they were "hard to rise" then increasing their speed only added to their danger'. It is an interesting theory, but in the case of the *Thetis*'s faulty hydroplanes, some new facts have only just come to light.

Shortly after her aborted diving trials in Gareloch the *Thetis* returned to Cammell Laird so that Vickers-Armstrongs, the hydroplane builders, could gauge what, if anything, had gone wrong when she refused to dive. Laird's employee H. T. Cragg accompanied Vickers' Dock Foreman Mr Ankers for his survey of the bow hydroplanes. His first action was to put the hydroplanes under primary power with the unit at 'hard to dive'. Under a telemotor pressure of 1,400 lb, the bow hydroplanes jammed fast. Several clearances were checked between moving parts and Ankers found that a piston operating the hydroplane was not properly seated at the end of its hydraulic cylinder. After adjustments the piston was soon working properly.

A badly fitted piston was not the only fault. Cragg later confirmed, 'Due to a misunderstanding on the part of our erector, the secondary power piston control valves, forward and aft, had not been completely erected. These were finally completed and adjusted to give satisfactory results'. To ensure they were in full working order, the hydroplanes were tested under Admiralty and Cammell Laird's supervision in Laird's Wet Basin. Two-ton weights were placed on each forward plane while the pistons were made to operate under both local and central control. At 1,500 lb they worked well. The after hydroplanes were given the same rigorous testing and they, too, worked perfectly.

Cragg added, 'The main alignment of the gears was good, but the importance of the final adjustment of the gear has not been appreciated by our erector, also the misunderstanding regarding the secondary power piston controls'. He then concludes, 'It is requested by the Admiralty that the zero angle of the aft hydroplanes, which was fixed by Admiralty officials on trial at 9° Rise to be altered to 6.5°'. This proves that the hydroplane gear was not reversed, at least after the aborted Gareloch trial. There was no reason for the hydroplanes to be any different when the *Thetis* dived in Liverpool Bay about a month later, but when she was salvaged the forward hydroplanes were *still* set at 'hard to dive' and the after hydroplanes *were* also in the dive position. This is a little odd, especially after Bolus had tried to surface and failed to do so shortly after the *Thetis* hit the bottom. Perhaps the hydroplanes, like the ASDIC gear, were damaged when she hit the seabed? There is no way to prove this now, except that they were completely overhauled, or possibly replaced, when she was re-fitted to become the *Thunderbolt*. As an added safety precaution, Ankers took part in the *Thetis*'s dive trial on 1 June, and never returned.

Although Carr's Navy books found a good popular market, his attempts to prove a conspiracy theory surrounding the *Thetis* loss was part of a whole new direction he had been nurturing for some years. After retiring he published many more works on alleged communist, capitalist and, in the spirit of Count Michael Alexander, Anti-Semitic works on how all these organizations were out to control the world in their own special ways. Such titles as *Red Fog over America* said it all. Another called *Pawns in the Game* covered his pet subject of how the *Illuminati*, a conspiratorial organization, are really controlling the world. In fact, although he probably got it from another source, author Dan Brown repeats some of Carr's work in his 2001 novel *Angels & Demons*. Carr eventually became one of America's leading conspiracy theorists where, at his death in 1959, he was writing of how the Synagogue of Satan was controlling all of our everyday lives. Altogether perhaps it could be said that in his case, conspiracy theories really were just that.

Another conspiracy theory developed within the Royal Navy among a few ASDIC operators working in Liverpool Bay. In August 1939 ASDIC operator Joe Lynch joined HMS *Eaglet*, the Mersey Division of the Royal Naval Volunteer Reserve, to undergo training in Liverpool Bay. Lynch recently recalled in a letter published on the internet that, steaming through the Liverpool Bay, he picked up the *Thetis* on his ASDIC, as the salvage operation was still in effect. He then went on to make a rather startling admission. HMS *Brazen*, he said, had already picked up the *Thetis* on her ASDIC when the submarine was first missing. He explained that because ASDIC was so secret the *Brazen* could not go straight up to the *Thetis* somewhere in the Irish Sea, or a possible enemy would know that D Class destroyers had the ability to locate submarines. Not a very good position when war was imminent.

So how could Lynch possibly know what had occurred aboard the *Brazen* on 1 June when he claimed to be in Rosyth, Scotland, aboard the W Class destroyer called HMS *Wallace* at the same time? ASDIC operator Harry Rainer aboard the *Brazen* was a close friend of Lynch's, and later recounted the events to him. Lynch said that Rainer was even the Coxswain aboard the whaler that pulled Oram, Woods and later Arnold out of the sea. Rainer told his friend how Arnold had explained all the details of what happened inside the *Thetis* and what the situation was when he left.

Without a doubt the secrecy of ASDIC's potential had to be maintained – a fact made all too clear by the *Brazen*'s captain, Lieutenant Commander Robert Mills prior to his being called to give evidence at the *Thetis* Tribunal. In the Tribunal correspondence leading up to the actual court investigation Mills stated quite adamantly that he would not, under any circumstances, discuss the use of ASDIC in open court.

All he said under oath was, 'I now started to carry out a search of an area about three miles in each direction from the *Grebe Cock* which was anchored. I stopped frequently to investigate positions where I suspected the submarine might be'. Clearly, knowing the submarine was on the seabed, he is referring to such 'positions' having been located using ASDIC. But just where did he search? What was his search pattern? What type of ASDIC did the *Brazen* have, and what was its range?

On 1 June the *Brazen*'s log begins at 6 am when she weighs anchor in Belfast bound for Plymouth. Her watch officers record, on nearly every line of the log, events such as lights sighted, weather conditions, sick list and other details necessary to record the smooth day-to-day running of the destroyer. At 18.50 hours the log records, 'Rec'd orders to proceed to search for s/m *Thetis*'. The log goes on to note the *Brazen*'s engines working up to full speed, and sighting the *Grebe Cock*. At 21.18 hours the log reads, 'commenced A/s sweeping'. 'A/s' means 'Anti-submarine', or ASDIC sweeping.

The *Brazen* continued sweeping until about 23.00 hours at least, a full hour after Admiral Nasmith was certain the destroyer would find the submarine. Mills' decision, based on what he thought was sound information, to search to the west of the *Grebe Cock* meant the *Thetis* would not be found for several more hours. If, that is, Mills had stuck to his original plan and not diverted south-south-west to investigate the buoy that Flight Lieutenant Avent later spotted, pulling the *Brazen* even further away from the real position of the *Thetis*.

From 22.35 hours when the *Brazen* first deployed her searchlight, until finding the *Thetis* at 07.50 hours the next morning there is some discrepancy between her 'official' log and the copy used during Bucknill's Tribunal. Her original log covers this nine-hour period of frantic activity with one sentence with blank lines either side up and down the log, stating, 'Searching for Submarine *Thetis* and investigating various reports including positions of marker buoys and oil etc.'. Once the *Thetis* is sighted the log again picks up a much more detailed minute-by-minute account of events until she stands down and continues her route back to Plymouth.

The Tribunal copy of the log is in much greater detail with entries on the five lines before and ten after those in the original. These show an incredibly detailed account of where the *Brazen* was and what was being done to help find the *Thetis*. '03.40 hours Stopped to investigate area where oil was reported'. '04.00 hours Watch correct'. '04.05 hours

188

Proceeded as required. No reported position of buoy'. And so it goes on down to 07.50 hours recording, 'Sighted HM Submarine *Thetis*'. Every movement the *Brazen* made throughout the night on what would later transpire as a wild goose chase around Liverpool Bay is there, but not in the original. Perhaps there was simply no time to record each event at the time. And there is certainly nothing out of the ordinary in either version to suggest the *Brazen* found, and then blatantly ignored, finding the *Thetis* in a bid to protect her ASDIC capabilities.

Without a doubt she was carrying out an ASDIC search from 21.18 hours on 1 June, right through to sighting the *Thetis* at 07.50 hours the next day. No other information has been located to back up Lynch's assertion either one way or the other, but the *Brazen* was clearly out of ASDIC range of the *Thetis* until after daylight on 2 June and so she was very unlikely to have picked up the stricken submarine.

On 1 June 1939 eighteen-year-old telephonist Samuel Gothorp was on duty at the Liverpool Hatton Garden Police Station. Fifty years and one day later he broke his silence during a press interview with *The Guardian*, claiming that he took a call from the Admiralty, who refused to allow a hole to be cut into the submarine, saying, 'The vessel must not be touched'. According to Gothorp a Naval Liaison Officer present objected to the order and said they could be ready at low tide to cut the hole. 'There has been a hypocrisy of silence over the years', he told *The Guardian* in 1989, 'I told the naval officer "you're not going to take any notice of those people are you?" He just said, "It's more than my job's worth. I have to obey orders".' During the call the officer was told, 'We regret the vessel must not be touched'.

After Gothorp's article appeared, he claimed he was visited by the Ministry of Defence who informed him that the incident was still under the Official Secrets Act and could not be discussed. Of all the conspiracy theories to develop around this disaster, Admiralty resistance to damaging the submarine to save the men has stood the test of time while all others have since been more or less forgotten or never widely known at all.

Chapter 17

'If Blood be the Price of Admiralty . . .'

Accusations against the Admiralty began the day after their official announcement that all life was lost. On Sunday, 4 June, one of the first newspapers to demand answers was the *Sunday Express*. The tabloid ran damning headlines demanding, 'COULD THESE MEN HAVE BEEN SAVED, WHY SO LATE?' and adding that public opinion wanted prompt and full clarification of what had gone wrong. 'Why was there not enough salvage equipment available in time? Why was Thomas McKenzie not called sooner? Why was it not possible to cut a hole in her stern, which had been above water for nearly twenty-four hours?' No official answers were forthcoming. Then the letters of complaint from angry and frustrated members of the public poured into Whitehall.

Some of them were nothing more than emotional outbursts from angry people who could not grasp what had gone wrong. The day after the *Sunday Express* raised the national temperature, and before other newspapers followed suit, Mr M. D. Goodson of Acton, London, wrote to Their Lordships in the strongest possible terms, 'I feel I must lodge a protest regarding the *Thetis* disaster and like the rest of the public I demand an answer to the questions asked on the front page of yesterday's *Sunday Express*. It is quite obvious that you did not do all that was possible to rescue the men on board and it is plain that your inactivity was due to "red tape".' It was not the Admiralty's finest hour.

Captain Hart was also heavily criticized, privately at least. He received fifteen letters, explaining how he could have got the trapped men out of the submarine long before they died. Again some were misguided cranks, while others were not. Hart was resigned to the fact that he would be damned for his actions, regardless of Admiralty

191

inclusion, but he always maintained that it was all too easy to judge after an event. He said, 'It was all working on a time factor over which there was no control'. Under the circumstances he always believed he did the best he could with the tools at his disposal. His peers did not share this view, nor did the Admiralty behind closed doors.

HMS *Thetis* was the twenty-seventh submarine accident to have occurred worldwide since just before the end of the First World War. She was one of three vessels to successfully get one end or another above sea level to aid rescue, and the first to fail in the attempt. Unlike many other country's submarine rescue mandates Great Britain's was both lagging behind and entrenched in a flawed logic based on too much emphasis with too little proven knowledge. Such a philosophy had been developing throughout the 1930s, culminating in Rear Admiral (Submarines) Admiral Sir Dunbar-Nasmith's crisp comment on the subject during Bucknill's Tribunal in 1939, that the Admiralty must concentrate on the efficiency of the submarine and its fighting qualities rather than studying methods of getting out of it. 'Our only business in going into the submarine' he told Bucknill, 'is to use it as a weapon of war against a possible enemy. That is the submarine view'.

One of the many ways the Admiralty was lagging behind was in the use of soda lime to absorb the increasing levels of carbon dioxide. The Admiralty could only see that if soda lime was going to be used, vast areas of much-needed space would be taken up storing the chemical. And if their mid-1930s rescue plan was correct, any submarine lost in home waters would be found within twenty-four hours while plenty of air was still available. So, the logic ran, soda lime was not necessary. To keep carbon dioxide levels down to less than three percent for forty-eight hours, some 12,000 inches^2 of soda lime were needed, that is an area of about 2 feet 6 inches by 2 feet 1 inches, by 1 feet 5 inches. It was not that big, but as Mediterranean First Submarine Flotilla Commander, Captain Ruck-Keene said, 'In modern war you must have your submarine so light and not bigger than is absolutely necessary. In addition to that, the men have to live in that craft sometimes up to six weeks and two months, and you have to draw the line somewhere'.

Then, to deploy it to its full use, the soda lime had to be fitted into specially adapted ventilation ducts, taking up more space, to ensure that it was wafted throughout the submarine. But such extravagant methods were not necessary. When the USS *Squalus* sank off New England the week before the *Thetis*, her surviving crew sprinkled soda lime on the deck plating and it was effective enough. The use of a diving bell to rescue the *Squalus* survivors was also a much more advanced life-saving technique than anything available in the Royal Navy. The method allowed for external rescue, should the trapped submariners fail to escape by their own hand, an extra card to play that would undoubtedly have greatly helped the *Thetis* rescue operation.

After many years of submarine disasters the Admiralty decided that to try to salvage a submarine to save life was just not practical. This was a very bold move, which was likely to inflame public opinion. The chosen time to announce the move was during the First Lord's Commons speech on naval expenditure in March 1934. First Lord Bolton Meredith Eyres-Monsell, First Viscount Monsell, stood to address Parliament in what he knew would be a highly emotive issue. He said that the Admiralty had to face facts in making the decision, and it was a fact that there was no hope of saving life by salvage.

He added, 'We have to make up our minds as to that, and we have come to our decision because we are convinced that it is in the best interests of the personnel of submarine service. Waiting for hours, perhaps for days, under most intense strain, might so weaken their strength and their will that eventually they might not be able to make use of that escape gear at all. Escaping by DSEA is an act, which requires great resolution and coolness. It must not be postponed too long if it is to be a success.' It was considered that if men knew that the DSEA was their only chance of rescue they would have the requisite nerve to escape provided they escaped before their morale had been weakened by waiting and foul air. He, 'Recommended emphatically that no provision should be made to salve submarines for the purpose of saving life, the DSEA being relied on to fulfill this duty and that this should be accepted policy.'

At the same time air connections fitted to each compartment in existing submarines to aid rapid salvage were dispensed with 'in the interests of fighting efficiency'. The more the pressure hull was pierced with such fittings the greater became the vulnerability of the submarine during depth charge attack, but the removal of such a safety asset further limited the men's chances of survival. Shortly after the *Thetis* disaster Nasmith chaired a six-man committee to decide whether any changes needed to be made to current Admiralty thinking. Its two main functions were to confirm whether DSEA was the best method to get trapped men out of a submarine or not and whether salvage, as a means to save life, was still viable. His 100-page report also made fifty-two recommendations for change, some key ideas having already been put forward at Bucknill's Inquiry by Scapa Flow salvage engineer Ernest Cox.

Firstly all twenty-six submarine accidents were reviewed, after which Nasmith, like Raikes, came to the conclusion that the DSEA escape method was still the one and only way forward, and salvage to save life was still not an option. He went on to praise the DSEA as the only worthwhile method of aiding trapped submariners. That was all well and good, but in the case of the *Thetis*, like several other peacetime submarine disasters before and since, the use of DSEA relied heavily on there being a rescue vessel directly above to pluck the survivors out of icy water within twenty-four hours. This, of course, had to be achieved before hypothermia or a flood tide did what carbon dioxide would have done had they stayed where they were. Not to mention the system jamming as it did aboard the *Thetis*.

In light of the successful HMS *Poseidon* submarine escapes in the South China Sea, Nasmith was adamant, 'It was clear that even if every conceivable salvage appliance were built the DSEA would inevitably be a more certain method of escape, if for no other reason than that we cannot control winds and tides. Escape by DSEA requires courage and it is more than probable that men, already in a highly nervous condition in the comparative safety of an end compartment, will hesitate before making that escape if they think there is the smallest chance of the submarine being raised. Men in such a condition have a sublime faith that those on the surface will be able to rescue them. If, however, they know there is no possible escape, except by their own efforts, they will not hesitate to run any risks'. That was it; cast in stone, the DSEA would remain the primary escape method. Granted, the system proved that a few men and a Chinese steward had survived aboard the *Poseidon*, but its reliance had just cost ninety-nine lives, and twelve years later when HMS *Truculent* sank in the Thames another fifty-seven men would also perish after being swept away, believing that had they stayed aboard, the *Truculent* accident would become a second *Thetis*.

Rescue-by-salvage was deemed as impracticable as it was back in 1934, even after Oram decided in the case of the *Thetis* that salvage was the only method necessary to save all her men quickly and efficiently. His rationale was simple, and reflected the very essence of salvage philosophy. No two salvage operations are the same and must be treated on individual merit, *not* by default assume that all cases are the same. But one disaster never made the Admiralty's list of inter-war submarine losses. In 1919 the Chilean submarine *Rucumilla* was on a routine training exercise in the Bay of Talcahuno, facing northwest into the Pacific Ocean. She began a standard dive procedure, but unbeknown to her captain, Arstides del Solar, a valve for the battery ventilator was open. Being an ex-US Navy H Class vessel the valve was threaded anticlockwise, causing confusion among the crew in a country where to close such a valve it must be turned in the opposite direction. Twenty-five men were now trapped on the seabed. Captain Arstides immediately blew all ballast tanks.

The *Rucumilla* did surface, but only momentarily before again going down under the increasing weight of the inrushing water. A passing cargo ship spotted her erratic behaviour and reported the incident to the Chilean navy. The authorities reacted immediately, sending three heavy-lift cranes and other assorted salvage vessels to the scene. Within two hours the *Rucumilla* had been found and salvage measures started. Only seven hours after the *Rucumilla* went down she broke the surface. Although shaken, all twenty-five men came out through the fore hatch, half suffocated, choking from the early effects of chlorine gas, but alive.

Nasmith's report highlighted design and procedural flaws, which were never made public. A great deal of evidence was gathered both by the Naval Inquiry, and by Bucknill's somewhat neutered Tribunal findings, to see whether early attempts to enter the flooded compartments to close Number Five tube could have worked or not. Both, in their own ways, concluded that the plan would never have worked, but deeper investigation by Nasmith's Committee found evidence to the contrary. When attempts were made to force enough air into the two flooded torpedo compartments the rear door of Number Five tube could have been closed without the need for Woods or anyone else even having to enter the compartments using DSEA to prepare them for blowing. No one would have suffered acute pain, nor would their attempts have failed, and the *Thetis* would have stood every chance of surfacing. A pressure of 3 lb to 5 lb above sea pressure, which was the amount of internal pressure that the fore hatch would stand, was sufficient to allow Lieutenant Woods to keep his head in the air once he had 'locked himself through the forward escape chamber under pressure'.

Some of the *Thetis*'s design characteristics were also examined, especially the alteration, against recommendations, to change the watertight doors in Number Twenty-five bulkhead. 'It is most regrettable that consideration of torpedo loading led to a departure from the important decision of 1935 that all doors should be quick-closing. Evidence has shown that the failure to close the door in Number Twenty-five bulkhead was a contributory cause of the loss of the submarine. Quick closing doors and bulkhead valves were essential, for not only do they enable the survivors to reach an end compartment, but they may prevent the accident occurring'. The Committee strongly recommended going back to quick-closing doors throughout a submarine, which was put into immediate effect.

A T Class submarine has four high-pressure air groups, one located at the fore end, two equally spaced around the midships section, and one near the stern. On 15 November 1939, while the *Thetis* was dry docked in Holyhead, a more thorough examination was made before she was towed around to Birkenhead. HP (High Pressure) air groups One, Two and Four were empty. Group Three showed 125 psi. However, various gauges throughout the submarine showed a pressure of at least 250 psi, double the pressure available.

The report concluded, 'This may point to a certain leakage of air having taken place in the last five months'. Director of Naval Equipment Commander Roderick Edwards believed that the gauges had rusted at the 250 inches^2 mark. It might be a small error, but Lieutenant Commander Bolus had every right to expect that the relevant Admiralty Overseer would have ensured that there was a full supply of compressed air before embarking into the open sea, and that all his instruments were working as they should aboard a brand new submarine. Such an error, as well as the blocked test cock that formed the heart of Mabel Craven's and Rose Duncan's negligence case, strengthens the view that the *Thetis* was not fit for the open sea, although they, and their legal team, never knew about the faulty HP air gauges.

Operating the DSEA was seen as being too complicated for the wearer, especially if he was in a confused and/or distressed state. The correct operation of breaking the seal of the oxygen bottle by a clockwise movement of the handle, followed by an anti-clockwise movement to charge the bag was liable to be overlooked in the stress of escaping. There was also little doubt that had the officers and men been trained to use the DSEA from 100 feet, as in other navies around the world, they would have used the forward escape chamber as well. Even when the after escape chamber had jammed so early on 2 June, when many men were still fit enough to escape, no one thought to use the forward one. Nasmith said, 'The fact the apparatus appears to have been considered unsafe to use at this depth was due to ignorance of the capabilities of the gear and the effects of pressure'. Had the Royal Navy trained their officers and men to a higher standard, the senior officers, crew and the civilian workers would have been more fully aware of just how easy it would have been to escape. After this tragedy the Admiralty did build a 100 feet escape training tank at Fort Blockhouse, which is still in use today.

Lieutenant Woods' comments on the three men who failed to stand the pressure of the chamber while attempting entry into the flooded compartments was also criticized. 'If men are unable to clear their ears while flooding up, the fact that the pain is temporary and would disappear when on the surface should maintain confidence as those below would not see or know that those in the chamber were suffering pain in their ears. There would be no question of stopping flooding and thereby delaying escape for the remainder'. Nasmith then added rather oddly, 'If necessary, one end of the submarine can be raised to facilitate escape, which may be particularly useful'. It was very useful, but no one, other than civilian salvage engineers like Cox and McKenzie, were able to grasp this.

In theory the chambers offered the men every means of escaping certain death, but the *Thetis* disaster proved this to be a false expectation. Perhaps it was time to scrap the escape chamber altogether. Nasmith's committee put forward another suggestion, which is still in use today, albeit with the added safety margin of a coldwater survival suit. The idea of a collapsible twill trunk suspended from the submarine's deck-head, or ceiling, that could drop down to about half way to the floor had positive advantages. Although the whole compartment needed to be flooded, this is only to just above the bottom of the twill trunk, thus eliminating the possible panic among men who knew their heads would soon be submerged as well. The air is captured inside and held in place while each man ducks under and pops through the hatch and up to the surface in rapid succession. The only real disadvantage was to ensure that lighting and other electrical circuits were put out of action to prevent possible electrical fires and electrocution.

The whole concept of marker buoys was also reviewed. The reason why the *Thetis*'s marker buoy got tangled around the submarine was because it was designed to deploy without any form of control over the wire paying out as it shot to the surface, so that, although she was about 125 feet down, all 300 feet of wire ran out. There was no control over how much wire to release. Cox's idea of blowing oil to attract attention was given detailed consideration, although he was told it was not practical; at the same time Nasmith's Committee agreed that this method was a quick and reliable way to alert rescue craft to a location.

Nasmith's committee wanted the air connections reinstated. These could be used to top up the high-pressure air bottles, blowing tanks and also to vent foul air from the outside. Cox's somewhat eccentric idea of putting simple fittings to enable a diver to secure himself to a stricken submarine was given careful consideration. 'Handholds must be provided', said the report. 'The connection should be carefully and clearly marked'. Small changes in attitude aboard a stricken submarine could have a dramatic effect on air conservation. All unnecessary crew should lie down and not move. Walking around doing nothing in particular could consume air half as quickly than a man lying down. Only a small amount of food must be eaten. Avoid at all times raising the metabolism above basal rate. All domestic waste such as vegetable matter must be covered as it absorbs oxygen and lets out carbon dioxide. Keep wet rags out of contact with air, to keep down humidity. No smoking. No cooking. No artificial heat, then with any luck the air will last much longer.

So many lessons had been learnt for such a heavy loss of life, but some questions on how those in the *Thetis* died were and never will be answered. Why was a bow cap open to the sea? Many theories were put forward. Perhaps it was left open in Birkenhead? This was not possible, as the sharp 90° angle of the bow shutter would have affected the steering, and those in the torpedo room would have been aware of the bow wave hitting the open space. Then, once the tube was full after a few seconds, the continuing inbound seawater would have overflowed into the open AIV (Automatic Inboard Vent) tank in the bow to about four tons by the time she was ready to dive. Apart from adding much needed weight to the bow for her first dive, the inflowing water would have been seen and heard by those working so closely to it. Woods also maintained that until at least about ten minutes before he opened the tubes, all the bow cap indicators were at, 'Shut, Shut, Shut'.

There was also the possibility that the bow cap crept open. This could well happen, if the lever was more than 10° towards the open position, but all the starboard side levers, that is those controlling torpedo tubes One, Three and Five were set at neutral, $5/32$ inch, $5/32$ inch and $3/32$ inch respectively, towards the open position, quite clearly not enough to cause any of the bow caps to open of their own accord. Assistant Director of Naval Construction Lawrence Collingwood Williamson developed what he called the 'bump' theory. He maintained that at some point between Laird's Wet Basin and the point of sinking someone inadvertently bumped into the lever of Number Five bow cap, then put it back into its previous position. It was the last and lowest lever of the three. The Tribunal did not accept the bump theory at first because Woods was adamant that no one other than fully trained personnel were in the tube space at any time during the trial. However, as more and more evidence was collated, Williamson's theory began to look likely.

Somebody at some time must have tampered with it. There was no other explanation. If the lever was knocked or placed at or near its open position and then put back to the neutral position just prior to the power being put on to the bow caps, the cap would automatically reset back to its last known position. Who would have made such an obvious blunder? Certainly not Woods, Hambrook or any of the other highly trained personnel in the torpedo room. They knew the consequences of such an action and would not have gone ahead and opened the rear doors, knowing what was sure to happen. But, as Bucknill said, 'It did not open itself'. Hambrook did set the levers to neutral, further enforcing the view that he did not knock the lever and put it back. Perhaps someone entered the torpedo room and tripped or fell against the lever and innocently put it back, thinking that was enough during the run out to the dive site. Whatever the cause, the lever to Number Five bow cap was opened and then closed by someone.

For all Bucknill's assertions that his Tribunal was instructed not to apportion blame, he did admit in a discussion with Attorney General Somerville, 'It may well be that the tube was filled at a much earlier stage. Of course, the only plausible explanation about the bow cap, apart from negligence, is a desire to flood the tube, which was part of the plan. Once the tube is flooded there does not seem to be any explanation except negligence'.

'Or accident', replied Somerville'

'Accident amounting to negligence – inadvertence', added Bucknill. 'I do not think anybody would suggest that it was deliberate'.

During the Tribunal hundreds of pages of examination and analysis were spent trying to identify who was responsible, but it was an impossible job. Too much emphasis was placed on *who* rather *what* had led the bow cap to be open. The *who* was irrelevant. The *'what'* was an inherent culture within one of the two groups of men aboard for the trial, those being the Royal Navy personnel and the civilians, including mainly Cammell Laird's men. Laird's workers always filled tubes for ballast via the WRT (Water Round Torpedo) tank. It was slower, but they believed much safer. It was most certainly a Royal Navy procedure to fill the tubes via the bow cap because it was much quicker, mere seconds, and thus a submarine could be trimmed more quickly under war conditions. Indeed, putting the power on to the bow caps for possible filling should the trim chit be wrong was carried out under Navy Order with the full intention of opening the bow caps of Numbers Five and Six tubes, should the trim chit be wrong.

Such actions cannot, under the House of Lords ruling be called 'negligence' because no Navy personnel involved in the trimming operation could have foreseen what was about to happen under Viscount Simon's, Lord Russell of Killowen's, Lord Macmillan's, Lord Porter's and Lord Simonds' judgement on Mabel and Rose's action. So, if not 'negligent', then perhaps the Admiralty could be called 'responsible', both for the bow cap opening, regardless of who tampered with the lever. There are eleven dictionary definitions of the word 'responsible'. The first one states, 'Answerable or accountable, as for something within one's power, control, or management'. Then how far is responsible from being liable?

Finally just how far-reaching might that accountability really be, and did the Admiralty really have an ulterior motive in not rescuing the men sooner, regardless of the many conspiracy theories surrounding the disaster? On 9 February 1940 Prime Minister Neville Chamberlain received a memo signed only 'J. R. C.' He was, in fact, Private Secretary Sir John 'Jock' Rupert Colville, an outstanding civil servant who went on to act as private Secretary to Winston Churchill and later to Clement Atlee. Colville précised Bucknill's Tribunal to give Chamberlain an insight into what the report contained. Ever the conscientious employee, Colville also attempted to inform his boss, saying, 'I have made a brief summary of this report, in which I have tried to include answers to the following:

(1) Why did the disaster occur?
(2) Was anybody to blame?
(3) Why were more people not saved?

He goes on to give an accurate, although brief, account of how the disaster was caused by the opening of the rear door to Number Five torpedo tube while the bow cap was open and how this action was exacerbated by the blocked test cock. With regards to blame he details how the Wailes Dove painter blocked the test cock hole and how Admiralty Overseer, Grundy, did not check it, nor did Woods or Laird's men consider it their duty to ensure the cock was not blocked. The reasons why more men were not saved, Colville informs Chamberlain, was because of the delay in finding the vessel and how the occupants were becoming weaker as the hours passed. The five-page memo contains more than sixty facts taken from Bucknill's report to give Chamberlain a rounded version of events from the time the flooding occurred until she finally disappeared beneath the waves. All the facts he gives are in every way accurate to the letter.

Towards the end of his account Colville tells how difficult it was for the salvage vessel, *Vigilant*, to keep the stern of the submarine up, work which was made even harder by the strong tides. He describes how, had the *Thetis* been lashed to one of the surface ships, and an earlier attempt been made to cut a hole in her, more men would have probably been saved. That much is known and accepted, but then Colville adds the only piece of information not in Bucknill's report, or the Inquiry's 2,000-page transcript, or any of the supporting correspondence and files on open access across the many, many thousands of pages in the public domain. He informs Chamberlain, regarding cutting the hole:

> This was not attempted until matters became desperate, in order that the submarine might be as little damaged as possible.

This is the only official written admission known to exist, proving that there was a concerted effort to save the ship over the men until it was too late. Colville was a highly accomplished civil servant. It is equally highly unlikely that he made a mistake, especially considering that the other sixty facts in his memo are accurate, literally in every sense of the word. But if not from Bucknill, who or what were his sources? Unless further records are de-classified, it may never be known. Bearing in mind that the last *Thetis*-related file was released as recently as November 2007, there could still be more to come. It is still hard to accept that somewhere between senior Royal Navy personnel at the wreck site, and the highest levels of authority in Whitehall, someone decided to let ninety-nine men die for the sake of saving the battle integrity of the submarine.

It is much more likely that this decision was taken without truly appreciating just how 'desperate', as Nicholson said, the situation really was. At least one would hope so. Then again it must be borne in mind the full implication of the sick state of the four survivors so early in the botched rescue operation, and the certain knowledge that there was not enough time left to get everyone out, using the heavily relied upon DSEA system. Either way this tragedy is made all the worse because, thanks to Colville, Neville Chamberlain knew this piece of damning information about two months before Bucknill's report was made public in the House of Commons – and thus to the British public – in the Prime Minister's name.

Appendix

When a book such as this covers a major disaster such as the *Thetis*, it is customary to list those who perished. All too often these lists of the dead give no more information other than name, rank and serial number, which gives the reader no real feeling that these were men who died either doing their job, or trying to stay alive.

Many times I have seen lists for the ninety-nine men who died aboard the *Thetis* give such scant details. These were living people who loved, were loved in return, and had aspirations for themselves and those for whom they cared. In compiling this remembrance, as much information as possible about each man is listed to give a more rounded understanding of who he was just prior to boarding HMS *Thetis* on 1 June 1939, and who was left behind to grieve for his loss:

ALLEN, William, Leading Telegraphist, husband to Mary

ANKERS, Thomas, Civilian Contractor, husband to Martha

ARMSTRONG, James, aged fifty, Civilian Contractor, husband to Lillian

ASLETT, William, Admiralty Civilian, husband to Mabel

BAILEY, Frank, Admiralty Civilian, son of Agnes, husband to Dorothy and father to Doreen aged eighteen, Sheila aged fifteen, Michael aged twelve

BAMBRICK, Thomas, Stoker, son of William, husband to Mary and father of little Thomas William aged two months

BATH, William, aged forty-seven, Civilian Contractor, husband to Bessie and father to Elsie aged eight

BATTEN, Francis, Leading Signalman, son of Martha, husband to Gladys and father of Roy aged four

BEATTIE, William, aged forty-five, Civilian Contractor, husband to May and father of Jean aged nine

BOLUS, Guy 'Sam', Lieutenant Commander of HMS *Thetis*, husband to Sybil and father of Martyn aged nine

BRESNER, Frank, aged fifty-five, Civilian Contractor, husband to Wilhelmina and father of Minnie aged seventeen

BROAD, Samuel, aged thirty-eight, Civilian Contractor, husband to Mary and father of Margaret aged one and Mary aged eleven months

BROOKE, Robert, Leading Stoker, husband to Lilian

BROWN, William, aged thirty-two, Civilian Contractor

BYRNE, Alan, Electrical Artificer

CHAPMAN, Harold, Lieutenant, husband to Inez and father of Felicity aged two

CHINN, Arnold, aged twenty-five, Civilian Contractor, husband to Vera

CORNISH, George, Chief Petty Officer, husband to Mary

COSTLEY, James, Able Seaman, husband to Ada and father of James aged eleven and Maurice aged five

CRAGG, Horace, Civilian Contractor, husband to Sarah

CRAIG, James, Stoker, husband to Elizabeth and father of William aged six

CRAVEN, Archibald, aged thirty-nine, Civilian Contractor, husband to Mabel and father of John aged ten

CREASEY, Jack, Engine Room Artificer

CROMBLEHOME, Stanley, Able Seaman, son of Jane

CROUT, Robert, aged forty-eight, Civilian Contractor, husband to Gladys

CUNNINGHAM, David, Acting Leading Stoker

DILLON-SHALLARD, Harold J., Chief Stoker, husband to Mabel and father of Harold aged seven and David aged five

DOBELLS, Gilbert, aged sixty-three, Civilian Contractor, husband to Jessie

DUNCAN, David, aged twenty-seven, Civilian Contractor, husband to Rose

DUNN, Alfred, Stoker, husband to Emily

ECCLESTON, Harold 'Dixie', aged thirty-eight, Civilian Contractor, husband to Ellen and father of Allan aged twelve and Maureen aged five

FEENEY, James, Leading Stoker, partner of Vera

FRENCH, Howard, Engine Room Artificer, husband to Doris

GARNETT, Richard, Lieutenant Commander of HMS *Taku*, husband to Mary

GISBORNE, Edward, Admiralty Civilian, husband to Mary

GLENN, Roy, Commissioned Engineer, husband to Marie and father of Jan aged sixteen, Brenda aged fourteen and John aged twelve

GOAD, Thomas, Petty Officer, husband to Doris and father of Doris aged ten, Geoffrey aged six and Elizabeth aged four

GRAHAM, C. T. W., Telegraphist, husband to Vera

GREEN, Louis, Stoker, son of Florence

GRIFFITHS, John, aged thirty-nine, Civilian Contractor, husband to Rose

HAMBROOK, Walter, Acting Leading Seaman, son of Matilda Ann

HAMILTON, Clifford, aged thirty-six, Civilian Contractor, Husband to Mary

HARWOOD, George, Acting Petty Officer, Husband to Alice

HAYTER, Reginald, Commander, husband to Elizabeth and father of Eve aged nine and George aged eleven months

HENDERSON, Colin, Lieutenant,

HILL, Albert, Admiralty Overseer, son of Elizabeth, husband to Ethel and father of Leslie aged twelve and Peter aged eight

HILLS, Albert, Stoker, husband to Gladys and father of Evelyn aged fifteen, Albert aged fourteen and Leslie aged ten

HOLE, Wilfred, Stoker, husband to Caroline and father of Eugene aged six months

HOMER, Richard, aged thirty-three, Civilian Contractor, husband to Edith and father of John aged nine, David aged five and Malcolm aged eleven months

HOPE, John, Acting Petty Officer, stepson of Kate and father of 'Miss E.'

HORNE, Charles, Admiralty Civilian, husband to Lottie

HORSMAN, Harry, Admiralty Civilian, husband to Ethel

HOWELL, Harold, Engine Room Artificer, son of Edith

HUGHES, Joseph, Petty Officer Cook, son of Catherine and husband to Doris

HUNN, Leslie, Admiralty Civilian, husband to Florence

JACKSON, Peter, Acting Chief Engine Room Artificer, husband to Jessie and father of John aged fourteen, Peter aged nine and Gladys age seven

JACKSON, Stanley, Engineer Captain, son of Thomas,

JAMISON, Antony, Lieutenant, of HMS *Trident*

KENDRICK, Edward, Able Seaman, husband to Dorothy and father of Stanley aged six, Albert aged four and Robert aged one

KENNEY, Thomas, Leading Stoker, husband to Frances and father of Sheila aged one

KIPLING, Robert, aged thirty-eight, Civilian Contractor, husband to Mary and father of Mary aged nine, Jean aged eight, Robert aged seven and Evelyn aged one

LEWIS, Edward, aged twenty-nine, Civilian Contractor

LLOYD, Thomas, Lieutenant Commander of HMS *Trident*, husband to Marie and father of 'new baby' aged two months

LONGSTAFF, Norman, Able Seaman, son of Grace

LUCK, Walter, Leading Seaman, son of Jessie and Walter Senior

MATTHEWS, William, Stoker, son of Alfred

MITCHELL, Ernest, Petty Officer, husband to Bertha and father of Frederick aged fourteen

MORGANS, James, Able Seaman, husband to Mary

MORTIMER, Thomas, Telegraphist, son of Alfred

ORMES, William, Chief Engine Room Artificer, husband to Florence and father of Pauline aged nine

ORROCK, William, Stoker, son of Annie

OWEN, Walter, aged thirty-two, Civilian Contractor, son of 'Mrs C.'

PAGE, James, aged forty-one, Civilian Contractor, husband to Doris and father of John aged four

PENNINGTON, Lionel, Commander, husband to Barbara and father of Evelyn aged fourteen

POLAND, William, Lieutenant

QUINN, Philip, aged thirty-six, Civilian Contractor, husband to Ada and father of John aged four and Margaret aged ten months

READ, John, Leading Seaman, husband to Phyllis and father of John aged six

ROBINSON, Arthur, aged forty-six, Civilian Contractor, husband to Muriel and father of Eileen aged fourteen and Barbara aged ten

ROGERS, Frank, Able Seaman, son of Emmie

ROGERSON, Richard, aged twenty-seven, Civilian Contractor, husband to Clara and father of Alan aged six months

RYAN, Patrick. Lieutenant, of HMS *Trident*, husband to Rosemary and father of David aged two

SCARTH, George, aged thirty-one, Civilian Contractor, husband to Edith and father of Joyce aged three and 'new baby' aged four months

SMITH, Alfred, Leading Seaman

SMITH, Cornelius, aged twenty-seven, Civilian Contractor, husband to Eleanor and father of Adrienne aged one and Cornelia aged four months

SMITH, William, aged eighteen, Civilian Contractor, son of 'Mrs J.'

SMITHERS, Cecil, Acting Petty Officer, son of Minnie, husband to Edie and father of 'new baby' aged one month

STEVENS, Stanley, Leading Seaman, son of Rosa

STOCK, Francis, Leading Steward, son of Florence

SUMMERS, George, aged thirty-three, Civilian Contractor, husband to May and father of Agnes aged seven, Elizabeth aged five and William aged two

TURNER, John, Acting Leading Seaman

TYLER, Donald, Civilian Contractor, aged forty-two

WATKINSON, Arthur, aged fifty, Civilian Contractor, husband to Marjorie and father of John aged seventeen and Richard aged fourteen

WATTERSON, William, aged thirty-five, Civilian Contractor, husband to Elizabeth and father of Marjorie aged twelve

WELLS, James, Stoker Petty Officer, husband to Isabella

WILCOX, Norman, Mersey Pilot, aged twenty-five

WILSON, Thomas, Able Seaman, son of Ellen

YATES, Albert, Stoker, husband to Doris and father of Robert aged two and Allan Roy aged five months

YOULES, Edward, Acting Leading Stoker, husband to Matilda

YOUNG, John, husband to Florence and father of Joan aged nine and Hugh aged eight

Bibliography

Interviews:

Taped interview with David Keys, son of *Thetis* diver Nelson Victor Keys

Taped interview with Dr Bill Barker on the effects of carbon dioxide poisoning

Taped interview with Ian Murray Taylor, grandson of Thomas McKenzie

Interview with Robert Furniss, based on his guided tour of HMS *Thunderbolt* in January 1942

Books:

Alexander, Count Michael, *SOS* Thetis, Franz Müller Verlag, Dresden, 1944

Bailey, Catherine, *Black Diamonds*, Viking, London, 2007

Burcher, Roy and Rydill, Louis, *Concepts in Submarine Design*, Cambridge University Press, Cambridge, 1994

Harris, Wendy, *The Rogue's Yarn*, Leo Cooper, London, 1993

Hart, Sydney, *Discharged Dead*, Odhams, London, 1956

Kemp, Paul, *The T-Class Submarine: The Classic British Design*, Naval Institute Press, Annapolis, USA, 1990

Maas, Peter, *The Terrible Hours*, HarperCollins, London, 2000

Masters, David, *Up Periscope*, Eyre & Spottiswoode, London, 1942

Roberts, David, *HMS* Thetis: *Secrets & Scandal*, AVID Publications, Merseyside, 1999

Ryder, Stephen P., short biography of Count Michael Alexander in 'Der Teufel von Whitechapel' ('The Devil of Whitechapel') by Alexander, Nürnberg, 1944. This edition, 2001

Warren, C. & Benson, J., *'The Admiraluty Regrets ...'*, George G. Harris & Co. Ltd, London, 1958

Weir, Gary E. and Boyne, Walter J., *Rising Tide, the untold story of Russian submarines that fought the Cold War*, NAL Caliber, New York, 2003

Werner, Herbert, A., *Iron Coffins*, Pan Books, London, 1969

National Archives, Kew, London:

ADM 1/10229	HM Submarine *Thetis*: salvage arrangements
ADM 1/10368	HMS *Thetis*, liability for cost of salvage
ADM 1/10403	Salvage of HMS *Thetis*, report to US Naval Attaché
ADM 1/11842	Estimates and Finance, Memorial Grave HM Submarine *Thetis*
ADM 1/20878	Funerals, Burial Grounds, Memorials
ADM 1/15076	HM Submarine *Thetis*: memorial to be erected on the grave at Holyhead
ADM 1/15258	Inquiry by C. T. Culverwell MP on German broadcasts
ADM 53/107837	HMS *Brazen*, June 1939
ADM 116/2900	Submarine *M-2*, salvage operations
ADM 116/2909	Submarine *M-2*, foundering and loss
ADM 116/4115	HMS *Thetis* salvage operations
ADM 116/4311	HMS *Thetis* salvage and funeral arrangements
ADM 116/4342	HMS *Thetis* insurance arrangements
ADM 116/4429	HM Submarine *Thetis*: post mortem examinations, escape problems, Nasmith Committee.
ADM 116/6358	Loss of HM Submarine *Thetis*, 1939, legal action for compensation claims
ADM 298/499	HMS *Thetis*, report on events surrounding the submarine disaster of 2 June 1939
PREM 1/417	Navy: Tribunal Inquiry into the loss of the *Thetis*
TS 27/472	*Thetis* disaster Relief Fund
TS 32/102	Submarine *Thetis* Inquiry: correspondence 1939–1941
TS 32/103	*Thetis* Inquiry: telegrams, signals, messages etc.
TS 32/104	*Thetis* Inquiry: brief & witness statements
TS 32/105	*Thetis* Inquiry: report of the Tribunal 1939–1941
TS 32/107	*Thetis* Inquiry: shorthand notes of proceedings 1st to 10th days
TS 32/108	*Thetis* Inquiry: shorthand notes 11th to 20th days

TS 32/112	Claims for damages, exhibits, photographs etc.
TS 32/113	HM Submarine *Thetis*: claims for damages; proceedings in Court of Appeal
TS 32/114	HM Submarine *Thetis*: claims for damages, proceedings in House of Lords
TS 36/258	HM Submarine *Thetis*: Duncan and another v. Cammell Laird, production of documents
TS 36/259	HMS *Thetis*: report of the Tribunal

Royal Navy Submarine Museum, Fort Blockhouse, Portsmouth:

A1939/9/001	Report of Admiral Nasmith's Committee of methods of saving life in sunken submarines.
A1939/005	The cause of the loss of HMS *Thetis* Letter from Captain Oram, a personal narrative Account by Lieutenant Woods taken in hospital, 4 June 1939
A1939/9	Problems associated with Nasmith's report
A1939/22	Various reports on loss of HMS *Thetis*
A1939/024	*Thetis*, signals and action taken when she was overdue
A1939/025	*Thetis*, signals, letters, etc.
A1939/032	News cuttings about loss of HM Submarine *Thetis*
A1939/67	Assorted files including survivor accounts, judge's comments, newspaper cuttings.
A1984/014	Material collected on HM Submarine *Thetis* for presentation
A1985/054	Plastic binding folder containing typewritten extract from Brassey's Annual 1940 – The Salvage of HM Submarine *Thetis*, by G. R. Critchley, 1940
A1988/032	Original script by Captain J. S. Steven of his Naval career Account of burial of Lieutenant Woods Account of recovery of dead by Cannock Mine Rescue Team
A1991/308	RN transcripts of German propaganda broadcasts
A1993/067	Various copies of evidence and personal accounts from survivors
A1995/087	Bound copy of *SOS* Thetis by Count Michael Alexander

| A1996/372 | Collection of documents re. recovery of bodies from HMS *Thetis* |
| A1995/446 | Detailed typed account with images of salvage operation |

Wirral Archives, Birkenhead:
Financial accounts of Cammell Laird 1937
Financial accounts of Cammell Laird 1938
Financial accounts of Cammell Laird 1939
Legal papers regarding various lawsuits filed against Cammell Laird and their outcome
Original cross-section plans of HMS *Thetis*
191. *Thetis* Vessel No. 1027 Inquiry Statements etc.
191. *Thetis* Vessel No. 1027 Salvage
191. Submarine '*Thetis*' V. 1027 PADS Whilst in course [of] Construction SPEC.
191. *Thetis* Vessel No. 1027 PADS whilst in Course [of] Construction
191. *Thetis* Vessel No. 1027 Lord Mayor's Fund General, Suggestions re. Salvage, Condolence Letters, Press
191. *Thetis* Vessel No. 1027 Staff & Burial

Assorted newspaper articles:
The Times
New York Times
Liverpool Daily Post
Liverpool Echo
The Guardian
Daily Mirror

Picture archives:
ITN Archive
ITN Stills
Mirrorpix

Other:
British Newspaper Library at Colindale, London
Hansard

Index